Greg L denby III

Trevor Scarfull

Martin Ashwin

BALLS

Sorry I missed you in Washington.
Phil Mackaden.

Barry Lamkin
Neil Edwards

Eric Kensett

Chris Heaton

DEBTORS

TO THEIR

PROFESSION

DEBTORS
TO THEIR
PROFESSION

A History of
The Institute of Bankers
1879–1979

EDWIN GREEN

PUBLISHED FOR
THE INSTITUTE OF BANKERS
BY METHUEN & CO LTD

DEBTORS TO THEIR PROFESSION

ISBN 0 416 72290 3
*First published March 1979
by Methuen & Co Ltd,
11 New Fetter Lane, London EC4P 4EE*
© *1979 The Institute of Bankers
Designed by Charles Whitehouse,
set in 'Monotype' Bell, printed on
Motomatt coated cartridge
& bound in Winterbottom
book cloth by
W & J Mackay Ltd,
Lordswood, Chatham
Kent*

Frontispiece: *Sir John Lubbock, MP, a partner in the banking firm of Robarts, Lubbock and Co., London, served as the first President of The Institute of Bankers between 1879 and 1883. In addition to his distinguished career as a banker and as a man of letters, his achievements in the House of Commons included the successful introduction of the first Bank Holidays Act in 1871 and the Bills of Exchange Act in 1882. Sir John Lubbock, later Lord Avebury, was President of the Central Association of Bankers from 1897 until his death in 1913.*

I hold every man a debtor to his profession,
from the which as men of course do seek to receive
countenance and profit, so ought they of duty to
endeavour themselves by way of amends,
to help and ornament thereunto.

FRANCIS BACON, *The Elements of the Common Lawes of England* (1630)

I owe the Institute a great debt, and know that
this feeling is shared by many. I have just
heard from a friend who has been eight years in India,
and who still continues his membership. He expresses
his indebtedness to the Institute, and, as a
matter of fact, the turning point of his
career was the day when he
joined its ranks.

FRANK STEELE, FIB, *Journal of The Institute of Bankers* (1898)

CONTENTS

[vii]

CONTENTS

ILLUSTRATIONS

ACKNOWLEDGEMENTS

I N the preparation of this history of The Institute of Bankers I have relied heavily upon the cooperation and support provided by the Institute itself. My first thanks are due to the Council of the Institute for inviting me to undertake the project and, through the secretariat of the Institute, for allowing me freedom of access to the Institute's archives. I am especially grateful to Malcolm Wilcox, MBE, President of the Institute, for help and encouragement throughout the preparation of the book; Geoffrey Dix, OBE, Secretary-General of the Institute, both for advice and for providing introductions to members and former officials of the Institute; David Whelpton and Eric Glover, Deputy Secretaries, for valuable guidance on the recent history of the Institute; and the Library and Registry staff of the Institute for their patience in dealing with research enquiries and checking references.

Although the main research sources for this history are located at the headquarters of The Institute of Bankers, a number of other archives, libraries, and individuals have supplied information or given access to records. I am grateful to Rosemary Ashbee, Archivist of Williams and Glyn's Bank; Kathleen Bryon, Archivist of Barclays Bank, for permission to consult the records of Martins Bank; Dr Angus Buchanan, University of Bath; the late Margaret Campbell, Archivist of the National Westminster Bank, whose sudden death in November 1978 removed one of this project's kindest and most helpful friends; Chris Cooper, Keeper of Manuscripts at the Guildhall

Library, London, for permission to consult uncatalogued records; Dr
Philip Cottrell, University of Leicester, for permission to read the
manuscript of a forthcoming study of the finance of industry in the
nineteenth century; W. R. Dunsmore, Manager, Domestic Training
Branches, Midland Bank; Basil Greer, Secretary of the Institute of
Bankers in Ireland; R. A. Harvey, Archivist, King's College, University of London, for advice on the career of Leone Levi; E. Holland-
Martin, who kindly allowed access to the papers of the Holland-Martin
family; Eric Kelly, Curator, Museum and Historical Research Section,
Bank of England; Brian McKenna, Secretary of the Institute of
Bankers in Scotland, and Evan Williams, Assistant Secretary, for
their hospitality and helpfulness during research into the origins of
the Scottish Institute; George Mahon, formerly of the Provincial Bank
of Ireland; Leif Mills, Secretary-General of the National Union of
Bank Employees, and Jon Robinson, Research Officer, for their assis-
tance in unravelling the early history of the Bank Officers' Guild;
Joan Milne, Senior Bursar, St Hugh's College, Oxford; D. B. Nash,
Department of Printed Books, Imperial War Museum; Dr John
Orbell, of the Business Records Advisory Service, Business Archives
Council; M. D. Roberts, Archivist of Lloyds Bank, for his help and
efficiency in dealing with a number of complex enquiries; J. P.
Sassoon, Secretary for External Students, University of London;
A. Scott, Bank of Scotland, Glasgow; Miss M. Skipp, Librarian,
Institute of Chartered Secretaries and Administrators; Miss E.
Talbot Rice, National Army Museum; Max Taylor, Chief Executive,
Building Societies Institute; Charles Tennant, for guiding me to
some fascinating documents in the Charles Gairdner papers at the
Bank of Scotland; Margaret Thoren, Editor, *The Bankers' Magazine*;
Margaret Torrance, Archivist of the General Accident Fire and
Life Assurance Corporation, Perth, J. Pugh of the General Accident,
London, and H. W. Sheppard, Manager of the Guarantee Society,
for arranging access to the records of the Guarantee Society, and
Chris Watkins, British Association for Commercial and Industrial
Education.

In the final stages of the project a number of members and former
officials of The Institute of Bankers kindly agreed to read the manuscript version of the history. I am particularly indebted to Philip
Chappell, CBE, a member of the Council of the Institute, for valuable

comments on the recent development of the Institute; W. F. Crick, CBE, Hon. FIB, a former Deputy Chairman of the Institute, for illuminating and detailed suggestions and for his comments on the main trends in the development of business education; Henry Eason, CBE, JP, Hon. FIB, formerly Secretary-General of the Institute, for his help and hospitality as well as his comments on the evolution of the Institute in the 1950s and 1960s; Maurice Megrah, QC, Hon. FIB, formerly Secretary of the Institute, for explaining important aspects of the Institute's work in the 1930s and in the post-war period; Cedric Muxlow, a former Deputy Chairman of the Institute, for detailed guidance; Michael Pitcher, General Manager's Assistant, Barclays Bank, for drawing attention to some neglected themes in banking history, Eynon Smart, for his keen interest and expert advice; W. J. Thorne, formerly Economic Adviser of the Westminster Bank, for reading early versions of the manuscript and for providing authoritative comments on trends in banking employment; and Derek Vander Weyer, Deputy Chairman of the Institute, for his helpful comments on the contemporary history of the Institute.

The preparation of this history for publication depended heavily upon the technical advice of Jane Hunter, Carol Somerset and Charles Whitehouse, and I am grateful to them and to their colleagues at Methuen. I also wish to thank Messrs W. Photoprint Limited, J. R. Freeman & Co., and Ernest Greenwood for their efficiency in preparing illustrations for publication.

I owe special thanks to the following for their support and guidance throughout the preparation of this history: Evelyn Brown, who has patiently and efficiently taken on the tasks of typing and reorganizing each draft of the manuscript; Professor Sydney Checkland and Olive Checkland of the University of Glasgow, who in addition to giving detailed comments on the text offered invaluable guidance on the history of banking in Scotland and the history of the other business professions; Michael Moss, Archivist of the University of Glasgow, who made many constructive suggestions both on the choice of material and the editing of the manuscript, and Lynne Moss, whose hospitality during this and other recent projects has been lavish; Guy Rippon, whose cheerful and sure-footed work as research officer has been a major contribution to the history; Jean Saunders, Archivist of The Institute of Bankers, who has ensured that the author, manuscript, and illustrations have been in the right place at the right time; Peter Spiro, Assistant Secretary and Librarian of the Institute, whose energy and enthusiasm have been vital not only in editing the manuscript but also in the management and direction of the project from its outset; and my wife Hilary, whose understanding and practical advice have been indispensable to the completion of this history. Any errors of fact or interpretation in the following pages are of course my own responsibility.

EDWIN GREEN

I am grateful to the following companies, institutions, and individuals for their permission to reproduce photographs and other illustrations:

The Bankers' Magazine, Figures 5, 18, 21
Barclays Bank Limited, Figures 12, 38(a)
Henry Eason, Esq., CBE, JP, Hon. FIB, Figure 36
The Folio Society, Figure 3
Guildhall Library, London, Figures 4, 7
King's College, University of London, Figure 11
Lloyds Bank Limited, Figures 22, 38(b)
Lord Avebury and Bromley Borough Council, Frontispiece
Midland Bank Limited, Figures 10, 13, 15, 17, 20, 38(c)
National Westminster Bank Limited, Figures 2, 9, 23, 24, 33, 38(d)
Williams and Glyn's Bank Limited, Figures 30, 38(e)

All other photographs and illustrations are reproduced from items in the records of The Institute of Bankers.

FOREWORD

BY THE PRESIDENT OF THE
INSTITUTE OF BANKERS

THE Institute of Bankers, with a total membership of over 110,000 banking men and women in over one hundred countries, is one of the largest professional associations in the business world. Its rapid growth, especially since the 1950s, makes it increasingly important that it should explain its function to all who are concerned with the role of banking in modern society, and the Institute's centenary is an ideal opportunity to do this within a general survey of its origins, its objectives and its activities.

This history, by attempting to identify and describe the emergence of 'the professional banker', is set in the context of the development of the banking industry as a whole and, against this background, it is clear that the establishment and growth of The Institute of Bankers has relied heavily upon an adaptable approach to changes in the structure and methods of banking. While never moving away from its responsibilities as the educational focus of the banking community, the Institute has, at different stages in its life, shown a readiness to assume other tasks – for example, as a source of opinion on the form of new banking legislation (in the 1880s), as administrator to a series of banking charities (in the 1920s and 1930s), as publisher (particularly since the 1950s), and, more recently, as the centre of post-qualifying activities for bankers in mid-career.

Essential as this flexibility has been and will continue to be in responding to new banking developments, there are strong threads of continuity in the aims and organization of the Institute and, in this regard, the Institute's members owe a significant debt to the permanent secretariat. Its contribution is vital: it helps to promote debate on topical issues, it implements policy decided by the Council, it controls the examination system and it services a widespread and varied programme of activities for qualified bankers. It is similarly important that, throughout the century of its existence, the Institute's qualified members – at all levels of business seniority – have given so much of their own time and energy to the sponsorship and support of activities in local centres in the United Kingdom and overseas and in the administration of examinations. Without this voluntary participation, The Institute of Bankers could not possibly have built up such a large and representative membership within which interest is sustained.

This blend of adaptability to change and continuity of performance will be an invaluable asset as the Institute seeks to fulfil its commitment to the maintenance of high standards and relevant knowledge in professional education. As new developments in financial services continue to affect the range and content of the Institute's activities, this firm and well-proven commitment – to members, to their employers and to the community at large – should ensure that the Institute retains its distinctive role. Through his research and his existing connections with a major banking institution, Edwin Green has acquired a deep understanding of our forbears and their achievements. The Council of the Institute, which commissioned this work, is grateful to him for recording its history with such skill and sensitivity.

MALCOLM WILCOX
August 1978

INTRODUCTION

IN the history of modern banking, the role and importance of bank personnel has often been neglected or forgotten. Inevitably, histories of individual banks concentrate on questions of organization and business performance, interpreting innovations in banking or major alterations in balance sheets in terms of decisions taken at the very highest levels of management. Yet explanations of the development of banking are incomplete without some attempt to bring the contribution of management and staff into clearer focus. In day-to-day business at the moments of great change in banking, the competence and efficiency of managerial and clerical staff is a vital ingredient in the effectiveness of a bank's services; the quality of the recruitment, training, and experience of a bank's personnel obviously affects its business progress. The Institute of Bankers, which was established in London with some 2,000 members in 1879 and now has a membership of over 110,000 banking men and women in England, Wales, and over 100 other countries, has an especially important place in the history of banking staff. Through its responsibilities for professional qualifications in banking and a wide range of other educational facilities, the Institute is central to any review of the history of professional banking.

In the contemporary business world, most occupations are represented by their own professional institutes. The scope of the activities of these institutes varies considerably, largely in response to the demands of the business or industry in which their members are employed. While some professional organizations act mainly as a meeting place for the exchange of ideas and business contacts, other institutes operate with a full range of qualifications, research facilities, and disciplinary procedures for controlling the standards of business conduct. The effectiveness of these different types of institute necessarily depends upon the active support of large numbers of members over a long period. In many salaried occupations, this support is decisively influenced by the attitude of employers in the relevant business or industry, particularly if an institute is striving to win recognition for its qualifications and other educational services. The long-term achievements of an institute, however, are also measured by its success in creating a sense of the identity, common interests, and shared expertise of a professional group. In the early history of The Institute of Bankers, this function was a key factor not only in attracting support throughout the banking community but also in determining the type of responsibilities which the Institute should undertake.

Banking was not widely regarded as a profession before the third quarter of the nineteenth century. Traditionally, commentators on banking in England and Wales had always described the business as a trade rather than as a specialist professional skill. In the later seventeenth century, for example, Sir William Petty, the political economist, explained that 'the Trade of a Banker' was 'the buying and selling of Interest and Exchange'. The business was 'a beneficial Trade, founded upon a good Opinion of the World, which is called Credit'.[1] This treatment of banking as a category of trade clearly reflected the structure and practices of the business. Like many other trades, banking was carried on in a small way by large numbers of private partnerships, and it was not unusual for the partners to maintain their banking interests alongside other commercial ventures.[2] As a result the term 'banker' denoted ownership or part-ownership of a banking firm rather than any distinctive expertise; the private bankers of Petty's time operated with only a rudimentary knowledge of accountancy and law, and the training of newcomers to the business was on the same footing as working apprenticeship in other trades.

With the important exception of the Bank of England, the banking system of England and Wales continued to be dominated by private banking partnerships until the 1820s. The survival of this pattern restricted the range of skills which were required for banking work, mainly because the private firms concentrated their business in a small geographical area and dealt with a limited variety of financial transactions. After 1826, however, when new company legislation permitted the formation of joint stock banks with publicly quoted shares,[3] the salaried managers of the new banks began to emerge as a recognizable occupational group. Unlike the private bankers, managers in many of the joint stock banks were faced with the responsibility of controlling relatively large networks of branch offices as well as supervising the routine work of head office departments. Economic expansion during the railway booms of the 1830s and 1840s was an exacting test of managerial and technical competence, but the managers of the joint stock banks were also required to master a complex framework of company legislation and to exercise close control over their banks' balance sheets. The development of these skills, partly by learning from the joint stock banking tradition in Scotland,[4] enabled the new banks to displace or to absorb many of the old private bankers and to open offices in areas where there was no previous link with banking. By winning the confidence of their shareholders and customers, the managers and branch managers of the new banks now took their place alongside other groups of professional people in the cities and towns of England and Wales.

By the mid-nineteenth century the directors and shareholders of joint stock banks expected to see men of proven ability and experience filling senior management posts. Managerial appointments were often open to competition, and it was increasingly important that managers or potential managers should show evidence of their abilities. This growing emphasis upon managerial and technical expertise was clearly identified by the founders of the short-lived Banking Institute of 1851–3 and the proposed Incorporation of Bankers of 1862 (see Chapters 1 and 2). Despite the eventual failure of these two ventures, their recognition of the value of qualifications was a sign that banking skills were becoming more generally accepted as part of a complex business profession. The transition was also mirrored in the changing use of the designation 'banker'. The title was effectively reserved to private bankers before the mid-nineteenth century, and the 2,000 'bankers' listed in the 1841 census represented no more than 10 per cent of the total number of banking employees.[5] In the second half of the century, this distinction was abandoned as more and more managers and other senior officials in joint stock banks described themselves as bankers. George Rae's *Country Banker*, for example, compiled between 1850 and 1885, was primarily intended for the instruction of branch managers of joint stock banks.[6]

Although the rise of the joint stock banks opened up new career opportunities in banking, many of those working in the banks realized that the growing awareness of technical skills could be harnessed to a system of banking qualifications. By the 1870s the initiative and much of the support for the introduction of qualifying examinations came from the junior managers and clerks of the banks. Their arguments were partly inspired by the conviction that qualifications in banking subjects would be helpful to the banks in the selection of managers and other senior officials. The career structure of appointments in the joint stock banks, for example, made it possible for employees to advance steadily up the ladder from junior clerk to general manager; this opportunity was in marked contrast to the limited scope for promotion in the private banks.[7] At the same time, those who favoured the use of qualifying examinations recognized that the role of the bank clerk was rapidly changing. In the 1860s and 1870s bank clerks were required to take on a heavier burden of responsibilities, including clerical work connected with the growing expansion of overseas banking business, the greater use of the cheque clearing system after the 1850s, and the growing complexity of book-keeping and legal documentation. The performance of these duties demanded a minimum standard of technical competence throughout the clerical staff of the banks, and it was increasingly important to the directors and shareholders of banking companies that these standards of knowledge and efficiency were maintained to keep pace with changes in banking business. For these reasons, the introduction of qualifications for the assessment of bank officials' practical knowledge was of great concern to the clerks as well as to their employers and their managers.

When The Institute of Bankers was established in 1879, this breadth of support for its proposed qualification was a major advantage. The founders of the Institute, including senior bankers and the clerks who had advocated the introduction of a banking qualification in the 1870s, made certain that its role as a professional body was not in any way restrictive. In contrast to professional associations which used their membership and qualification as a 'licence to practise', the Institute was launched on the understanding that its qualifications would be accessible to many thousands of bank employees. This willingness to monitor standards, award qualifications, and provide study facilities at all levels of banking work quickly drew the Institute to the centre of the banking community in England and Wales and gave it important links in overseas banking. With a deliberately broad base of membership, it was soon clear that the Institute's development would be closely adjusted to changes in bank employment and banking business as a whole. This history of The Institute of Bankers attempts to throw light on these changes by examining the objectives, membership growth, and the main alterations in the role of the Institute in modern banking.

1

PROLOGUE:
THE BANKING INSTITUTE
1851–1853

*The world is wide enough for us all, and when our interests
are in common, why should we not fraternize?*

GEORGE RAE, *The Bankers' Magazine*
(February 1851), p.72

WHEN the modern Institute of Bankers was established in 1879, it
was the culmination of over thirty years of debate and experiment within the banking community of England and Wales. Many of the advantages of an association of professional bankers had been recognized as
early as the 1840s, but without sustained support the initial attempts
to form an institute were inconclusive or short-lived. This long period
of gestation was similar to the experience of other professional
institutes in nineteenth-century Britain: the Institution of Civil Engineers, the Royal Institute of British Architects, and the Institute of
Chartered Accountants in England and Wales were all preceded by
serious efforts to form central or local societies.[1] In the case of the
bank officials the most whole-hearted of the early attempts to launch
an association was the formation of 'The Banking Institute' in 1851.

In the 1840s neither the banks nor their officials were represented
by permanent associations or societies for promoting their common
interests. The development of this type of cooperation was hindered by
deep divisions in the banking system of England and Wales. There
was no single association or agreement, for example, for supervising

[1]

the conduct of business, for dealing with questions of employment, or for negotiating with governments or parliamentary committees on banking matters. The long-standing distinctions between London bankers, who had met together in the London Clearing House since the 1770s, and the country bankers, who were represented by a series of *ad hoc* committees in the early nineteenth century, preserved fundamental differences between day-to-day business in London and the provinces.[2] In the second quarter of the nineteenth century this lack of cohesion in the banking community was maintained and complicated by division and rivalry between the private and joint stock banks. The Banking Co-partnerships Act of 1826, which defined joint stock companies as 'any Body Politic or Corporate, or any Number of Persons exceeding Six', permitted the formation of joint stock banks in England and Wales for the first time for over 100 years. The new legislation was bitterly resented by the private banks as well as the Bank of England, whose charters had given it a monopoly of joint stock banking in England and Wales since 1709.[3] Disputes over privileges were particularly frequent in London, where the private bankers steadfastly refused to admit joint stock banks to their Clearing House for cheque payments until 1854. In the 1830s and 1840s this prohibition was a formidable obstacle to cooperation between the private bankers and the 'Committee of Deputies' which represented most of the joint stock banks.[4] As long as this divergence of interests within the banking community was maintained, the opportunities for bank officials to find common ground for the discussion and study of banking were severely limited.

Disunity within the banking system was paralleled by uneven standards of banking practice. Within twelve years of the Banking Co-partnerships Act of 1826, no less than 114 joint stock banks had successfully opened for business in England and Wales.[5] Many of these concerns had been established to meet the growing demand for financial resources, especially in the railway sector in the late 1830s. Some of the new banks operated on rudimentary or unsound principles, often employing networks of agents who doubled as stockbrokers, accountants, or solicitors. When a number of banking companies closed after the collapse of the railway boom of the mid-1840s, commentators attributed the failures to the inexperience or ignorance of the officials and agents as well as to the prevailing economic conditions:

Though possessed of an ample paid-up capital, numerous and influential shareholders, and a fair business opening, as was the case with the Northern and Central Bank of England and the Agricultural Bank of Ireland,* still these advantages could not counterbalance the want of proper officers; and the thousands who were ruined by the failure of these establishments were victims more of the ignorance than the bad conduct of the men they entrusted with the management of their affairs.[6]

The remaking of Britain's commercial life after the traumas of the mid-1840s was slow and painful. The survivors of the crash were faced with the task of restoring public confidence in Britain's financial institutions, a task which was made more difficult by the continued fragmentation of Britain's banking system. In the popular mind there was much concern with the quality and competence of many of the men employed by commercial undertakings, including the banks. Customers' anxieties about the credentials of bankers were aptly summarized by the author of *The City*, an early survey of financial institutions in 1852:

A wide difference exists between the class of people employed in joint stock banks and those employed in private banks. Instead of meeting in the former, as you do in the latter, cashiers and clerks peering through spectacles, with a steady and staid appearance, whose only enquiries are respecting the weather and the prospects of business, you find yourself in the company of sprightly young gentlemen, who talk about new operas and the other amusements of the town with all the ease of connoisseurs on high life; and whose chief study is to give effect to chequered neckerchiefs showing chains and mogul pins. This, no doubt, is the march of improvement, but to the quiet man of business . . . the modern improvements do not facilitate the counting or weighing of sovereigns, crossing cheques, or balancing ledgers.[7]

If these criticisms of the composition and practices of banking business were to be answered, it was clear that the public status of the banks

* The Northern and Central Bank of England, established at Manchester in 1834, failed in 1837. The Agricultural and Commercial Bank of Ireland, Dublin, which was also formed in 1834, collapsed in 1836.

and their officials had to be raised. This ambition could be achieved both by increasing the external prestige of banking and by ensuring that the quality of routine banking work was brought to a uniformly high level.

The progress of other professional groups became an important influence in the search for an improved status for banking work during the 1840s. The civil engineers, lawyers, and architects had formed representative associations early in the nineteenth century; new societies for chemists, veterinary surgeons, mechanical engineers, and actuaries were all successfully launched between 1840 and 1850.* These societies provided meetings for members, published their proceedings, and represented their professions whenever legislation was likely to affect working conditions or the conduct of business. In the 1840s many of these bodies began to look at ways of regulating entry to their professions. For example, the actuaries demonstrated that serious professional study and the examination of candidates for membership could be of great value to the business world; the life assurance companies actively encouraged their actuarial staff to participate in the new institute's affairs.[8] Senior bankers did not share this preference for using qualifications to control entry to a banking career, but they recognized the success of these associations and the progress of learned societies (including the Royal Statistical Society, founded in 1834).[9] By the mid-nineteenth century the growth of the new professional associations was a challenge to the banks and their employees to form an institute of their own. As one influential banker pointed out, 'every other science, art, or profession, has its institute or society, and with the very best results to the progress of the particular branch of knowledge, or the particular interests, which it is the object of the institute to investigate'.[10]

In the 1840s these ambitions for raising the professional status of banking were combined with an increasing awareness of the flaws in the existing methods of training bank officials. Banking in the mid-nineteenth century was a labour-intensive business, with large numbers of clerks under the supervision of a relatively small band of

* The Institution of Civil Engineers was founded in 1818, the Law Society in 1825, and the Royal Institute of British Architects in 1834. The Pharmaceutical Society was established in 1841, the Royal College of Veterinary Surgeons in 1844, the Institution of Mechanical Engineers in 1847, and the Institute of Actuaries in 1848.

managers and chief clerks. Neither the private banks nor the joint stock companies envisaged any form of middle management to carry out their comparatively narrow range of banking duties, and it was to be many years before the banks considered the recruitment of specialist staff for legal or company secretarial work. In these circumstances internal training programmes were too costly and too complex a proposition for individual banks in the United Kingdom. Private bankers and the managers of joint stock banks could offer only rudimentary in-service training for their new employees. This period of learning by experience could continue for up to six years before the clerk's practical education was complete, but in the heady days of the 1830s, when a large number of joint stock banks were formed, the rate of recruitment and advancement had inevitably increased.[11] The outcome, to the horror of some contemporaries, was the banks' dependence upon large numbers of young, inexperienced officials: 'It is remarkable what a large class of juveniles the joint stock banks have in their service; at the counter the cashiers are usually young, in the counting-house they are younger, and in the interior offices many of them are mere boys who have just left school.'[12]

As the training of clerks depended so heavily upon word-of-mouth instruction, there was always a risk that the apprentices' understanding of the business of banking would be partial or haphazard. In the first half of the nineteenth century there were few aids for young clerks anxious to fill gaps in their knowledge of the routine tasks of banking. A small number of handbooks on banking practice were available, notably James Gilbart's *Practical Treatise* and John Dalton's *Banker's Clerk*,[13] but apart from the basic education provided by mechanics' institutes and commercial schools there were no formal arrangements for tuition.[14] For those who were keen to study the available textbooks, as an alternative to 'the trashy contents of the country circulating library', there was little encouragement from their employers; the first library for banking staff, for the clerks of the Bank of England, did not open until 1850, and the other banks were slow to follow suit.[15] John Dalton, Editor of *The Bankers' Magazine*,* argued in 1846 that

---

* John Sparks Dalton had established *The Bankers' Magazine* as a monthly journal for news and comment on banking and finance in 1844. In addition to his banking duties at the London office of the Provincial Bank of Ireland, he also edited the financial column in *The Atlas* newspaper.

Figure 2 *Joint stock banks took an increasingly large share of banking business in England and Wales in the 1830s and 1840s. The purpose-built banking hall of the London and Westminster Bank at Lothbury, London, shown here in 1845, was in marked contrast to the informal bank parlours of the older private banking firms.*

young bankers who wished to build up their technical knowledge were also obstructed by the high costs of specialist books. When a clerk needed to buy textbooks, Dalton suggested, would it not be sensible for the banks to offer a subsidy as an incentive? One of the magazine's readers agreed that there was a shortage of cheap and useful books available to young bank clerks: '. . . the heads of the banking profession are therefore morally bound to do all in their power to incite their juniors to aim at a high standard of general as well as official acquirement'.[16] These difficulties, which put the reputation and efficiency of banking at risk, could not be solved by any one bank; cooperation between the banks in the instruction of their employees was badly needed.

In the history of the professions in nineteenth-century Britain, the

search for higher public status and the improvement of business practice was the chief motive for the formation of professional associations
and study societies.[17] Less commonly, occupational groups on the lines
of the British Medical Association (originally formed in 1832) or the
National Union of Teachers (established in 1870) were brought together with the specific task of improving the working environment
and remuneration of their members.[18] Among bankers the value of
this type of cooperation was fully admitted in the 1840s. *The Bankers'
Magazine*, for instance, began to campaign for improvements in the
conditions of employment. Like the arguments in favour of more
systematic training of bank officials, the magazine's suggestions were
directed at raising the status and professional standards of banking as a
whole. Support for this approach came from James Gilbart, General
Manager of the London and Westminster Bank and one of the pioneers
of joint stock banking, who urged bankers to accept that the price was
worth paying: 'If an advance of salary quickens the attention or the
zeal, or strengthens the fidelity of a party, or induces him to cultivate
those talents which add to his efficiency . . . an outlay becomes probably
one of the most profitable of [a banker's] investments.'[19]

The Bankers' Magazine's interest in working conditions came at a
time when few bank clerks or commercial clerks were either well-paid
or secure in their jobs. Although a bank clerk's salary was normally
higher than that of a clerk in the office of a commodity broker or a
utility company, it was hardly commensurate with the loyalty and
trustworthiness expected of him. For clerks entering a bank on a
salary of £50 and rising to an income of £250 per annum, 'the
progress of twenty or thirty years cannot put them in a very com-
fortable position'; with their salaries paid in quarterly instalments in
arrears, many clerks were continually in debt (see Appendix 1).[20]
After payment of debts to tradesmen and friends, as one of *The
Bankers' Magazine*'s readers explained, a quarterly salary of £40
could easily be wiped out before the beginning of a new quarter,
leaving the bank clerk 'embarrassed to the end of his days'.[21] At the
same time the clerks' prospects of advancement were not bright. Of
those entering the service of the North and South Wales Bank between 1850 and 1875, when the bank was developing its relatively
large network of branches, only 30 per cent reached managerial status
by 1875.[22] Before the mid-nineteenth century, both in the private

banks and in the joint stock banks, the chain of promotion stopped short of partnership or membership of the board of directors; when James Rhodes was elected to the board of the London and County Bank in 1851, he was the first official of a joint stock bank to cross the frontier between management and direction.[23]

By the mid-1840s, as part of a campaign to improve the position of bank officials, *The Bankers' Magazine* was recommending the foundation of a central body for recruiting staff and looking after their interests. The banking community, it was argued, needed 'some proper institution or society for protecting the interests and forwarding the views of such persons; for rescuing them from the danger of want, and procuring them appointments adequate to their abilities and experience'.[24] Of these tasks, the security of clerks and their dependents attracted the most interest, and serious efforts were made to establish a central provident fund for bank officers.

Early schemes for a provident fund had depended upon the pooling of the resources and experience of the banks themselves. A small number of banks, led by the British Linen Company in Edinburgh in 1808, had set up their own in-company provident funds,[25] and many of the English private banks had a reputation for generous treatment of their old clerks. Yet in the development of this type of benefit, the banks had been left behind by the formation of the independent Provident Clerks' Mutual Benefit Association in 1840.* The Association provided endowment and benefit insurance, but it also opened a separate benevolent fund for clerks. The experiment attracted the interest and encouragement of the banking community, and at the annual general meeting of the London Joint Stock Bank in 1845 shareholders urged the bank to open a staff pension and sickness fund of its own.[26] The proposal was turned down by the directors, who were worried by the complexity of the plan. As an alternative, the Editor of *The Bankers' Magazine* suggested the formation of a provident fund: 'we have long thought that a benefit fund for bankers' clerks, if it could be made general and equitable, would be eminently

---

* The company was established as the Provident Clerks' Mutual Benefit Association and Benevolent Fund in 1840, renamed Provident Clerks' Mutual Life Assurance Association and Benevolent Fund in 1849, and renamed Provident Clerks' and General Mutual Life Assurance Association in 1903. The company's modern title, Provident Mutual Life Assurance Association, was adopted in 1917.

serviceable'.[27] After canvassing the views of leading bankers, *The Bankers' Magazine* published plans for a superannuation fund exclusively for bank officials and their dependents. The fund was to provide life assurance cover and loans to members, as well as annuity benefits for both married and unmarried bank employees. The financing of the fund would rely upon the support of the joint stock and private banks and, knowing that London banks had subscribed £10,000 to the Provident Clerks' Association, the magazine wondered 'what may not be expected from the bankers throughout the whole Kingdom when the object is to provide for their own officers exclusively?'[28] The initial response to the proposal was disappointing, but the concept of a provident fund was to influence many subsequent plans for associations of bankers.

One of the most serious risks to the public reputation of banking in the early nineteenth century, especially in the new joint stock banks, was defalcation or fraud by employees. Before 1840 banks, insurance companies, and other institutions required employees who were appointed to positions of trust to name personal sureties or guarantors. A surety undertook to make good to the employer any loss, up to an agreed limit, arising from the conduct of the person guaranteed; in the case of the banks, the guarantees were for sums as small as £100 for porters, rising to £1,000 for clerks and more than £5,000 for managers.[29] The inadequacies of this arrangement were obvious. If the surety died or failed to fulfil his agreement, the employer was left unprotected. The insistence upon sureties also narrowed the opportunities for employment, as 'persons of the highest respectability have been obliged to forego valuable appointments, from either the great difficulty of obtaining security or a repugnance to place their relatives or friends under the obligations involved'.[30] By the 1830s and 1840s, when the banks were drawing most of their work-force from the growing and increasingly mobile populations of the cities, the task of finding satisfactory sureties had become markedly more difficult.

After 1840 many of the drawbacks of the surety system were overcome by the introduction of fidelity guarantee insurance. The Guarantee Society, which began business in London in 1840, offered to stand as surety 'to persons holding places of trust' on payment of a premium. By putting the surety on a commercial basis, with employees paying premiums adjusted according to underwriting experience, fidelity

Figure 3 *Catching the 'bus for the Great Exhibition. The Industrial Exhibition of 1851 attracted tremendous interest throughout the United Kingdom: many senior bankers were impressed by its popularity, and their reports were an influential factor in the formation of the Banking Institute in 1851.* From an etching by George Cruickshank.

guarantee insurance released the employee from his dependence upon a private guarantor, and gave the employer the protection of guarantee by a legally constituted company. *The Bankers' Magazine* was impressed by the Guarantee Society's initiative, and throughout the 1840s the magazine stressed the advantages of guarantee insurance for bank employees.[31] The Bank of England, quickly recognizing the advantages of guarantee insurance for bank officials, launched a fidelity guarantee fund for its own employees in 1840.[32] Elsewhere, however, the initial progress of guarantee insurance was slow. The London Joint Stock Bank was not the only company to refuse to accept the Guarantee Society's policies in the 1840s,[33] and by 1850 less than 1,000 bank officials were insured by the Society (see Appendix 2).

All these proposals for lifting the status of banking and improving the conditions of bank employment meant little without the sustained commitment of the banks and bank officials. The ideas put forward in *The Bankers' Magazine* in the 1840s were not enough. An extra spark of incentive was needed before the bankers and their employees could meet together in a common association.

In the excitement of the preparations for the Great Exhibition of 1851, few branches of British business failed to seize the opportunity of promoting the sale of their own goods and services in an international marketplace. Three small shows of 'Art Manufactures' had been mounted under the direction of Henry Cole, with the help of the Society of Arts, in 1847, 1848, and 1849, but the plans for the Exhibition of 1851 were far more ambitious. With Prince Albert and Henry Cole at their head, the promoters of the Exhibition planned 'a Great Collection of Works of Industry and Art . . . for the purposes of exhibition and of competition and encouragement'.[34] Five thousand exhibitors from all over the world dispatched over 100,000 items for display, and, after the completion of the Crystal Palace exhibition hall in less than nine months, Queen Victoria opened the Great Exhibition in Hyde Park, London, in May 1851.

Bankers throughout the United Kingdom, while recognizing that the Exhibition was primarily intended for displaying the marvels of manufacturing industry, were keen to show their approval and enthusiasm for the project. The Liverpool Union Bank presented £10 to each of its clerks and apprentices to cover their expenses in visiting the Exhibition, 'it being understood that the Bank of Liverpool and the Borough of Heywood would do the same'.[35] Many of the country joint stock and private banks announced similar allowances, while the London banks gave additional leave or free tickets for the Exhibition.[36] Nevertheless, without a range of products to put on display, bankers were in danger of missing the opportunity to publicize their own business and to build upon the current enthusiasm for experiment and innovation. The banking industry needed a showplace of its own.

Inspired by Joseph Paxton's descriptions of his 'Industrial Palace' under construction in Hyde Park, the first serious proposal for a joint effort by bankers appeared in an anonymous letter in *The Bankers' Magazine* in December 1850. The letter argued that the Exhibition would include designs and equipment which might have practical application to banking. The design of buildings, methods of lighting and heating, and the printing and engraving of documents were all essential parts of banking business, and it was certain that the Exhibition would feature relevant new or improved techniques. The author of the letter, anxious that the lessons of the Exhibition were not lost on the world of finance, suggested that the banks should offer a prize of £100 or £200 for the best essay on the question 'In what way can any of the articles collected at the Industrial Exhibition of 1851 be rendered specially serviceable to the interest of practical banking ?'[37]

This imaginative plan for an essay competition was quickly adopted. In January 1851 *The Bankers' Magazine* announced that James Gilbart, General Manager of the London and Westminster Bank (possibly the author of the anonymous proposal in December 1850), had agreed to donate a £100 prize for the competition. The regulations opened the competition to bankers and non-bankers, and entries from British or foreign candidates were permitted.[38] By May 1851, the date of the opening of the Exhibition, judges for the competition were already appointed.* The prize was subsequently awarded to Granville Sharp, an accountant at the East of England Bank at Norwich, for his 'Essay on the Adaptation of Recent Discoveries and Inventions in Science and Art to the Purposes of Practical Banking'. Sharp's essay, which was a remarkable encyclopedia of contemporary techniques in printing, stationery, building design, and security, was published in 1854.[39]

In the meantime the essay project had been overtaken by a more ambitious programme. Early in 1851 the publicity for James Gilbart's prize focused interest on the prospects for long-term cooperation between bankers. A number of suggestions were put forward, but the broadest and most influential of the new proposals came from George Rae, General Manager of the North and South Wales Bank, Liverpool. Writing to *The Bankers' Magazine* under the pseudonym of 'Thomas Bullion' in February 1851, George Rae advocated the setting up of a bankers' institute with a status and function parallel to the existing institutes for the sciences, arts and other professions. 'By the collection of facts, the reading and discussion of papers, and the periodical publication of such papers', he argued, 'the knowledge and practice of banking would be advanced and improved'. He also offered the first serious arguments in favour of examinations for bankers, which would give credence to the representation of the banking industry's interests:

> I can imagine an Institute of this nature, when fully developed, having within itself an honorary committee, or Court of Examiners, before whom it would be competent, at stated periods, to any officer in a bank to appear and be interrogated as to the range and accuracy of his banking knowledge, and to obtain a testimonial or diploma . . . to promote the advancement of the really talented and deserving . . . Carry the idea a step further, and let the Institute be the natural headquarters of the Committee of Deputies and of Associated Bankers, and you will thus invest it with the high function of watching over and

* The judges were P. F. Aiken, Managing Director of Stuckey's Banking Company, Bristol; C. Brown, Director of the Cumberland Union Bank, Workington; and P. M. James, Director and Manager of the Manchester and Salford Bank, Manchester.

protecting our interests and render it the centre and focus of action when any great monetary question is to be discussed in Parliament.[40]

George Rae's ideas took the banking community by surprise, and no other scheme could offer such a wide base for cooperation between the banks. A plan for a 'Banking Convention' in May 1851, for instance, offered only a conference on questions of banking law and practice.[41] Fortunately, John Dalton, Editor of *The Bankers' Magazine*, was impressed by the arguments put forward by Rae. In August 1851 he published an appeal for support for a 'Banking Institute', basing his appeal on the potential value of an association for 'the discussion and publication of its proceedings, on a similar plan to that adopted by the various learned and scientific societies'. This objective had the subsidiary aim of opening both a provident fund and a guarantee fund for the exclusive use of bank employees. The notion of a learned society was uppermost in John Dalton's mind, and he reminded his readers that bank officials should not be seen as exceptions 'when every other profession has its society or institute'. The new institute, Dalton argued, should be responsible for periodical meetings (on the model of the Statistical Society), the publication of a journal, the formation of a library, and the reprinting of rare books on banking. He was also anxious that the new institute should represent the banking community as a whole, both in negotiations with government and in 'educating public opinion'; like George Rae, Dalton saw no reason why a single institution should not represent the interests of both the banks and their employees.[42]

John Dalton had struck exactly the right note. His readers and the financial press were strongly in favour of the plan. *The Economist*, comparing Dalton's objectives with the aims of the Institution of Civil Engineers and the other professional associations, welcomed the news on the grounds that 'the public at large require to be informed of the utility of bankers to society'.[43] Amongst the bankers themselves, support came from far and wide: G. Waterson of the Caledonian Bank

Figure 4 *The inaugural meeting of the Banking Institute was held at the London Tavern in Bishopsgate, London, in October 1851. The tavern, which was a popular location for meetings of City institutions, was demolished in 1876.* From a watercolour by Thomas Shepherd.

in Inverness, and Tenison Collins, writing from Tipperary, were not at all discouraged by their distance from the London base which John Dalton had recommended. The idea of provident and guarantee funds was also favourably received. At the same time bankers came forward with additions or modifications to the scheme. The advantages of branch centres for the proposed institute were canvassed, and Edward Jones, of the Union Bank of Manchester, urged the promoters to link up with bankers in Europe. Another Manchester reader saw the institute in the role of an employment agency for bankers, with employers giving preference to officials who were members of the institute. *The Athenaeum* magazine, following George Rae's lead, cautioned that the safest ground for an institute lay in the supervision of examinations for bank clerks and the award of 'certificates of proficiency'.[44]

In the event *The Athenaeum*'s warning was put aside while John Dalton pushed ahead with his original plan. By October 1851 more than fifty country bankers had applied for membership of the proposed institute and both the private and joint stock banks in London were 'ready to cooperate. The first applications for membership included the general managers or managers of seventeen English country banks, eight Irish banks, and two Scottish banks.[45] With this backing John Dalton announced an inaugural meeting at the London Tavern, Bishopsgate, on 22 October 1851.

The preparations for the Great Exhibition, the announcement of the Gilbart Prize, and the editorials in *The Bankers' Magazine* had put bankers of the United Kingdom into an enthusiastic mood. On 22 October 1851 no less than 300 bankers attended the meeting at the London Tavern. There they heard William Prescott, of the firm of Prescott, Dimsdale and Co., and chairman of the meeting, announce the foundation of 'The Banking Institute'. The government of the Institute was put in the hands of a council representing private and joint stock banks with John Dalton as its Honorary Secretary.* Membership was opened to any bank official on payment of an annual

---

* The original Council comprised Messrs G. Chambers, E. Smyth, and N. J. Williams of Barnett, Hoares & Co., H. T. Fairland, J. W. Weldon, and C. Reeve of the London and Westminster Bank, J. A. Barnard and a Mr Gardner of the Royal British Bank, H. Ely of the Provincial Bank of Ireland, T. P. Lowell of Lubbock & Co., and W. J. Norfolk, Inspector of the London and County Bank.

Figure 5 *The formation of the Banking Institute in 1851
was largely the work of John Dalton, who acted as its
Honorary Secretary. Dalton was also Editor of* The Bankers'
Magazine *from 1844 until his death in 1852.*

subscription of one guinea (£1.05p). To loud applause, Prescott and
Dalton explained that the new Institute would be devoted to 'the
extension of sound knowledge on commercial, banking, and monetary
subjects' and the promotion of cooperation between the banks. Yet for
those who remembered the original proposals for launching the
Banking Institute, there were disappointments in store. Although the
Honorary Secretary gave a persuasive description of the advantages of
a special guarantee fund for bankers, which was to form part of the new

[17]

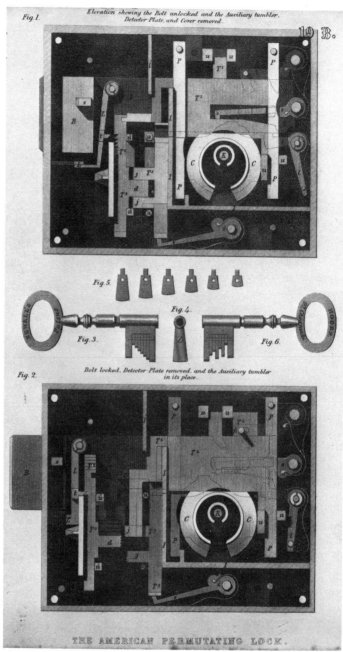

Figure 6 *The patent lock manufactured by Messrs Day and Newell, which was illustrated in Granville Sharp's Gilbart Prize Essay, was at the centre of 'the lock controversy' at the Great Exhibition in 1851. The different merits of British and American locks were debated at the first monthly meeting of the Banking Institute in November 1851.*

Institute, the earlier plans for a provident fund were inexplicably dropped. The idea of the Institute as a representative association for bankers was also kept well in the background, perhaps in deference to the attitude of James Gilbart. Gilbart, whose presence at the meeting was a great boost for the promoters of the Institute, argued that the members of the new association represented nobody but themselves; the objects of the Institute should be literary and scientific rather than political or social. In James Gilbart's view, the protection of the interests of the banks was best left to *ad hoc* committees of London and country bankers.[46]

For those who had supported John Dalton's initial campaign for a bankers' association, a more worrying aspect of the meeting at the London Tavern was the confusion over the educational function of the new Institute. Prescott, Dalton, and Gilbart were satisfied that the 'intellectual standard of the profession' could be raised by debate and publication. Equipped with no more than a library and reading room, the Institute would follow the pattern of other learned or literary societies: '. . . several gentlemen, eminent as writers on the currency, have promised to contribute papers to the earlier meetings of the Institute; several gentlemen have kindly offered the use of rare and curious tracts on banking affairs for republication'.[47] On the other hand, a number of delegates at the meeting were keen that the Institute should become an examining body, along the lines proposed by George Rae. William Newmarch, the eminent economist and the then Secretary of the Globe Insurance Company, pointed out that the new Institute was bound to influence the future status of banking as a career. 'He saw no reason why . . . the Institute might not be made the means of promoting the progress of scientific and practical banking, by the establishment of certain examinations, through which, if a young man passed with credit, he might receive a certificate of proficiency.' This approach won support from J. R. Rogers, of the National Provincial Bank. Rogers made it plain that many bank clerks would give their support to the new association in the belief that 'a prospect was now held out that a proficient education in banking matters could advance the salaries of the clerks'.[48] Although these ideas were well received at the meeting, they were far removed from Dalton's ideal of a learned society for bankers. These differences of purpose, which were either forgotten or overlooked in the excitement of the first

[19]

meeting, were to become a serious handicap for the new Institute.

After the meeting at the London Tavern the direction and organization of the Banking Institute depended heavily upon Dalton, the Honorary Secretary, and his preference for discussion and publication soon emerged as the controlling influence. For the first monthly meeting on 25 November 1851, he staged a debate on 'the lock controversy'. It was a topical choice, both because it was of practical interest to bankers and because the different designs of lock had been given prominence at the Great Exhibition earlier in the year. The controversy had been sparked off when A. C. Hobbs (representing the American firm of Day and Newell) had claimed that locks manufactured by Bramah and Prestage or C. Chubb and Son could be picked open. News of the competition between the British and American manufacturers drew a large attendance for the Institute's meeting, and A. C. Hobbs, Charles Chubb, and a representative from Bramah and Prestage all spiritedly defended their products.[49] For John Dalton, who had opened the debate with a review of banking security, the meeting confirmed that the discussion of technical developments in banking was a means of building up cooperation among bankers. It was an encouraging start for the new Institute.

By the end of November 1851 nearly 200 bankers had enrolled as members of the Banking Institute, including Thomson Hankey, Deputy Governor of the Bank of England.[50] James Gilbart, William Prescott, and other senior bankers had made donations to its funds. At first this enthusiasm was sustained by the programme of monthly meetings. After the success of the November meeting John Dalton arranged discussions on bankers' cheques and on guarantees for bank officials, and in April Dalton himself read a long paper on currency and the effects of the gold discoveries in California and Australia.[51] After January 1852 all these meetings were held at the reading room which the Institute had rented at the Hall of Commerce, Threadneedle Street, London.

While the monthly gatherings continued to attract a large attendance, the other objectives proposed at the formation of the Banking

Figure 7 *The reading room of the Hall of Commerce in Threadneedle Street, London, served as the headquarters of the Banking Institute between 1852 and 1853. The Hall of Commerce, shown here soon after its completion in 1842, was subsequently the head office of the Bank of London.*

Institute were being neglected. The founder members had enrolled on the understanding that the Institute would open its own guarantee fund, but little progress had been made by the time the first annual general meeting was held on 6 April 1852. The original plans for a library had also been deferred. To many members, especially those who could not attend the monthly meetings in London, this delay was a major disappointment, and it was the principal reason for the introduction of a half-price 'country' subscription of 10s. 6d. ($52\frac{1}{2}$p) in 1852, on the model of many London gentlemen's clubs.

The delay in setting up the Banking Institute's guarantee fund scheme and the deferment of the publication programme and library plans were partly the outcome of a slow growth of membership. The membership, in spite of an encouraging start, had reached only 253 by April 1852, and total donations and subscriptions in the first six months of operation stood at a meagre £435.[52] This enrolment was well below the forecast membership of 1,000 and tiny in comparison with John Dalton's estimate of a total of 20,000 bank officials in the United Kingdom.[53] Apart from a meeting of bankers in Limerick in April 1852, when a number of new members were enrolled,[54] little effort had been made to publicize the new Institute or to recruit from the ranks of country bankers. The Council of the Institute, dominated as it was by London bankers, was not alarmed by this slow rate of growth, insisting that its support came from 'gentlemen of high standing in the commercial world', but the low level of subscriptions inevitably restricted the prospects for the guarantee fund and the opening of the library.

Of more serious concern was the Banking Institute's dependence upon John Dalton. Like so many small voluntary or charitable associations in Britain,[55] the members of the Banking Institute assumed that one man's energy and willingness could sustain both the intellectual efforts and the administrative work. In John Dalton's case his first interest was the organization of the monthly programme, and this contribution, apart from his editorship of *The Bankers' Magazine*, left him little time to develop the other responsibilities of the Institute. Consequently when Dalton became seriously ill in the summer of 1852, the development of the Institute came to a halt. Although monthly meetings were resumed in October after the scheduled summer break, the Council of the Institute was soon forced to admit that all work on the guarantee fund and the organization of a library had been postponed.[56]

The death of John Dalton on Christmas Eve 1852, at the age of only 37, jeopardized the prospects of the Banking Institute. As a measure of his importance to the project, the career of the Institute was over within a few months. The winter season of meetings was completed according to plan, and papers read by Leone Levi (who lectured in commercial law at King's College London) and Henry Stephens (a partner in the firm of Stephens, ink manufacturers) continued the tradition of debates on practical banking.[57] Yet after the paper by Stephens in March 1853, the chairman of the meeting 'expressed a hope that, on future occasions, they would see a larger number of members present'. The decline in attendance was matched by a sharp reduction in the Institute's publicity. The second annual general meeting in April 1853 merited only four lines of comment in *The Bankers' Magazine*, and although it was reported that 'the objects are in a fair way of being carried out' there is no further record of any Institute meetings or publications. The reading room had closed by the end of 1853.[58]

The abrupt decline of the Banking Institute after the death of John Dalton marked the end of the first concerted effort to 'raise the intellectual standard of the profession' and to improve cooperation among bankers. Dalton's death was a decisive factor in the failure of the experiment, but there were inherent long-term weaknesses in the Institute which made it unlikely that it would take a firm foothold in the banking community. In spite of the blessings of James Gilbart, William Prescott, and Thomson Hankey, the Institute never enjoyed the full active support of influential bankers. Although members of the Council were drawn mostly from the London-based banks, they were chosen from the second or third ranks of management in their own companies. The Honorary Officers and Council members were rarely present at the monthly debates after November 1851, and at a number of meetings the nominated chairmen failed to put in an appearance.[59] Without this commitment, the Institute's Council could not pretend to represent the banking community as a whole. In a period when many of the old divisions and rivalries within the banking system remained, the Institute needed positive support at a senior level before it could draw in and maintain the loyalty of all sections of the banking community.

THE BANKING INSTITUTE.
52, THREADNEEDLE STREET, LONDON.

HONORARY OFFICERS.

THE RIGHT HONOURABLE THOMAS CHALLIS, M.P., LORD MAYOR.

SIR MOSES MONTEFIORE, BART., F.R.S.

JAMES WILSON, ESQ., M.P.

JAMES HELME, ESQ.

JOHN SADLEIR, ESQ., M.P.

THOMAS EDWARD JONES, ESQ.

ARTHUR HENRY HEYWOOD, ESQ.

JAMES RHODES, ESQ.

JAMES WILLIAM GILBART, ESQ., F.R.S., General Manager, London and Westminster Bank.

THOMAS HEWAT, ESQ., Secretary of the Provincial Bank of Ireland.

H. I. CAMERON, ESQ., General Manager, Royal British Bank.

JOHN BATES, ESQ., General Manager, West of England Bank, Bristol.

JAMES RAE, ESQ., North and South Wales Bank, Liverpool.

HENRY LUARD, ESQ., General Manager, London and County Bank.

WILLIAM NEWMARCH, ESQ., Secretary of the Globe Insurance.

COUNCIL.

MR. J. A. L. BARNARD (Royal British Bank).

MR. GEO. CHAMBERS (Messrs. Barnett, Hoares, and Co.)

MR. HENRY ELY (Provincial Bank of Ireland).

MR. S. O. GRAY (Bank of England).

MR. JOHN LIDDELL (Messrs. Glyn and Co.)

MR. T. P. LOWELL (Bucklersbury).

MR. W. J. NORFOLK (Inspector, London and County Bank).

MR. C. REEVE (London and Westminster Bank, Bloomsbury).

MR. J. R. ROGERS (National Provincial Bank of England).

MR. G. F. STANTON SMITH (Bank of England).

MR. EDWARD SMYTH (Messrs. Barnett, Hoares, and Co.)

MR. GEORGE TAYLOR (Messrs. Prescott and Co.)

MR. J. W. WELDON (Chief, Country Department, London and Westminster Bank).

MR. ROBT. YEAMAN (Union Bank of London).

MR. J. S. DALTON, Honorary Secretary.

MR. GEO. J. SHAW, Honorary Solicitor, 8, Furnival's Inn.

(WITH POWER TO ADD TO THEIR NUMBER.)

BANKERS.

MESSRS. PRESCOTT, GROTE, CAVE, & CAVE, 62, Threadneedle Street.

AUDITORS.

MR. F. KIDD
(Provincial Bank of Ireland).

MR. J. J. JAY
(London and Westminster Bank).

THIS INSTITUTE offers the following advantages to its Members:—

Monthly Meetings during the winter season, when papers on subjects connected with Banking and Commerce are read and discussed.

The Publication of the Proceedings of the Institute, including the papers read at the meetings, on a similar plan to that of the *Statistical Society,* &c.

A *Reading and News Room,* supplied with the daily papers, and publications of general interest and importance.

A *Banking and Mercantile Library,* for reference and circulation.

SUBSCRIPTION:

Life Members £10 10 0

Annual Members in London 1 1 0

Ditto   in Country 0 10 6

NOTE.—Country Members are admitted till the end of the year 1852, upon payment of 10s. 6d., after which their subscription will be £1 1s. for the first year, and 10s. 6d. annually.

J. S. DALTON Hon. Sec.

From the outset of the Banking Institute's short career the continued narrowing of its objectives steadily reduced its chances of winning general support from bank officials. The negative approach to banking education was the most serious of these drawbacks. In comparison with the Pharmaceutical Society and the Institute of Actuaries, for example (both of which had been established as examining bodies in the 1840s),[60] the Banking Institute was reluctant to act as a central qualifying association. Despite persuasive evidence that certificates of proficiency were needed to raise the standard of training, the organization and finance of an examination system was beyond the capability of the Banking Institute. Instead, John Dalton chose the limited role of the debating club or learned society. This choice offered little hope of a general improvement in banking education, and without the incentive of qualifications the meetings of the Institute could not attract those bank officials who were in search of practical training as an avenue to promotion. In the same way the decision not to open a guarantee fund for bankers under the auspices of the Institute, at a time when the independent fidelity guarantee companies had hardly found their feet, removed one of the main attractions of the original plans for the Institute. The idea of the guarantee fund, providing members with a cheap and safe form of surety, enjoyed strong support throughout the United Kingdom, and it gave the Institute the chance to establish a solid membership base among the bank clerks. The collapse of the scheme during 1852, alongside the decision not to offer examinations, ensured that the Banking Institute's membership was never more than a small minority of British bank officials.

Figure 8 *Advertisements for the Banking Institute described its plans for monthly meetings, publications, reading room, and library. Notwithstanding the approval of many leading figures in the banking community, few of these aims were carried out before the Institute closed in 1853.*

[25]

2

PLANNING FOR
A PROFESSIONAL
INSTITUTE
1853–1879

A S if nervous that another effort to form a professional association would meet the fate of the Banking Institute of 1851–3, the banking community did not seriously attempt to create a new association until the 1870s. In the intervening period there were signs that the banks badly needed leadership in the education of their officials. Although many of the tasks which the Banking Institute had set itself could be taken on by individual banks or by independent provident and guarantee funds, bankers and their employees became increasingly aware that the question of professional education could only be resolved by independent supervision: '. . . what are our colleges of advocates, our inns of law, our colleges of physicians, surgeons and apothecaries, but evidence of the same want of some trustworthy and responsible association, primarily for the mutual instruction and support of their members?'[1]

In the 1860s and 1870s these attitudes were influenced by significant changes in the structure and manpower needs of the banking industry. The stringent registration conditions prescribed in the banking legislation of 1844, especially the limitations on the issue of bank notes, caused a lull in the formation of new joint stock banks. In 1857, however, the Joint Stock Bank Act was repealed after it had been found to be both clumsy and inadequate as a control over the banking system. Following the introduction of simplified banking legislation in 1857–8, no less than 46 new domestic banks were launched between 1860 and 1866; another 26 banking companies were promoted between 1870 and 1875.[2] These new banks were only part of the response to the renewed confidence of both investors and bank customers as the economy expanded in the middle years of the century. The total paid-up capital of the London joint stock banks, in particular, was raised from barely £2 million in 1844 to over £8.3 million by 1874. Their deposits, which had multiplied from nearly £8 million in 1844 to over £88.6 million in 1874, showed 'an enormous augmentation, even if allowance be made for the absorption of several large private banks'.[3] The total capital of and money lodged with the private banks in the same period was not regularly recorded, but from returns collected in 1875 it is clear that even the country joint stock banks had experienced an average increase of about 250 per cent in the level of their deposits.[4] As part of this growth many banks had sought business through new branch offices, and between 1858 and 1878 the total number of bank offices in England and Wales rose from 1,212 to 2,195. Throughout the period the branches of the joint stock banks, which were concentrated in areas of new or growing population, decisively outnumbered the offices of the private banks. Most of the new banks formed after 1862, for example, assiduously built up their branch representation in suburban districts.[5]

These changes quickly affected the pattern of employment in the banking industry. The new branch networks left little room for the part-time agent who had been the mainstay of country banking in England and Wales in the first half of the nineteenth century. With their other professional interests and their inadequate offices, such agents were not equipped to carry forward the expansion of the joint stock banks. In their place, full-time professional branch bank managers were given the task of bringing in new customers and maintaining existing business at purpose-built or converted local offices. By the late 1870s bank managers had emerged as a recognizable professional group in the local business community, playing their part along with doctors, lawyers, and clergymen in parochial activities. Answerable to a head office, a branch manager was required to undertake a formidable range of duties. Before the general introduction of the telephone by the banks in the late 1890s, all business was conducted by hand-written or copy correspondence, with branch managers providing daily business reports and seeking head office permission for allowing loans or overdrafts to customers. This heavy routine did not excuse the branch manager from learning or developing techniques for assessing the creditworthiness of customers (including the largest industrial customers as well as private clients).[6] In the meantime the branch system could only be enlarged by a corresponding increase in the number of bank employees, both in the branches themselves and at head offices. The work-force of the London and Westminster Bank, for example, grew from only fifteen at its formation in 1836 to 200 by 1860; this strength had increased to 460 (including 259 head office clerks but excluding messengers) by 1879.[7]

The duties of bank clerks were also altered by the expansion and diversification of routine banking business. At the counter, cheques rapidly replaced bank-notes as the most common medium of exchange, and throughout the later nineteenth century bank tellers were required to handle an assortment of different types of transaction, including post bills and composition bills as well as notes and cheques.[8] In the supply of credit facilities, however, the growth of deposits made the rediscounting of bills of exchange relatively less important to the banks as a source of earnings; by the 1870s the significance of bills of exchange was already in decline. In these circumstances the use of bank loans and overdrafts on customers' accounts was more widely adopted both in London-based and country banks. Bank officials, to keep pace with this trend, were required to build up their expertise in the assessment and control of securities. In the same period the work of the London banks was also altered by the expanding market for the acceptance of foreign bills.[9] For the bank officials the acceptance business required familiarity with the names and standing of foreign acceptors and special skills in book-keeping and the handling of inter-national shipping documents. In step with changes in the management of railways, local government, and insurance companies, the slow but steady improvement in accounting methods placed new demands and re-sponsibilities on banking staff, and in some cases techniques of financial control were already becoming more complex and labour-intensive.[10]

Inevitably, the expansion of banking business in the 1860s and the early 1870s sharpened the rivalry among banks both in London and in

Figure 9 *James Gilbart, General Manager of the London and Westminster Bank between 1833 and 1859, was a powerful influence on the development of joint stock banking in England and Wales. He supported the Banking Institute, and in 1872, under the terms of his will, the Gilbart Lectureship in Banking was founded at King's College London. Gilbart's many publications included* A Practical Treatise on Banking *(1828) and* History and Principles of Banking *(1866).*

the provinces. To some commentators, including the economist William Newmarch, the new phase of competition carried great risks; banks were 'running after deposits with the offer of advancing terms on the one hand, and after active and borrowing accounts with too keen an appetite on the other'.[11] The more realistic observers accepted that competition for new business often helped to widen the market for banking services without necessarily damaging the older-established banks. 'The newcomers from Bolchester, on their own behalf, will give the banking soil of your district a fresh turn-over, so to speak; but this may serve indirectly to fertilize your business as well.'[12] In districts where new banks opened offices in competition with older-established companies the success of a new branch was dependent upon the recruitment and efficiency of its managers and staff. Any shortcomings in the salaries, working conditions, and training of bank officials, as James Gilbart had pointed out in the 1840s,[13] could quickly lead to failure or fraud. As a guard against these dangers, during the period of intensified competition in the 1860s and 1870s, many banks agreed that the growth of banking business should be matched by improvements in the welfare and education of bank employees.

The position of bank officials, as measured by their annual salaries, did not greatly alter between the 1850s and 1870s (see Appendix 1). The purchasing power and method of payment of these salaries was again a controversial issue. Answering an enquiry from a Fellow of the Statistical Society, who could not understand how a bankers' clerk could 'support a wife and family (as many certainly do) upon £80 a year', readers of *The Bankers' Magazine* explained that even a salary of £120 per annum was not enough to save a clerk from deficit or debt. The problem was partly a matter of the gap between income and social status:

> I do not say that a man and a wife and a family cannot live on £80 per annum. It may be done . . . by people who live on brick floors, who dress in fustian, who scour their own doorsteps, take their toad-in-the-hole to the baker on Sundays, eat cold bacon on other days when there is any in the cupboard, and a herring and potatoes when there is not; but it is not done by gentlemen who put on a clean shirt and an 'all-rounder' [collar] every other morning.[14]

Although there were no substantial improvements in the salaries of clerks, there was compensation in the greater security and improving conditions of banking work. The numbers of bank failures in the third quarter of the century, although they included the closure of Overend, Gurney & Co., a major discount house, were less disastrous for the banking work-force than the series of closures in the 1830s, partly because the demand for trained bank officials from newly established or overseas banks remained high during the 1850s and 1860s. Over twenty major foreign and colonial banks were launched in London in the third quarter of the century, including the Chartered Bank of India, Australia and China (1853), the Hongkong and Shanghai

Banking Company (1856), and the Standard Bank of South Africa (1862).[15]

As John Dalton and his supporters had anticipated, the job security of bank employees was improved by the more systematic development of provident and guarantee funds and the reduction of premiums required from bank employees for guarantee insurance. The London and County Bank, for example, opened its own provident fund and compulsory guarantee fund in January 1853; these internal funds, with their original capital subscribed by John Sadleir, MP, Chairman of the bank, had the declared aim of promoting 'a better standard of service from those in their employ . . . who are able so materially to influence the *tone* and manner in which the business of public companies is conducted'.[16] A similar scheme, based on compulsory membership of a provident fund, was organized at the Bank of England in 1854, and by the 1870s the Bank's Provident Society was able to offer rates of insurance which were 'certainly more economical to the insured than the rates of any of the public companies'.[17] Outside the banks the Provident Clerks' Association made vigorous efforts to persuade bank employees to join its life assurance scheme; relying heavily upon its policyholders in the London banks and merchant houses, the Association had issued policies valued at a total of £880,000 by 1855, and by 1880 this total had reached £2.25 million.[18]

Parallel to the development of the provident funds, fidelity guarantee insurance for bank clerks came into more widespread use during the third quarter of the nineteenth century. As well as simplifying the recruitment of bank officials (by reducing the banks' dependence upon private fidelity bonds), the growth of guarantee insurance also helped to reduce the clerks' current expenses. The number of bankers insured by the Guarantee Society, for instance, rose from only 951 in 1850 to 6,136 by 1870 and, because the rate of default on bankers' policies was markedly lower than for the other clerical occupations, the Society was able to reduce bank clerks' premiums in 1865.[19] Even lower premiums were offered by the Bankers' Guarantee and Trust Fund, which was formed in April 1865. The Fund was set up exclusively for bankers and was supervised by representatives of the banks themselves.[20]

There were signs of other improvements in working conditions in the banks during the 1860s and 1870s. At the London Joint Stock Bank, one of the largest metropolitan banks, salaries of clerical staff

[31]

were paid on a monthly basis after 1860, and a formal salary scale and pension scheme (yielding between 33 and 66 per cent of retiring salary) was devised in 1867–8.[21] Employees of all banks welcomed the introduction of statutory bank holidays after 1871, giving them an additional four days of paid leave each year.[22] At the same time the working environment was markedly improved when many of the banks built or rebuilt their offices to purpose-built designs in the third quarter of the century. The old and patchily converted offices used by banks both in London and in the provinces in the early nineteenth century now gave way to the more spacious banking halls of the High Victorian period.[23]

For the banks each improvement in working conditions was justified by its 'favourable influence in promoting steadiness of character and general uprightness of conduct'.[24] None the less, by the 1870s the alterations in the structure and character of the banking business had turned the attention of both the banks and their employees to the strengthening and standardization of banking education. This goal became the centrepiece of new attempts to form a professional association in the third quarter of the century.

James Gilbart, whose sponsorship of a prize essay competition had been an important factor in the opening of the Banking Institute in 1851, was not prepared to shelve his own ideas for banking education when the Institute was wound up in 1853. Throughout his career Gilbart was a consistent advocate of practical and theoretical training and he was unhappy that the British banks underestimated the value of private study:

> The time is gone by when it was a reproach for a young man to be bookish, as he was supposed to abstract so much more time and attention from his official duties. It is now well known that the general cultivation of the intellectual powers renders them more effective in every operation in which they may be exercised. It is a great advantage to public companies to have educated servants.[25]

After the closure of the Banking Institute Gilbart was one of the few British bankers with the seniority and influence to call for renewed efforts to upgrade banking education. He was convinced that the industry should be led by example and he now suggested a new

King's College, London.

GILBART LECTURES.
1879.

1. How do you appreciate the different degrees of risk incurred in discounting Commercial Bills, the result of different operations of Trade, and on what portion of the rate of discount charged, will such difference act?

2. What is the difference in the security offered by a Share, a Bond, or a Debenture, in a Railway Company?

3. What sciences are respectively required for the professions of an Actuary and Accountant?

4. What is the difference between the power of a particular and a general agent? Is a Director of a Banking Company a general or a particular agent?

5. In what cases does a Banker act as agent in relation to his customers?

6. What are the reasons in favour. or against Limited Liability in Banking?

7. What is the difference between paying money, in deposit, or in open account, to a Banker, and entrusting securities in his hands for safe keeping, in so far as concerns the power of the Banker over the same?

8. Who is a Contributory in the winding up of a Joint Stock Company?

9. What are the principal requirements of a good Audit of accounts?

10. On what ground are Trustees made Contributories to the City of Glasgow bank, and personally liable apart from the trust estate?

Figure 10 *Apart from interruptions during the two world wars, the Gilbart Lectures have been given each year since 1872. Examinations in connection with the lectures were offered from 1875. This examination paper of 1879 includes topical questions on limited liability in banking and the consequences of the City of Glasgow Bank failure.*

scheme for teaching the principles and practice of banking. In November 1856 he wrote to nine of the principal literary and scientific institutions in London inviting them to establish their own programme of lectures on banking. Any society which announced a course of banking lectures before March 1857 would receive a donation of ten guineas, in return for twenty free tickets to the lectures for distribution 'among the clerks of the London and Westminster Bank or other persons engaged in banking'. In response the organizers of the Young Men's Evening Classes arranged for a programme of six lectures on the principles of banking by Leone Levi, who had now become Professor of the Principles and Practice of Commerce at King's College London. The Society of Arts subsequently gave its support to this venture. A similar course, with Professor Levi as lecturer, was announced by the Islington Library and Scientific Society in January 1857.[26]

Leone Levi was well suited to the task of developing and publicizing the study of banking. In 1853 he had given the first of a series of invitation lectures on commercial law at King's College London; the College had planned to offer a course on 'mercantile instruction' as early as 1832, but it was not until Leone Levi's first appearance at the College* that commercial law became part of the curriculum.[27] These lectures, and his lectures to the Young Men's Evening Classes under the chairmanship of the Lord Mayor of London, drew large audiences of 'bankers, shipowners, general merchants, underwriters, commission agents and clerks'.[28] James Gilbart, impressed with Leone Levi's teaching, was keen that the lectures should become a regular part of the bankers' curriculum; although Gilbart himself died in 1863,[29] under the terms of his will his trustees founded a lectureship in banking at King's College. After long negotiations between the trustees and the College, the first series of four 'Gilbart Lectures on Banking' was given by Leone Levi in 1872. These evening lectures were open to the public and to the College's students of commerce, and from 1875 those attending the course could enter for competitive examinations.

* Levi was not appointed to the teaching staff of King's College until 1855. On his arrival from Italy and after naturalization as a British subject, Levi had joined the Free Church of Scotland but, in accordance with the rules of King's College, he was not officially a member of the College until he became an Anglican. Levi held the Professorship of the Principles and Practice of Commerce from 1855 until his death in 1888.

Figure 11 *Leone Levi, who was appointed Professor of the Principles and Practice of Commerce at King's College London in 1855, consistently advocated the extension of banking education. His contributions included lectures to the Banking Institute in 1853 and to the Institute of Bankers in Scotland in 1879–80. Leone Levi held the Gilbart Lectureship in Banking at King's College from its inception in 1872 until his death in 1888.*

The lectures were a rare opportunity to study topics which were of both practical and theoretical value, and the choice of subjects reflected this range of interests. Leone Levi's 1872–3 lectures, for instance, included papers on Scottish banking, foreign exchange rates, and the law of guarantee. By 1877 the course attendance already exceeded 100 and the lectures rapidly became an influential and prestigious contribution to banking education. Apart from interruptions during the First and Second World Wars the Gilbart Lectures have been presented every year since 1872.[30]

By including examinations which were open to bankers as well as to students of commerce, the Gilbart Lectures were an early example of voluntary, self-improving education among the professions—in contrast to compulsory entry requirements. They were also introduced at a time when university extension courses were becoming accepted as a serious contribution to adult education. The idea of extension courses had been devised between 1867 and 1873 by a Cambridge don, James Stuart, and the University of Cambridge had appointed a syndicate to organize formal courses throughout the country from 1873. A similar programme was opened by the University of Oxford in 1878.[31] In London, from 1876 onwards, university extension courses were supervised by the London Society; the syllabus included political economy, constitutional history, and philosophy. The Society had been formed in 1875 with the purpose of extending 'university teaching in the metropolis in as close a connection with the universities of Oxford, Cambridge and London as may be possible'.* The Society and its lectures were open to all comers on payment of a nominal subscription, and voluntary examinations were set at the end of each course. By the autumn of 1879 the attendance at London Society courses already exceeded 1,200.[32]

These developments, alongside the Gilbart Lectures and other sponsored courses for professional people, were a sign of increasing public interest in voluntary education and voluntary qualifications. Nevertheless, the Gilbart Lectures needed coordinated support from the banking community. They could not become fully effective until banking education as a whole was put on a more systematic basis. Unlike the voluntary examinations set by the Royal Institute of British Architects since 1863, the Gilbart Lecture examinations were not linked to qualifications of a professional association.[33] In addition, although some of the London banks contributed to a prize fund for the

---

* The first Secretary of the Society was Walter Leaf, a prominent classical scholar, subsequently Chairman of the Westminster Bank and President of The Institute of Bankers between 1919 and 1921 (see also p. 96).

examinations, there was no guarantee that students of the lectures would be given special recognition or advancement by their employers. There was also a problem of access to the lectures; in the 1870s it was impracticable for country banking officials to attend the courses.[34]

During the 1860s the principle of professional examinations, which would be open to bank staff throughout the country and recognized by all the banks, emerged as the platform for demands for the formation of a professional institute. With another period of expansion in the industry already under way, this preoccupation was closely bound up with the question of the economic and social status of bank employees. In 1862, for example, plans for an Incorporation of Bankers were announced by W. H. Logan, a banker from Berwick-upon-Tweed.* The long-term aims of the association, Logan claimed, were to 'confer a status upon the profession' and to give shareholders and depositors confidence in the management of the bank. Logan sought a Royal Charter for his incorporation and proposed that membership should be restricted to 'those who for five years and upwards have pursued the business of bankers in the United Kingdom, whether as managers, agents, clerks, or on their own private account'.[35] Within these limits, under the supervision of local committees and local secretaries, Logan envisaged courses on the principles of banking and a set of qualifying examinations. Successful candidates would be awarded a certificate of competency which would 'stamp the holder as a man of merit, and stimulate him to achieve a higher position'.[36]

Logan's initiative was widely applauded in the banking press. For bank employees, although there was no question of applying for 'a licence to practise', it was a chance to give their profession the status already enjoyed by members of the oldest qualifying associations. In England and Wales by 1862 only the surgeons, lawyers, pharmacists, veterinary surgeons, and actuaries could obtain professional qualifications by examination; the distinction of a Royal Charter was similarly rare, with only seven professional associations holding a Charter in 1862.[37] From the banks' point of view the advantages of the plan included the education and examination of their officials on general

---

* W. H. Logan was managing partner in the Scottish Border Bank of Berwick-upon-Tweed, which had been founded in 1857. The bank was wound up in the 1860s. Logan was also connected with the London Bank of Scotland, which was formed in 1863 and wound up in 1864.

and banking topics. The examination results 'would draw a line of demarcation between the clerk who aspired to the first rank of his profession, and the one who had no ambition beyond obtaining the bare means of subsistence'.[38] Despite these promises of goodwill, the opportunity was allowed to slip. Logan himself was reticent about the ways and means of launching the incorporation and it is doubtful whether he would have been able to call upon influential support in London. He was still working on the proposal as late as 1871 but there is no record of formal meetings, examinations, or any other activities of the proposed incorporation. When the Managing Director of the Bank of New Zealand asked for news of the incorporation in February 1872, for example, the Editor of *The Bankers' Magazine* admitted that 'we have no certain information on the subject'.[39]

The search for leadership and standardization in banking education, which was a guiding influence in the formation of the Gilbart Lectureship and in the abortive attempt to establish the Incorporation of Bankers, was instrumental in the development of the banking profession in Scotland. In contrast to the banking community south of the border, there was already a strong literary and debating society tradition in the Scottish banks. Since 1863 the Scottish Bankers' Literary Association had brought together a voluntary membership for 'the consideration of banking and literary subjects, by means of essays and debates, or otherwise'.[40] By 1874 members of the Association were admitting that the incentive of qualifying examinations was needed before banking education could be significantly reformed. Andrew Kerr, Secretary and Treasurer of the Association, argued that 'some systematic action should be taken for the better training of young bankers by the institution of classes and lectureships with examinations, in connection with which certificates of merit should be awarded'.[41]

Kerr's proposal, which was published in May 1874, soon bore fruit. A provisional committee of the Association, with the concurrence of the Scottish banks and representatives of banking staff, recommended the setting up of an independent association to organize qualifying examinations.[42] The recommendation was quickly accepted at meetings of bank staff in Edinburgh and Glasgow, and on 6 July 1875 the Institute of Bankers in Scotland was formally established 'to improve the qualifications of those engaged in banking and to raise their status and influence'.[43] With its headquarters in Edinburgh, the new Institute was governed by a council of senior Scottish bankers and financed by members' subscriptions and a small subsidy from the Scottish banks. Within a few months the Institute had organized courses of lectures and classes, with contributions by leading economists and lawyers at the universities of Edinburgh and Glasgow. The Institute's own examinations for admission to membership were inaugurated in the spring of 1876, when the total number of members and Associates had already reached about 600; of this total, over half were regularly attending the courses of lectures. Libraries and reading rooms were opened in both Edinburgh and Glasgow before June 1876.[44]

The formidable progress of the Scottish Institute in its first year was closely watched by banking men of England, Wales, and Ireland. J. Lindsay Reid, of the London merchant house of J. A. Forbes and Co., was consulting Andrew Kerr about the plans of the new Institute as early as August and September 1875, and Kerr declared that he would 'be glad to hear that a similar movement is going on in London and shall have great pleasure in giving you any further information'.[45] The Irish bankers were offered similar support: Kerr assured R. Farquharson of the Munster Bank in Dublin that the Scottish Institute would 'rejoice to see the formation of an Irish sister institution'.[46]

Prompted by the success of the Gilbart Lectures and the formation of the Institute of Bankers in Scotland, Lindsay Reid began to investigate ways of introducing a banking qualification in England and Wales. Early in 1876, for example, he was considering a scheme for introducing examinations under the control of the Society of Arts; on Andrew Kerr's advice he also sought the help of William Newmarch, who 'is much interested in this movement'.[47] *The Bankers' Magazine*, in the meantime, reported the activities of the Scottish Institute in detail, and by 1877 it was urging London's prominent bankers to open an institute. Impressed by the high attendance at the Gilbart Lectures, the Magazine saw 'signs of an increasing desire amongst bank employees to avail themselves of opportunities for education'.[48] The major obstacle to the formation of a new institute was the magnitude of the banking community. Even in London a single institute might not be able to cater for such a large and dispersed work-force. This worry was shared by *The Bankers' Magazine*'s readers outside London.

[39]

G. Lawson Brown of Sheffield agreed that a qualifying association for bankers was badly needed, but felt that the banks themselves should take on the responsibility of providing bank employees' education at local level. Each bank, Lawson Brown argued, could 'do something for their [clerks'] intellectual welfare' by providing a library and by inviting outside lecturers to present courses on banking law. Alternatively, as another reader suggested in September 1877, banking education could be extended throughout England and Wales by repeating the Gilbart Lectures and examinations in the major provincial cities.[49]

In spite of these anxieties, the new campaign for a banking institute brought encouraging results during 1877 and the early part of 1878. Readers of *The Bankers' Magazine*, in contrast to their predecessors in 1850 and 1851, were more or less unanimous in their approval of the plan. Above all they sought a recognized banking qualification which could be linked to career prospects in the industry. 'Unitas Vis', writing to the Magazine in December 1877,[50] selected three main advantages of a qualifying association:

I. That it would raise their social position in the estimation of the public, by making education one of the necessary elements of success.

II. That it would afford the means of bringing to the notice of employers of clerks' labour, men who, having proved themselves masters of routine duties, are competent to fill positions when that routine ceases and more intellectual work begins.

III. That private influence would thereby be diminished and merit would be more generally recognized.

'Unitas Vis', who explained that he was himself a bank clerk, was primarily interested in banking qualifications as a door to promotion and higher social status for bank employees. Like most of those who wrote to *The Bankers' Magazine* in favour of an institute, he saw himself as part of a 'grass roots' movement, speaking for thousands of bank clerks. As a corollary of this approach, supporters of the plan for an institute felt that the senior London bankers were dragging their feet in organizing a banking association. J. M. Sutherland, writing from the Isle of Man Banking Company in July 1877, was 'at a loss' to understand why an institute had not been formed in London.[51] 'Unitas Vis' was also critical of bankers in the capital:

> Those holding the most important positions in banking here
> ... have as yet come forward with no practical suggestions on
> the subject. Is it that they have not sufficient interest in the
> prospects of those they employ to give the matter their serious
> consideration? Or is it that they are not sufficiently impressed
> with the necessity for, or the benefits to be derived from, a
> higher standard of commercial education than is more generally
> to be met with in those employed in banking?[52]

These criticisms were largely justified. Although the London banks had participated in the foundation of the Gilbart Lectures, they did not seem inclined to follow the example of the Scottish banks in supporting the formation of the Institute of Bankers in Scotland. As in the 1850s the London and County Bank was an exception when it introduced examinations for its officials in February 1877; new recruits to the bank's clerical staff were examined in orthography, English composition, and arithmetic, with options in algebra, geometry, French, German, and Latin.[53]

By the beginning of 1878, although the London banks were not ready to put their weight behind the movement, the objectives of the proposed institute were clear. *The Bankers' Magazine* summarized these aims in a circular to the London banks in January 1878,[54] explaining that the supporters of the plan were ready to form a committee of management:

> Among the objects of the institute may be mentioned . . . that
> of collecting a library of works upon banking and commerce, to
> be available to all members of the institute; also to have courses
> of lectures delivered by men competent to treat of banking matters; and to organize a system of examinations upon certain
> specified subjects, which it is hoped would considerably influence the appointment of bank clerks to higher posts.

As the banks were reluctant to contribute to this debate, the responsibility for putting this scheme into practice rested clearly upon the shoulders of the bank officials themselves. With this in mind, Lindsay Reid began to canvas support amongst the students attending

Figure 12 *The support of Richard Martin, MP, senior partner in the firm of Martin and Co., was an influential factor in the formation of The Institute of Bankers. In addition to his term as President between 1883 and 1885, Richard Martin served as Treasurer of the Institute between 1879 and 1883 and between 1897 and 1916. The treasurership has remained with officials of Martins Bank (now part of Barclays Bank) throughout its history. In this photograph Richard Martin (second left) was joined by his partners Frederick Norman (left), John Martin (second from right) and Edward Norman (right).*

the Gilbart Lectures. Sensing that the employees of the London banks would be vital to the membership of a new institute, Lindsay Reid sought the cooperation of Leone Levi at King's College London. Levi, whose Gilbart Lectures were already attracting an attendance of 500 each year, agreed to help. 'I am very glad to learn that Professor Levi has taken up the institute movement', Andrew Kerr wrote to Lindsay Reid in February 1878, 'and am sure that no one is more able to do justice to the question'.[55]

The alliance between Lindsay Reid and Levi soon proved its worth when, in March 1878, Levi's students at the Gilbart Lectures met to discuss the ways and means of launching an institute. Like the readers of *The Bankers' Magazine* they stressed the importance of a library, courses of lectures, and qualifying examinations, but they were not prepared to delay while the London banks decided whether to endorse the proposals. As a first step it was 'highly necessary to secure the concurrence in this project of as many bank clerks as possible'. The meeting agreed that if the bank officials gave their concerted approval, then the London banks would soon be convinced of the value of the institute. Those bankers who were prepared to support the plan were invited to write to Lindsay Reid or John H. Butt (of the Australian Joint Stock Bank, London). By May 1878, on the basis of enthusiastic encouragement from bank officials, Lindsay Reid and John Butt were able to circulate a draft constitution for the institute.[56]

As Levi's students had predicted, a number of senior London bankers were now impressed by the seriousness of the proposals. Lindsay Reid and John Butt were particularly encouraged by the interest shown by Richard Martin, a partner in Martin and Co.; Herbert Tritton, a partner in Barclay, Bevan, Tritton & Co.; and Henry Billinghurst, Country Manager of the London and Westminster Bank. With this influential endorsement, Butt and Reid convened an open meeting of bankers at the London Institution on 29 May 1878 under the chairmanship of Richard Martin. The meeting was unanimous in its approval of the foundation of an institute, and the delegates were impressed by the efforts that were being made to bring the officials of all types of banks (including foreign and colonial banks) into the membership.[57] This breadth of representation was reflected in the composition of the executive committee which the meeting elected to supervise the launch of the institute.*

The participation of Martin, Tritton, and the other prominent members of the banking community gave the proposed institute a valuable measure of prestige and influence. Nevertheless, almost as

* The executive committee comprised Henry Billinghurst; Hammond Chubb, Secretary of the Bank of England; Henry Ely of the Provincial Bank of Ireland; Robert Fowler, a partner in Dimsdale, Fowler and Co.; William Howard of the London and County Bank; A. G. Kennedy of the City Bank; Richard Martin; W. C. Mullins of the Chartered Bank of India, Australia and China; Inglis Palgrave, for the Association of English Country Bankers; Frederick Price of Childs Bank; D. T. Robertson, General Manager of the Chartered Mercantile Bank of India, London and China; L. G. Robertson of the National Provincial Bank; T. G. Robinson of the National Provincial Bank of England; Robert Slater of the Union Bank of London; and Herbert Tritton.

soon as Richard Martin was introduced to the movement, its objectives were re-examined. Martin was anxious that the constitution should not be dominated by the notion of qualifying examinations to the exclusion of lectures and discussions on the theoretical and technical aspects of the banking profession. He wished to see the new institute giving leadership over the whole range of banking studies. 'The first and most important part of the proposed institute', he told the meeting on 29 May, was

> to attach to the institute all those gentlemen who, whether as private bankers or heads of departments of joint stock or colonial banks, see the necessity of having a common place of meeting and a common medium of communication. It has, as you are aware, been thought advisable to do this in several other professions, such as the architects and actuaries and others, and I believe by whatever name they may be known, they proved to be very successful, and have done a great deal for the cohesion of the professions they represent.[58]

This approach, Martin argued, gave a positive role to 'the leaders of the profession' in the affairs of the institute, and at the meeting on 29 May his views were warmly endorsed by Tritton, Billinghurst, and the other senior bankers who were present. Martin also made it clear that the cooperation of the members of the new executive committee was based upon this wider interpretation of the institute's work. 'If you do not keep your eyes on what the newspapers insert concerning the proposed institute', he warned Lindsay Reid and John Butt on 31 May, 'we shall be in a difficulty. The first paragraph in the notice contained in the *Standard* of this day would lead the public to consider that the proposed institute is intended to be merely educational and in that case, few of the gentlemen whose names have been provisionally obtained for the committee would care to act'.[59]

This significant shift in emphasis in the aims of the institute and the increasingly important role of senior banking men did not mean that the campaign for a proper system of qualifying examinations was being abandoned. Richard Martin, well aware of the strength of feeling amongst the bank clerks, appreciated that a professional association would not win industry-wide approval without the incentive of qualifications for bank employees. 'The proposed institute', he reminded well-wishers, 'would enable those who pass such examinations to be known by their more or less distinguished abilities, and would at once give them a position within the circle of the profession'.[60]

This insistence upon qualification by examination kept open the prospects for a broadly based membership for the new association. In Ireland the promoters of a similar institute were not so fortunate. News of the meetings in London had soon reached Dublin, and in June 1878 an assembly of Irish bank officials agreed to form an institute on the model suggested by the constitution which had been drafted by Lindsay Reid and John Butt.[61] An Institute of Bankers in Ireland was duly established on 16 November 1878, but, in the interval since June, the question of qualifications had been forgotten. The new society was to open a reading room and hold lectures and courses but not examinations; it would 'increase the intelligence and improve the position of those engaged in banks . . . and establish a community of feeling. The Institute would be an invaluable blessing, if it could be so attractive to the younger officials as to induce them to avail of its advantages, instead of resorting to questionable places of amusement'.[62] Sadly, without the additional offer of a qualifying certificate, these aims were not fulfilled and in March 1879 the secretaries of the Irish Institute announced its closure. The lack of widespread support had made it impossible to continue, to the bitter regret of the Editor of *The Irish Banker*: 'The spirit of the dream has been changed. Energy has become apathy; zeal indifference; and the smiles and open arms have been transformed into frowns and shoulder-shruggings.'[63] After this setback, the successful birth of an independent Irish institute was to be delayed for another twenty years (see p. 85).

In London the executive committee stood by the commitment to professional education and examination which had been agreed upon at the London Institution in May 1878. Work on the examination syllabus began in earnest during June and July. Inglis Palgrave, as a member of the committee, obtained valuable guidance on the examinations of the Scottish Institute from Andrew Kerr, but Kerr warned that the first two or three years would be 'uphill work'. Kerr also suggested that cooperation between London and country banks and between private and joint stock banks would not be easy to achieve, and that the promoters of the institute 'should not be discouraged by obstacles thrown in their way by jealousy and indifference. Persistence will carry them through.'[64] The committee stuck to its task, and at the end of November Lindsay Reid and John Butt circulated copies of the revised constitution.[65]

The plans for the work and government of the institute were virtually complete. The revised constitution confirmed that the institute would organize lectures, discuss and publish approved papers, open a library, and issue certificates to successful candidates in the institute's examinations. Control of the institute would be vested in a president, vice-president, treasurer, and council to be elected by the membership. The membership itself was to include fellows and honorary fellows elected by the council, associates who had served at least ten years in banking or who had passed the examinations of the institute or a recognized university, and members who were on the staff of any banking concern. (The Scottish Institute, in contrast, had been formed for members and associates, both categories being admitted by examination.) Subscriptions, the committee proposed, should be set at two guineas for fellows, one guinea for associates, and five shillings for members.[66]

The response to the circular was encouraging, and by the beginning of 1879 large numbers of bankers in London and the provinces had volunteered their assistance. Confidence in the proposed institute was strengthened by the news that Sir John Lubbock had been invited to become the first president; Lubbock's name had been mentioned as early as May 1878, and the executive committee had canvassed his support during the autumn.[67] It was a shrewd choice of leader. Lubbock, a partner in the firm of Robarts, Lubbock and Co., had served as Secretary of the Committee of London Clearing Bankers since 1863, while as a Member of Parliament he had sponsored the highly popular Bank Holidays Act of 1871.[68] The invitation was readily accepted, and during February 1879 the executive committee arranged for an inaugural meeting at the London Institution in March 1879. The meeting was publicized in all the major newspapers and financial journals.[69]

The inaugural meeting of The Institute of Bankers on 11 March 1879, as Richard Martin noted simply in his diary, was 'a success'.[70] This was partly the outcome of careful preparation in the previous twelve months, but it was also the culmination of some thirty years of effort and experiment in bringing together an association for professional bankers. It was clear, moreover, that the long campaign had now created a solid basis for membership; as Martin pointed out from the chair of the meeting, over 1,000 names had been proposed as members before the formation of the new Institute. The depth of support was also a mark of strength, and Martin and his colleagues recognized that there was no good reason why 'a hard-and-fast line should be drawn as to bankers and bankers' clerks'.[71] Consequently the election of Sir John Lubbock as President, and the election of the vice-presidents and Council members, was designed to represent as many categories of banks and bankers as possible; the appointment of John Butt, Lindsay Reid and Luke Hansard (an official of Martin and Co.) as Honorary Secretaries ensured that the continuity of planning and administration was preserved.* Martin himself insisted that the new association would 'not exclude any person who took an interest in [the] proceedings', and he was confident that 'we shall receive a great accession of members before we have been at work very long'. With this promise, as soon as the election of the honorary officers was completed, The Institute of Bankers was formally established.[72]

The evolution of the objectives and constitution of The Institute of Bankers, especially during the 1870s, had been sustained largely by the bank officials' requests for some form of qualification by examination. This ingredient, which had been missing from the plans of many professional groups up to and including the 1850s, was becoming accepted both by employers and employees as a means of winning recognition and status for a profession during the third quarter of the nineteenth century. In some cases examinations were devised as a control over entry to a career or profession. The Civil Service, for example, based its recruitment on competitive examinations from 1855 onwards. In other cases, including the Institute of Actuaries after

---

* The first Vice-Presidents were William Beckett Denison, MP, of Beckett and Co., Leeds; Donald Larnach, Bank of New South Wales; Sampson Lloyd, MP, Alliance Bank; Sir Andrew Lusk, MP, Imperial Bank; George Rae, North and South Wales Bank; Thomas Salt, MP, Lloyds Bank; and Sir Sydney Waterlow, MP, Union Bank of London. The Council membership duplicated that of the executive committee with the exception of L. G. Robertson and with the addition of Howard Gwyther, Chartered Bank of India, Australia and China; G. H. Hopkinson, Hopkinson and Sons; Charles Praed, MP, Praed and Co.; Frederick Seebohm, Sharples and Co.; A. Strickland, Hoare and Co.; and Robert Williams, Williams Deacon and Co.

[47]

1850 and the Institute of Accountants from 1871, post-entry examinations were accepted as an essential part of membership of a professional body but without giving their members monopoly of practice.[73] The founders of The Institute of Bankers also envisaged examinations as qualifications at the professional level. Leone Levi, who had contributed so much to the teaching and examination of banking studies in this period, saw the new Institute of Bankers as a similar opportunity to recognize merit throughout the banking community. In a searching review of the prospects for the new association, Professor Levi reminded his students of the value of qualifications: 'At this moment, what a field lies before you . . . surely the Banking Institute will be able to exercise a powerful education influence among the many bright and talented youths still comparatively unknown in the profession, but ready to appear with minds equipped and hands prepared for any competition where real merit may have a chance'.[74]

3

PROFESSIONAL INSTITUTE
OR PRESSURE GROUP?
1879–1895

AFTER years of discussion and planning, The Institute of Bankers began its life at a time of sudden turbulence and depression in British banking. Early in October 1878 the financial world was shaken by the news that the City of Glasgow Bank had suspended payment; with its 133 branch offices in the West of Scotland and deposits of over £8 million, the company's total liabilities placed it as the fourth largest bank in Scotland. A prompt investigation of its affairs by nominees of the major creditors made it clear that the bank, which had been formed in 1839 on joint stock principles with unlimited liability, was the victim of a major cumulative fraud by the directors and manager. The City of Glasgow Bank's balance sheet, weakened by the failure of the Western Bank of Scotland in 1857, had been systematically falsified since the 1860s to disguise the effects of lending to highly speculative concerns in the United States of America and in New Zealand. The bank's luckless shareholders were faced with a charge of up to £2,750 per share to meet a total loss of over £6 million, and, after a long and bitter criminal trial early in 1879, the guilty directors and manager were sentenced to imprisonment for terms of between eight and eighteen months.[1]

Although the other Scottish banks were able to repair some of the damage by accepting the notes issued by the City of Glasgow Bank, the collapse dealt a heavy blow to public confidence in the British banking system. News of the failure hastened the demise of other banks which had been weakened by the downturn in the economy in the late 1870s, and within a few weeks Fenton and Sons of Heywood and Rochdale, Lancashire, and the Caledonian Banking Co., Inverness, had suspended payment. The West of England and South Wales District Bank followed them into liquidation in the same month after the discovery of losses of over £1.2 million.* A total of £23.8 million was wiped off the value of United Kingdom bank shares between September and December 1878, representing a fall of some 13.5 per cent of their aggregate market value of £174.5 million; Scottish bank shares were particularly hard hit, declining by roughly 30 per cent from a market value of £28.9 million in September to £19.7 million in December.[2] The unease shown by investors was shared by customers, and the banks saw a sharp fall in the level of their deposits in the immediate aftermath of the failure. In the first week of December alone the Bank of England's deposits fell by about £1.2 million when many country banks called in cash resources from London to guard against a run on their branch offices.[3]

The rapid decline in the level of deposits and bank share values after the City of Glasgow Bank failure left the banks and their employees in no doubt that fundamental reforms in banking business were required before confidence would return. Amongst bank customers, and on the London and provincial stock exchanges, the story of the failure raised questions about the competence and judgement of officials throughout the banking system. In the case of the joint stock banks, these questions were linked to a widespread conviction that shareholders in banks with unlimited liability were entirely unprotected. As one irate shareholder wrote to George Rae, Chairman of the North and South Wales Bank, 'the securities and advances should be scrutinized by the most experienced and honest auditor. . . . It is [to be] hoped the Bank's funds have not been employed on the Stock Exchange.'[4]

The shareholders and depositors were not the only losers. The collapse of confidence was a chilly warning to bank employees of the

---

* Fenton and Sons, established in 1819, failed with losses estimated at £600,000. The Caledonian Banking Co. had been formed in 1833, and its collapse was attributed largely to its liability on shares in the City of Glasgow Bank; the Caledonian Bank eventually reopened in August 1879. The West of England Bank, launched in 1834, held £4.5 million in deposits at the time of its liquidation.

insecurity of some banking appointments. Clerks of the West of England Bank, through no fault of their own, found it difficult or impossible to obtain appointments with other banks after the sudden closure of the bank's head office and 49 branch offices. In February 1880, for example, a group of the bank's employees wrote to *The Bankers' Magazine* to explain that since the suspension in December they had been 'retained by the Official Liquidators, subject to one month's notice to terminate the engagement. [They] will very shortly be thrown out of employment . . . and none can hope to be much longer retained.'[5]

The crisis diverted senior bankers' attention from the practical work of organizing and publicizing the Institute, but the turmoil and nervousness within the banking community in the late 1870s may have improved the long-term prospects for the new venture. Although the launching of the Institute had been agreed upon well before the failure of the City of Glasgow Bank, its formation in March 1879 was announced at a moment when the directors and managers of the banks were seeking reform and reorganization of the banking system. If the banks were to restore both their own confidence and the confidence of their depositors and shareholders, the technical and educational leadership of a professional institute would be a valuable, and perhaps an essential, new asset. From the point of view of the bank officials, in a period of renewed uncertainty over appointments, here was a chance to obtain a professional recognition which would win security and promotion. Professor Leone Levi of King's College London, in the Gilbart Lectures in 1879, emphasized these special reasons for joining the Institute:

> The Institute of Bankers will be most beneficial in that it will bring together men connected with the various classes of banks, for the discussion and ventilation of questions which from time to time arise, and which are at present in a more or less unsettled state; and also that bankers themselves, and heads of departments, may thereby have a common place of meeting, and a common means of communication.[6]

In these 'unsettled' business conditions, bankers and their officials quickly gave their backing to the Institute. The initial membership returns were impressive, rising from about 1,000 names on 11

March 1879 to 1,300 at the first general meeting in May 1879, increasing to 1,800 in June 1879 and about 2,000 by the end of the
year.[7] Applicants were drawn from banks throughout the country
(including Scotland and Ireland), and with explicit encouragement
from the Council of the Institute this number included officials from
the foreign and colonial banks and a small number of representatives
of the merchant houses. Overall, the London-based banks contributed
1,153 members when the first registration list was compiled in June
1879, with the remaining 752 members coming from the country
banks.* Of this membership 241 were elected Fellows by the Council
and 397 were eligible as Associates on the basis of at least ten years'
employment in a bank or by entering the Institute as graduates of a
British university; in future members who passed the Institute's
Associateship examinations would also be eligible for election as
Fellows or Associates. The remaining 66 per cent of the membership
was made up by the ordinary members, who were permitted to join
the Institute if they were 'on the staff of any banking establishment'.[8]
This participation from different sections of the banking community
compared well with the experience of other professional bankers'
associations. The Institute of Bankers in Scotland, after attracting a
total membership of 925 by 1878, was suffering a depletion of its
support by 1880. Although the Scottish Institute drew upon a banking
population no larger than about 6,000 (in comparison with upwards of
20,000 bank employees in England and Wales), senior Scottish
bankers were worried by a downward trend in membership which
continued into the 1880s.[9] Similarly the early expansion of The
Institute of Bankers was encouraging when contrasted with the
membership growth of the American Bankers' Association. That
Association had been launched to represent both banks and their
officials in July 1875, but the number of its subscribers did not exceed
1,500 until 1878.[10]

* The largest contingents were drawn from the metropolitan offices of the Union
Bank of London (130 members), the London and Westminster Bank (127), and
the London and County Bank (122). One hundred and fifty-four members were
officials of foreign and colonial banks, with strong representation from the
Chartered Mercantile Bank of India, London and China (31) and the Standard
Bank of British South Africa (20). Of the country banks, the out-of-London
branches of the National Provincial Bank (138 members) and the London and
County Bank (56) were followed by Gurney and Co. (33) and the Capital and
Counties Bank (32).

The new Institute's membership, bringing in total subscriptions of £1,365 by June 1880, enabled the Council to finance the activities which had been outlined in the prospectus and constitution of 1878. In March 1879 the Council appointed George Dayrell Reed, formerly of the Bank of England, as full-time Secretary, and in mid-April as office was opened at 11 and 12 Clements Lane, London (the headquarters of the Bankers' Guarantee and Trust Fund). The Institute's lectures, which Richard Martin, a managing partner in Martin and Co., had advocated so strenuously at the preliminary meetings, were successfully launched in June 1879 with papers by Sir John Lubbock, the first President of the Institute, and Inglis Palgrave, Editor of *The Economist* A full programme of lectures was promised for the following winter season.[11] In the meantime, as planned in the Institute's constitution, a library was opened at the Clements Lane offices and an appeal for donations of books was issued to members in June. A collection of basic reference books was brought together during the next few months, supplemented by duplicates purchased for circulation to country members; to make room for further expansion, the collection was rehoused at the London Institution in Finsbury Circus in November 1879.[12] The Council of the new Institute also turned their attention to the foundation of an annual prize fund for essays by members. Supervised and judged by Inglis Palgrave, Hammond Chubb (Secretary of the Bank of England), Herbert Tritton (partner in Barclay, Bevan, Tritton and Co.), and Robert Slater of the Union Bank of London, the first of the competitions attracted nineteen well-researched entries. The £20 prize, awarded to R. W. Barnett of Glyn and Co. for an essay on 'The Progress and Development of Banking', was the first of the many competition prizes to be administered by The Institute of Bankers.[13]

As the counterpart of these efforts to improve facilities and incentives for the study of banking, the Institute pressed forward with plans to provide legal and technical advice to its members. Following the example of other professional associations, including the Royal Institute of British Architects with its Proceedings (first published in 1835) and the Institute of Actuaries with its Journal (from 1851), the Council of the Institute agreed that the far-flung membership needed its own journal for the circulation of lecture papers, for the advertisement of lectures and examinations, and for an advisory service to bankers.

Remarkably, Dayrell Reed as first Editor was able to publish the opening issue of the *Journal of The Institute of Bankers* at the beginning of June 1879. This issue, with 56 pages mainly devoted to a transcription of Sir John Lubbock's inaugural address, was soon followed by a special edition for the first membership list. Under the distinguished editorship of Hammond Chubb between November 1879 and April 1884, the monthly appearance of the *Journal* made it possible to publish questions and answers on points of practical interest to members.[14]

In the early issues of the *Journal*, at Institute meetings, and in correspondence with the membership, the responsibility for giving practical advice ultimately rested with members of the Council. Henry Billinghurst, Country Manager of the London and Wesminster Bank, took the lead in this work, but on the suggestion of Herbert Tritton the London firm of Jansen, Cobb and Pearson, solicitors, was retained by the Institute for answering the more difficult legal questions.[15] Almost from the outset of the Institute's history, this combination of expertise was able to deal with problems ranging from the comparison of procedures for cheque payments to the legal definition of the status of notarial documents. As a natural extension of this advisory service, the Council urged the banks themselves to standardize their rules for documentation. In December 1879, for example, Dayrell Reed was instructed to write to the English and Irish banks recommending uniformity in dealing with the endorsement of cheques; the recommendation was accepted in 1881 when the Irish banks decided to follow the example of London banks.[16]

The Institute of Bankers owed much of its original support, especially amongst the ordinary members, to the promise of a qualifying examination in banking. The promise was kept, but not before misunderstandings over the purpose and management of examinations were overcome. In July 1879 the Council was divided on the question of whether the proposed examinations should be general and literary in scope or specifically linked to banking skills. The President, Sir John Lubbock, together with Luke Hansard, one of the Honorary Secretaries, preferred that the examinations should be kept as broad as possible. In their view, the syllabus should insist upon algebra, arithmetic, English language, geography, and modern languages, as well as book-keeping, political economy, banking and finance. Henry Billinghurst, in contrast, persuaded Richard Martin, Herbert Tritton,

John Butt, Hammond Chubb, and Hilton Price that mercantile law, political economy, and banking and finance were more important requirements for a professional qualification. This difference between the academic and practical interpretation of the role of examinations was resolved, on this occasion, in favour of the Billinghurst scheme. At the end of July, Henry Billinghurst, Hammond Chubb, and Luke Hansard were appointed as a sub-committee to devise a syllabus for the first series of examinations.[17]

The Council's rejection of Sir John Lubbock's advice on examinations may have been influenced by doubts over the progress of the broad syllabus devised by the Institute of Bankers in Scotland. The Scottish Institute's examinations, inaugurated in the spring of 1876, were based upon a multiple syllabus of arts, science, and financial subjects, supplemented by joint lecture programmes at the Universities of Edinburgh and Glasgow. With its declared emphasis on 'self-culture', in the tradition established by the Scottish Bankers' Literary Association since 1863, this syllabus was clearly designed for as wide an education as possible. In its early years, however, the promoters of the Scottish Institute were disappointed by the small number of entries for the examinations; declining attendances also forced the Institute to abandon its special courses on political economy and law.[18] Equally worrying was the reluctance of the Scottish banks to come forward with any proper recognition of the examinations and membership of the Institute, and it was not until the late 1880s that the Scottish banks agreed to enter the results of the Institute examinations in their staff records.[19]

At the London headquarters of the new Institute of Bankers the Council shared this uncertainty about the attitude of the banks towards the proposed examinations. Although most of the London and country banks were represented amongst the membership, it was not clear whether success in the examinations would be given any formal recognition. John Butt, a staunch ally of the ordinary membership throughout the preliminary meetings, wondered whether 'the certificates obtained by those who pass these examinations will serve as recommendations in their subsequent promotion'.[20] It was a question which could not be put to the banks until the examinations were successfully launched, but the need to convince the banks of the value of the new qualifications encouraged the Council to stress the importance of practical banking in the examination. Consequently, when Henry Billinghurst, Hammond Chubb, and Luke Hansard presented their syllabus for the Council's approval in October 1879, it was a workman-like combination of papers in arithmetic and algebra, book-keeping, commercial law, political economy, and practical banking. The certificate of the Institute, admitting a member as an Associate, would be awarded to candidates who could pass both a preliminary and a final examination in each subject. Like the qualifying examinations of the Institute of Actuaries and the Pharmaceutical Society, the new syllabus would not allow candidates to sit the finals before passing all the preliminary examinations.[21]

It was vital to the ordinary members of the Institute and to bank officials throughout the country that the new examinations should be a serious test of professional competence. If the Institute's certificate was to impress the banks themselves and stand comparison with the qualifications of the other professions, it would need authentication from independent examiners; it was equally important that the syllabus should be based upon a depth and range of knowledge which was not offered elsewhere. By and large the publication of the certificate regulations, syllabus and reading lists in November 1879 met these requirements. Candidates for the preliminary paper on political economy, for instance, were expected to cover questions on the definitions of wealth, production, the division of labour, fixed and circulating capital, theories of market value, and the principles of currency. The equivalent final examination would include questions on international trade, the theory of foreign exchanges, the money market, and the history of banking systems. The papers on practical banking, which were unique to the Institute's syllabus, included questions ranging from the note issue in England, Scotland and Ireland to the problems of managing banking investments. Comprehensive reading lists were recommended for each subject, devised or approved by external examiners. Initially the panel of examiners comprised Stanley Jevons, Professor of Political Economy at University College London, and author of *The Theory of Political Economy* (1871), for the political economy syllabus; John Whitcher, a Fellow of the Institute of Actuaries and the Statistical Society, for arithmetic and algebra; J. J. Saffery, a council member of the Institute of Accountants, for book-keeping; and Mackenzie Chalmers for mercantile law. The choice of these examiners from specialist disciplines outside the world of banking ensured that examination standards would be kept high. The papers on practical banking were examined by members of the Council, as it was felt that technical questions should be set and marked by experienced bankers.[22]

Under this regime the Institute's first examinations were held in May 1880. Candidates, each paying an entry fee of 5s. 0d. (25p), sat the evening examinations either in London (at offices in King William Street) or in the provinces (under the individual supervision of Fellows of the Institute). A total of 46 members entered the preliminary examination, and of these 14 passed in all subjects and another 11 were partly successful. On this one occasion, when a special paper was set as a substitute for the final examination, 2* of the 8 candidates did well enough to become the first Associates.[23] This group of candidates had relied largely upon the reading lists for their preparation and revision, but 'in response to the considerable demand' the Institute arranged for special evening classes at selected colleges for the following year. In London, Birkbeck College, City of London College, King's College, and the Young Men's Christian Association were specifically recommended; outside London, the Birmingham and Midland Institute, the Liverpool Institute, Owen's College in Manchester, and University College, Bristol, agreed to offer courses.[24] Despite these new facilities the number of candidates for the 1881 examinations fell alarmingly to only 22, and only one candidate qualified as an Associate. The entry recovered to 34 in 1882, but in comparison with the Scottish Institute, where the number of examination candidates was 60 in 1882, it was a disappointing result for a carefully planned syllabus.[25] These returns were not the only setback for the Council. The essay competition, which had again been won by R. W. Barnett in 1881, attracted only one entry in 1882 and 1883. A more fundamental problem was the evidence of resignations from membership. The first year's intake of about 2,000 members was reduced to 1,804 in 1881 and 1,758 in 1882.[26]

The Council of the Institute, questioned about the decline in the membership between May 1880 and May 1881, attributed the resignations to the decision in May 1881 to raise the subscriptions of

* The first certificate holders were George Amphlett of the Bank of New Zealand, London, and Henry Sowdon of the Stourbridge and Kidderminster Banking Company, Moreton-in-Marsh branch.

ordinary members from 5s. 0d. (25p) to 10s. 6d. (52½p). The new scale of subscriptions had been designed to pay for the publication of the *Journal of The Institute of Bankers*, which was costing approximately 10s. 0d. (50p) per member each year in 1879–80. Even after this increase the Council was forced to accept advertisements in the *Journal* in order to continue monthly publication, and in June 1881 the Council considered an amalgamation of the *Journal* with *The Bankers' Magazine*; in the event, the suggestion was not taken up.[27] The Council also admitted that the Institute had not been able to offer a lecture programme based on the examination syllabus. This gap in the Institute's activities inevitably contributed to the reduction in membership, and the Council issued an urgent appeal for lecture papers on practical banking, political economy, and commercial law.[28]

Important as these factors were, the disappointing trends in membership and examination entries in the early 1880s reflected the Council's uncertainties in establishing and maintaining priorities for the Institute's commitments. The main difficulty, which revived all the questions about its objectives, was the role of the Institute in banking and company legislation. Should the Institute take an active part in lobbying for changes in the banking laws, and was the Institute to be responsible for coordinating the interests of the banks as well as bank officials? In the early years of the Institute, while the Council attempted to resolve this dilemma, the administration of the Institute's membership services and examinations was bound to be affected.

Although the founders of the Institute had envisaged it as a forum for bankers to discuss new issues in their profession, they had not offered to represent the banking industry as a whole. This responsibility belonged to the associations representing the banks themselves, including the London Clearing House (which had been established in about 1770) and the Association of English Country Bankers (founded in 1874). In practice, the new Institute could not ignore major new legislation affecting the banks between 1879 and 1881. The Companies Act of 1879, amending the 1858 legislation on the liability of shareholders in joint stock banks, was introduced too early for the Institute to take a direct part in its preparation. Nevertheless, at a special meeting after the President's inaugural address in May 1879, the Institute was urged to keep a close watch over the new legislation on behalf of the banking industry. 'Our legislation in regard to companies', Sir John Lubbock told the members, 'is in an unsatisfactory condition, having been made at a time when we did not properly understand the working of the unlimited liability principle. So far as that part of the Bill is concerned I therefore think that it deserves the greatest possible attention on our part.'[29] The new Act came into force in August 1879, removing some of the inadequacies in company law which had been brought to light by the City of Glasgow Bank failure. Many of its clauses were the work of leading figures in the joint stock banks. George Rae, Chairman of the North and South Wales Bank and one of the Institute's Vice-Presidents, was prominent in the negotiations with Sir Stafford Northcote, Chancellor of the Exchequer, which led to the Act's provisions for auditing the balance sheets of joint stock banks; he also devised the principle of reserved liability, primarily for adjusting the reserve funds of limited liability banks.[30] Impressed by the effect of bankers' influence on the new legislation, the Council of the Institute unhesitatingly offered to represent the banks in preparing for further banking legislation in 1880 and 1881. Of this legislation, the bankruptcy bill emerged as the Institute's most time-consuming commitment.

Despite a major codification of bankruptcy law in 1869,[31] the British economy had been weighed down by a heavy incidence of bad debts in the 1870s. The banks were especially alarmed by the increasing number of 'liquidations by arrangement' and 'compositions' between debtors and creditors. Under these agreements, debtors and their trustees often escaped judicial examination, with the result that creditors could not always be sure that the settlement of an insolvent's estate was either full or equitable. The reports of the Comptroller in Bankruptcy confirmed that debts in this category had multiplied from 3,651 cases in 1869 to 11,976 in 1879, when total liabilities under liquidations and compositions reached over £25.3 million.[32] A series of amendments to the 1869 Bankruptcy Act had been put before Parliament between 1876 and 1879 in an attempt to strengthen the supervision of insolvents' estates, but in each case a congested parliamentary timetable had forced the Government to withdraw the amendment bill.[33] At the news of the reintroduction of an amendment in the 1880 session, however, John Smith of the London and Yorkshire Bank, a Fellow of the Institute, urged the Council to petition Parliament on behalf of the banking community:

[59]

That every debtor unable to pay his debts shall . . . submit his books for investigation, and himself to examination under oath, as to his past dealings and conduct before he obtains his discharge. . . . That such discharge should not be confirmed . . . if it is proved to [the Court's] satisfaction that the debtor has been guilty of reckless, extravagant or culpable conduct, or has failed to keep and produce proper books and accounts in the same manner as is provided in the case of an adjudication in bankruptcy.[34]

Smith's suggestion was accepted, and in July 1880 the Council circulated copies of a paper on 'Bankruptcy in Reform' by T. R. Davison of the Swansea Bank to all members of the House of Commons Select Committee on Bankruptcy. In the Commons itself Sir John Lubbock and Richard Martin agreed to watch the progress of the new amendment, and in a direct approach to the Board of Trade the Council insisted that the amendment should give full recognition to the interests of creditors in liquidations and compositions.[35]

By mid-1880 the Institute had entered uncharted waters. Although the Institute's members included a number of Members of Parliament and although it had opened up contact with the Board of Trade, it could not be sure of the attitude of the banks. The Institute represented individual members and not their employers; here was a case where the Institute was acting directly in the interests of the banks. The Council, none the less, knew that there was no single body which could represent the points of view of the different sections of the banking industry. In an effort to clarify the position, the Council approached individual banks in the autumn of 1880 for their authorization to petition the Government. It soon emerged that the Association of English Country Bankers was preparing a similar petition.[36] The Association had originally been brought together in May 1874 'to oppose the encroachments of the Scotch Banks in England' (the Glasgow-based Clydesdale Bank had opened three branches in Cumberland earlier the same year), but this task was subsequently overtaken by the work of watching over the political and legislative interests of the private and joint stock country banks.[37] On the issue of bankruptcy reform, the Institute and the Association were in broad agreement, and in November 1880 they planned a joint deputation to the Prime Minister for the presentation of their petitions. The consultations with the Association enabled the Institute's Council to speak for all the London banks. It was a convincing role for the Institute, and by mid-December 54 joint stock and private banks, 24 merchant and discount houses, and 36 colonial and foreign banks had signed a draft petition circulated by Dayrell Reed.[38]

The petition followed the line originally suggested by John Smith in February, and its emphasis upon the examination of debtors and the use of the bankruptcy courts alone for the discharge of debtors was comparable with the views of the Law Society, the newly established Institute of Chartered Accountants, and the influential *Statist* magazine as well as the Association of English Country Bankers.[39] The joint deputation was received by the Lord Chancellor on 15 December 1880 and, as the amendment bill moved slowly through Parliament over the next few months, the Council was regularly consulted by the Board of Trade. Procedural delays again held back the bill, but in 1883 Sir John Lubbock himself was able to guide the revised bill through the Commons.[40] This attention to the bill, time consuming as it had been for the Institute, brought to bankruptcy law the close supervision and stability which the Council had been looking for, and the 1883 statute was not significantly altered until the passage of the Insolvency Act of 1976.

The campaign for bankruptcy reform was not the Council's only foray into negotiations over banking legislation in the early 1880s. Of all its early adventures, the Institute was particularly proud of its contribution to the framing of the Bills of Exchange Act, 1882. At Council meetings in the first two years after the Institute's formation close attention was paid to the efforts of law reform groups (notably the Association for Reform and Codification of the Law) to simplify and consolidate major sections of common law. The Council of the Institute was considering ways and means of supporting reform of the law of negotiable instruments as early as July 1879, and in December 1879 Mackenzie Chalmers, a leading barrister, was invited to address the Institute on the question of codifying the mass of legislation on bills of exchange.

The prospect of a consolidation of this legislation was of obvious importance to all practising bankers, and in March 1881 a plan for guiding the reform of the legislation through Parliament was jointly formulated by the Institute and the Association of Chambers of Commerce. The two bodies gave instructions to Mackenzie Chalmers to prepare a parliamentary bill, and the Institute's Council appointed Sir John Lubbock, Herbert Tritton, Robert Slater, and Henry Billinghurst to give editorial assistance. By July 1881 Chalmers had prepared a bill which summarized the legal effect of no less than 18 statutes and about 2,600 decided cases on the usage of bills of exchange, cheque payments, and other negotiable instruments. The bill was introduced to Parliament by Sir John Lubbock, the Institute's President, in the summer of 1881, and it eventually received the Royal Assent in August 1882. Known as the Bills of Exchange Act, 1882, it was a measure which Mackenzie Chalmers described as 'the first piece of codification that has safely reached the harbour of the statute book. . . . While professors of jurisprudence, and congresses of divers kinds have been discussing the possibility of codification and its theoretical aspects, the Institute has taken the matter practically in hand.'[41] With only one major amendment the Act was to dominate the law and practice of modern banking, and it quickly became part of the staple diet for the training of young bankers. Admittedly, the Act needed complex and often abstruse interpretation, but few pieces of business law have ever enjoyed such a long working life.

In a period of hectic parliamentary activity in the 1880s, the Council also lobbied the Postmaster-General in an effort to simplify the arrangements for the encashment of postal orders, and became closely associated with the London Chamber of Commerce in the revisions of the Factors' Acts between 1884 and 1888.[42] In these cases the Council appeared to be representing the banking community, and there was no obvious attempt to distinguish its responsibilities to individual members from its responsibilities to the banks.

Throughout the nineteenth century pressure groups representing the business community were an important factor in the management of new legislation. The railway interest, with large numbers of Members of Parliament voting in its favour, was perhaps the largest and most organized of these groups, but in the case of doctors, lawyers, and accountants, professional associations were also successful in influencing Parliament or Government.[43] The Institute of Bankers was in a different position. Whereas the railway companies represented nobody but themselves, the Institute appeared to be representing the

Figure 13 *George Rae was one of the outstanding bankers of the second half of the nineteenth century. Rae, Chairman of the North and South Wales Bank from 1873 until 1898 and author of* The Country Banker *(1885), was a Vice-President and Trustee of the Institute from 1879 until his death in 1902. He also founded a prize for the Institute's essay competition in 1884.* From a portrait by Frank Holl.

banking industry as well as those working in the banks. Members could be forgiven for wondering whether the Council, which had devoted time, energy, and funds to its parliamentary adventures, had forgotten the constitutional objectives of the Institute. Valuable as its role in bankruptcy reform had been, there seemed to be confusion

[63]

about the Institute's identity and purpose within the banking community. The Association of English Country Bankers was especially worried by the situation. The Association was unequivocally representing the interests of banks rather than bank officials, and it was uncertain where the Institute's commitments began and ended. Tension came to the surface during the joint attempt to reform bankruptcy law. George Rae, a leading figure in the Association as well as a Vice-President of the Institute, was anxious that the work of the two organizations should not be duplicated. Writing to William Beckett, President of the Association, in the spring of 1881, he hoped that

> some friendly understanding can be come to with the 'Bankers Institute' whereby they need not trespass on ground properly occupied by our Association nor we upon their preserves. Or failing any more definite agreement could it not be arranged for their executive and our own to act *in common*?[44]

He was especially irritated that the Institute could launch into new campaigns without consulting the Association or the other representative bodies:

> The competition betwixt the 'Bankers Institute' and our Association increases. By this post, we receive the form of letter from the Institute, to be signed and sent to them or to the Postmaster General, agreeing to his recent concessions in respect of Postal Notes; and by the same post, we receive the annual report of our Association, in which we are requested to inform our Committee . . . whether we are content with the concession in question. The circumstance only strengthens my previous view that some agreement should be come to between the rival associations.[45]

Whether from anxiety not to intrude upon the Association's territory or from concern over the sluggish growth of the Institute's membership, the Council began to withdraw from legislative activities during the mid-1880s, especially after Richard Martin succeeded Sir John Lubbock as President in 1883. Differences between the Institute and the Association of English Country Bankers were resolved. George Rae, for example, founded a prize fund for the Institute's essay competition in 1884, and an annual Beckett Memorial Prize for the candidate winning the highest marks in the Institute's examinations was launched in 1892 to commemorate the work of William Beckett, the former President of the Association.[46] The attention of the Council now switched to the working conditions and prospects of bank officials, in the hope that intervention would bolster the membership and influence of the Institute. In March 1883, for example, senior members of the Council (notably Sir John Lubbock and Herbert Tritton) took the initiative in the formation of the Bank Clerks' Orphanage Fund for the protection of orphaned children of bank officials. Supported by voluntary contributions, the Fund was placed under the management of Institute officials (this link was to be maintained until 1935).[47] In the long run, however, the Council's most practical contribution to the welfare of the membership was to be its efforts to win the banks' recognition for the Institute's examination certificate.

Ideally, members needed an assurance that the Institute's certificate would lead to security and promotion in their appointments, as the founders of the Institute had hoped.[48] A number of banks were willing to adopt an arrangement whereby successful candidates for the Institute's examinations were rewarded with a bonus or salary increase. An early example of this type of incentive was adopted by the Worcester City and County Bank, where the directors decided in December 1885 that it was 'in the interests of the Bank as well as the clerks' to award a bonus of £10 to clerks passing either the first or final part of the Institute examinations. It was a pioneering decision, backed by a promise to purchase 'any books required in preparing for these examinations not present in the Bank's library'.[49] Similar schemes were adopted throughout the industry in the late 1880s and early 1890s, including bonus awards at the Capital and Counties Bank (from 1888), Lloyds Bank (from 1890) and Martin and Co. (from about 1890); a comparable bonus scheme was introduced for successful candidates in the Scottish Institute's examinations in 1890.[50] As a rule the bonus for passing either part of the Institute examinations was held at £10, but by the early 1890s a number of banks were ready to offer larger incentives. In 1892 the Liverpool Union Bank decided to award £10 for obtaining the first part of the certificate and £20 for the final part. In order 'to encourage among the staff the study of professional subjects', the bank also agreed to pay the membership fees of examination candidates and the Associate subscriptions of successful

IV.—PRACTICAL BANKING.

Final Paper.

MAY, 1890.

1.—Give a short account of the Bank Charter Act.

2.—Is there any limit to the rise and fall in the Exchanges? What are the pars and bullion points of Berlin, Paris and New York?

3.—Within what period must a charge creating an equitable mortgage be stamped, and, if a further advance is made on the same form, can it be legally stamped?

4.—Contrast the terms "market rate" and "bank rate." Whom, and what classes of security do both affect?

5.—Within what period must a banker present for payment cheques handed to him by his customer for credit, and if unpaid, when is a banker bound to return them?

6.—What are the rights of bankers in regard to Stock Exchange Securities upon which they have advanced, and how far are the bankers affected by recent legal decisions?

7.—Is noting, or, in the case of foreign bills, protesting, absolutely necessary, or purely optional? Is it legal to note or protest a bill which is presented for payment after the due date, or should it be noted or protested on the due date? What is the legal object in noting bills of exchange?

8.—Give some account of the Bullion Committee of 1810, and the conclusions they arrived at.

9.—What do you understand by Bi-metallism? State briefly any arguments for or against it, with which you may be conversant.

Figure 14 *The Institute's syllabus and examinations are an unbroken record of trends in banking education. While insisting upon high standards, the Institute has always ensured that its examinations tested knowledge of contemporary banking. This examination paper, set in 1890, demanded detailed knowledge of changes in company law.*

candidates.[51] The Commercial Bank of Australia was even more determined to support its staff candidates. As early as 1888 the bank was awarding salary increases of £25 per annum to new Associates, but it is probable that candidates continued to study for the examinations in their own spare time.[52]

The growing recognition of the examinations by the banks was paralleled by the Institute's own efforts to increase the size of the membership. W. Talbot Agar, who had replaced Dayrell Reed as Secretary in December 1881, was given permission to expand the Institute's publication programme as a means of improving the services available to members. The outcome in 1885 was the Institute's decision to publish *Questions on Banking Practice*, a compilation of the questions and answers which had appeared in the first five volumes of the *Journal*. Under Talbot Agar's editorship the book enjoyed widespread sales: over 1,000 copies had been sold by the end of 1885 and another four revised editions were produced between 1887 and 1898.[53] The success of this textbook, in the opinion of *The Bankers' Magazine*, improved the Institute's overall reputation for teaching and advice within the banking community:

> The publication of these opinions will, it is hoped, lead to complete uniformity of action among banks on many points. Questions frequently arise on practical matters . . . and the publication of the volume referred to has been of much service in diffusing the information needed.[54]

Similarly Talbot Agar was responsible for making the library services a more coherent part of the Institute's routine work. When the offices of the Institute were moved to St Michael's House, Cornhill, in 1884, the library was transferred from the London Institution to the new offices and Talbot Agar was given authority to increase book purchases for circulation to members. Attendance at the library soon increased, and by 1891 pressure on space made it necessary to move the offices to 34 Clements Lane, above the London office of the Clydesdale Bank; this was to remain the Institute's headquarters until 1923.[55] These changes were supplemented by renewed attempts to recruit new members to the Institute. Regular advertisements appeared in *The Bankers' Almanac* from 1887, and senior bankers were requested to introduce new members. As Talbot Agar wrote to

Figure 15 *Ledger keepers at the ready: this cartoon impression of
ledger clerks, each carrying a sword of office to denote the ledger
in his charge, was drawn by a bank clerk of the London Joint Stock
Bank in the 1880s. Many bank employees in the late nineteenth
century remained in the same appointments for the major part of their
careers, and it was not until the early twentieth century that a
greater variety of careers in banking became available.*

Charles Gairdner, General Manager of the Union Bank of Scotland, in
July 1888, 'a larger amount of support in the future will enable it,
more effectually, to further the interests of the profession and to
become, in fact, a central institution to which every banker should
belong'.[56]

These initiatives inevitably had their detractors. For some bankers, keenly aware that all study for the examination was undertaken in students' own time, the bonus offered for examination success was a 'paltry sum' which was not worth a clerk's sacrifice of 'several years of his entire leisure'; '. . . is a gratuity of £10 sufficient recompense for the time, trouble and expense in preparing for the examinations?'[57] These doubts were echoed in a series of criticisms of the Institute by J. M. Morgan, Editor of the *Banking World* journal. In 1888, Morgan was especially unhappy about the high standard required for the Institute examinations:

> It is notorious that the standard required by this Institute is far too high for practical purposes, and the value of the certificate too hypothetical for any widespread desire to acquire it. . . . We have not heard of one instance in which official advantage has been derived from the possession of the certificate.[58]

The short answer to these criticisms, in the Council's view, was the upturn in membership and examination numbers in the late 1880s and early 1890s. Bank officials appear to have welcomed the new bonus schemes and the consolidation of the Institute's facilities. Herbert Tritton, in his first term as President, between 1885 and 1887, noticed that 'the interest of the younger members of our profession in their work is increasing'.[59] The Institute's membership, which stood at only 1,790 in 1886 in comparison with the 2,131 members in 1880, had improved to 2,788 by 1894.[60] The multiplication of entries for the examinations was even more striking, reflecting the impact of the certificate bonus schemes within the banks. Whereas the total number of examinees had reached only 60 by 1886, the entry rose from 131 candidates in 1887 to 442 in 1895. Even the Council was astonished by this expansion: '. . . gratifying as this is as evidence of the value now placed upon the education of bank officials, it perhaps is hardly to be expected that the number of candidates can continue to increase in future years at the present rate'.[61]

These achievements helped to clarify the Institute's responsibilities towards its members. Throughout the late 1880s and early 1890s meetings of the Council and of Institute members were again dominated by educational and professional issues rather than by legislation and banking reform. Much of the Council's time was taken up with introducing additional subjects to the syllabus (notably commercial

geography and French) and alterations were made to examinations in arithmetic and algebra.[62] At members' general meetings this attention to the syllabus was given enthusiastic support. In 1892 Frank Steele of the London and County Bank expressed a widely held view of the Institute's work:

> There is growing up another class of men who see beyond the routine of their profession, and into the principles by which it is governed; . . . it is to this Institute, its Library, its Examinations, and *Journal* that a very large part of the credit for this altered state of things is due.[63]

As a corollary of this awareness of the growing educational importance of the Institute the Council was now deliberately avoiding opportunities to act as a pressure group for the banks. Early in 1891, hearing that the Association of English Country Bankers had retained counsel to work on the director's liability bill, the Council preferred to leave the question to the Committee of the London Clearing House. Three years later, a similar opportunity to review methods of income tax assessments on behalf of the banks was not taken up (despite the recommendation of Sir John Lubbock) on the grounds that the question 'should be dealt with by the Chamber of Commerce rather than the Institute'.[64]

Significant as these changes of emphasis were within the Institute, the commitment to an educational and technical role was not secure until the banking industry made up its mind to commit itself to a more coherent representation for all the British banks. In the 1880s both the Institute and the Association of English Country Bankers had claimed to be working in the interests of the banking community. More discreetly, but at least as effectively, the Committee of the London Clearing House had represented London private and joint stock banks (excluding the West End banks and the Scottish and Irish banks) since 1854. Yet none of these associations carried the authority or influence to speak up for all the private and joint stock banks of the

Figure 16 *The headquarters and library of The Institute of Bankers were housed above the London offices of the Clydesdale Bank, 34 Clements Lane, between 1891 and 1923. In the period of this tenancy, which was the Institute's longest stay at the same address, the total number of members rose from only 2,389 in 1891 to 17,687 in 1923.*

United Kingdom. There was clearly room for a central representative organization for the banks.

The prospects for closer cooperation within the banking system were decisively improved by the rapid and efficient rescue operation which was mounted when the merchant banking firm of Baring Brothers ran into difficulties in 1890 as a result of unfortunate investments in South America. On the initiative of the Bank of England, banks throughout the United Kingdom joined together to guarantee Barings' contingent liabilities, which were estimated at upwards of £21 million. Guarantees amounting to over £17 million were eventually subscribed, with the Bank of England acting as manager of the covering payments for the Baring bills. Financial panic was averted, and the business of Baring Brothers was restored on a solid foundation.[65] Apart from the effects of the crisis on the management of banking reserve funds,[66] the events of 1890 and 1891 helped to break down many of the long-standing jealousies and insularities between the different sections of the banking community. It was a short step from the formation of the Baring guarantee fund to a more permanent form of cooperation which could act as a mechanism for defence against similar crises, as an agency for inter-bank consultation, and as a representative association. By 1892 this approach was being advocated by *The Bankers' Magazine*, which favoured a 'Central Bankers' Association for the United Kingdom':

> It would be of great service to the business of banking and also to the public, if a central body existed which . . . could speak in the name of all the banks of the country. It should combine representatives of the London banks, the English provincial banks, the Scottish and Irish banks.[67]

The suggestion was sympathetically received, and in May 1895 the Central Association of Bankers was formed by representatives of the Committee of the London Clearing House, the West End banks, and the Association of English Country Bankers. The new Association's founders also hoped to have the support of the Scottish and Irish banks. Simply stated, the Association's objective was 'to safeguard the interests of bankers as a whole . . . without in any way interfering with the separate work of the older societies'.[68] It was a daunting task, but the authority and influence of the new Association could not be in doubt. With the backing of private and joint stock banks throughout the country the birth of the Association reflected sure progress towards greater cohesion within the banking industry.*

The Central Association of Bankers, with Talbot Agar as its Secretary, began its work in the certainty that misunderstanding or duplication of the Institute's activities would be kept to a minimum. From the point of view of the Council of the Institute, the purpose and status of the new Association ensured that the Institute could concentrate upon the professional and educational role which had been planned in 1878 and 1879. Because the new Association so specifically represented the banks rather than bank officials, the confusion over the respective responsibilities of the Institute and the Association of English Country Bankers was finally put aside. With this question resolved, the Institute could more easily turn to the tasks of raising the status and broadening the availability of qualifications for bankers.

* The founders of the Association, acting as representatives of their banks, included many of the senior members of the Institute. Lord Hillingdon of Glyn, Mills & Co. served as the first Chairman of the Association, with R. B. Wade of the National Provincial Bank of England as Vice-Chairman and Herbert Tritton as Treasurer.

4

A VOICE FOR
THE MEMBERSHIP
1895–1914

THE encouraging growth of the membership of the Institute in the late 1880s and early 1890s could not hide a number of long-standing questions about its future structure and management. After the foundation of the Institute in 1879 both the Council and the membership had wondered whether centralized control of all the Institute's affairs was the most efficient and fair means of promoting the interests of the profession. This was largely a problem of access to meetings and lectures, as Richard Martin had acknowledged at the inaugural meeting:

> We have been repeatedly asked what benefit country bankers will derive from this Institute. I think I may say that they will derive almost as much benefit from it as the London bankers, for although they may be only present occasionally, and do not personally take a part in the discussions which will take place, yet it is fully intended to publish and forward to them every paper and discussion of interest which we have.[1]

Even if this obstacle could be overcome, there was still no clear understanding with the banks over the recognition of the examination. Valuable as the bonus schemes were in encouraging bank officials to join the Institute and sit for its examinations, the status of the Institute's certificate as a supporting qualification for promotion had not been generally accepted by the mid-1890s.

As early as 1879 John Butt, one of the original Honorary Secretaries, had favoured a direct approach to 'banks whose clerks are members of the Institute asking if results of examinations will be recognized by them, and if the certificates obtained by those who pass these examinations will serve as recommendations in their subsequent promotion'.[2]

For bank clerks and for commercial clerks in general, the 1890s and the first years of the twentieth century were a period of renewed disquiet and disturbance. A sustained expansion in the volume of banking business lifted the aggregate value of bank deposits in England and Wales from an estimated £457 million in 1884 to £648 million (excluding the deposits of all but eight private banks) in 1904, while the total number of banking offices in England and Wales grew from 2,075 to 4,621 in the same period.[3] Unprecedented increases in the numbers of bank staff at all levels were needed to cope with the expansion, and, because the banks had no difficulty in filling the vacancies, the influx of thousands of newly recruited clerks revived and added to the old worries about pay and career prospects. 'It may be that in the course of another twenty years', *The Bankers' Magazine* had suggested in 1892, 'there will be *no* town or village that is not acquainted with [bank clerks]. . . . Whatever may be their future and prospects, this we know, that there are ever hundreds of recruits awaiting with anxiety a probable vacancy.'[4] This plentiful supply of applicants was a threat to the level of salaries in the 1890s, especially at the lower end of the scale:

> The market is well stocked with bank clerks—overstocked. Put an advertisement in the paper—
>
> > BANK CLERKS WANTED. Commencing salary £50. Must have good knowledge of book-keeping, French, German, shorthand. Apply 'Banker' c/o *Daily Telegraph*
>
> and we have no hesitation in saying there will be a couple of hundred, ay, three hundred, applications. Knock off some of the qualifications and reduce the salary to £20, and you will find almost an equal number of aspirants.[5]

With this chance to pick and choose their recruits the banks were able to insist upon a minimum standard of proficiency. In the 1890s entry examinations in arithmetic and English were being set by many of the

leading multiple-branch banks, including the London and Westminster
Bank, the London Joint Stock Bank, and the Union Bank of London;
the London and County Bank offered an optional examination for
clerks who were keen to 'single themselves out for future promotion',
in addition to compulsory papers in arithmetic, dictation, and composition.[6]

Along with falling bank profits, which were being squeezed as a
result of a downturn in economic activity combined with intensifying
competition between the large, multiple-branch banks, this over-
supply of suitable candidates for bank appointments was being blamed
for actual reductions in salaries in the later 1890s:

> There is a greater demand than ever for banking posts. The
> rate of remuneration is in process of reduction; has been, in
> many cases, already reduced . . . in cutting down salaries bank
> directors know that the supply of bank clerks is far in excess
> of the demand; that they can retrench to a certain extent with
> impunity.[7]

Salary scales were certainly unchanged or less favourable than they
had been twenty years earlier, with most of the London-based joint
stock banks paying their clerks an annual salary of between £30 and
£80 as apprentices and £200 to £250 as senior clerks (see Appendix 1).

These anxieties were compounded by the unsettled state of the
banking system as more and more small banks acknowledged economies
of scale by combining with other, larger concerns. The bank amalgamations of the 1890s transformed the structure of the industry by
concentrating the lion's share of banking business in the hands of a
relatively small number of joint stock banks, each with London headquarters but with branch office networks in several different regions of
England and Wales. In 1900 the National Provincial Bank, which had
been founded in 1836 and now controlled 240 branches, was joined
in London by Lloyds Bank, with 278 branches, and the London City
and Midland Bank, with over 280 branches. In the twenty years
between 1884 and 1904 the total deposits of London banks with
country business increased from £70 million to over £362 million,
while the deposits of the joint stock country banks grew only from
£135 million in 1884 to £150 million in 1904. The estimated

deposits of the remaining private country banks dwindled from £79 million to less than £20 million in the same period.[8]

Bank officials, in spite of the increase in the number of opportunities at branch offices, remained nervous about these developments. Each amalgamation of a London or country bank was followed by rationalizations of the head office staffs of the two merging banks, causing a reduction in the prospects of reaching the highest levels of management. Any dissatisfaction with pay and prospects was also magnified by bank clerks' worries about the bureaucratic and labour-saving methods which a centralized organization would be likely to adopt. By 1909, for example, the banking press was wondering whether the morale of the bank employees would suffer from the evolution of the new amalgamated banks:

> A bank clerk is becoming a cross between a type-writer and an automatic machine. At the same time, with the gradual absorption of country banks by the great joint stock institutions, the most important part of the business of banking—the lending of the bank's funds—has become centralized in the advance department at the head office of each bank, so that the managers and chief officials at the branches have been relieved of much of their responsibility. The natural result has been a reduction in the salaries paid . . . one effect of the modern centralization of banking had been to limit greatly the numbers of those who will in fact rise to well-paid posts.[9]

The changing structure of the banking system did bring some compensations to bank employees. The multiplication of branch offices improved the prospects of senior and middle-ranking clerks for promotion to manager or accountant in the new branch offices. Moreover, bank employees in general benefited from the introduction of pension schemes. Provident and pension funds had been established and partly financed by most of the British joint stock banks, including the London-based foreign and colonial banks, between 1870 and 1910.[10] In 1912 these schemes were supplemented by the opening of a sanatorium at Easthampstead, Berkshire. Wernher, Beit and Co., who had owned the sanatorium since its completion in 1901, now placed the purpose-built hospital under the management of The Institute of Bankers. Finance for the maintenance of the sanatorium was provided by contributions to a guarantee fund from all the major banks and finance houses. The sanatorium was equipped for the treatment of tuberculosis patients, and the Institute was able to reserve places for employees of the banks.[11] There was also a continuing reduction of working hours: arrangements for the London clearing, which since 1886 had allowed the banks to close at 2.30 p.m. on Saturdays, fixed the Saturday closing time at 1.00 p.m. from 1902. Spencer Phillips, Chairman of Lloyds Bank, pointed out in his presidential address to the Institute in 1905 that these developments placed bank employees in a relatively secure position; the bank clerk 'is personally exempt from the severe risks of business, and no part of losses falls to his share. He has practical "fixity of tenure" and almost universally now, a pension at the close of his career.'[12]

Despite these assurances the bank clerks of the 1890s and early 1900s showed increasing interest in some form of trade union representation for dealing with questions of pay and conditions. Clerks of the railway companies had formed a union as early as 1865,[13] but representative associations for the clerks of the banks, insurance companies and merchant houses were not seriously considered until the 1880s. The Scottish Clerks' Association, for example, which had been launched as a provident association in 1886, acted as 'a sort of trades union' in negotiations with the banks in the late 1880s.[14] Bank clerks in Australia advocated a similar association, and rumours of a union for English bank clerks were current by 1892: '. . . in these times, when each trade has its union, we should not be at all surprised at any time to hear that bank clerks had formed themselves into a union. Indeed we have already heard the subject hinted at.'[15] The movement made little further progress until 1907, when the formation of a 'federation of British bankers' was announced. Probably influenced by the successful formation of unions for taxation clerks, customs officers, post office clerks, and the Railway Clerks' Association,[16] the authors of the scheme believed that they could 'restore bankmen to the position they occupied some twenty-five years ago' by negotiating pay settlements, investigating grievances, and forming a benefit fund. The proposal was coldly received in the banking press. *The Bankers' Magazine* could not 'imagine that any bank clerk would be so foolish as to allow his relations with his employers to be the subject of negotiations between them and third parties'.[17] The announcement of

Figure 17 *By the early twentieth century many banks in England and Wales encouraged members of their clerical staff to join the Institute and take its examinations. This photograph, behind the counter at the Peckham branch of the London Joint Stock Bank in about 1910, shows the staff of the office surrounded by their ledgers, scales, and coin shovels; clerical work in the banks in this period remained an all-male occupation.*

the federation's objectives was treated with similar caution by the banks and their employees, and the new plans for representation were quietly shelved.

Although the prospects for trade union representation looked bleak, there were alternative means for bank officials to improve salary and prospects. Emigration became a popular route for many banking men during the late Victorian period. Clerks and apprentices from the Scottish banks, helped by the qualifications of the Scottish Institute, were recruited in significant numbers to banks in Canada, the United States, Australia, South Africa, and the Far East. They were joined by large contingents of clerks from banks in London, Manchester and Liverpool.[18]

In comparison with this movement in search of greater opportunities, additional qualifications were the most straightforward course for bank employees who wished to enhance their chances of promotion in an over-stocked British employment market. This argument was forcibly put by presidents of The Institute of Bankers whenever the question of pay and conditions arose. Spencer Phillips, in a presidential speech in 1905, agreed that promotion in the banks was perhaps slower than it might be in other business houses, but promotion 'is certain to any young man with the grit to persevere and an intelligent understanding of what passes before his eyes . . . some of our members have shown in an unmistakable way by their rapid rise to positions of authority in their banks that theory and practice are not necessarily divorced'.[19] In a small number of cases, the banks indicated that they might give preferment to the Institute's certificate-holders. Ahead of the field, the directors of the York City and County Bank issued a circular to its officials in 1896, offering to pay their examination fees, to buy their books, and to take 'the Institute certificate into account in future when considering questions of promotion'. Outside the United Kingdom the Institute's certificate was winning a reputation among the foreign and colonial banks, which badly needed well-qualified officials capable of managing remote banking offices. Recruiting most of their clerks from the British banks, they stressed the value of the Associateship of the Institute when considering applications:

> One of the Eastern banks is in want, for its London staff, of young men, not over the age of twenty, who have had a few years' of banking experience. Those who are appointed would, in due course, be sent to the East. The fact that an applicant held the certificate of The Institute of Bankers would tell in his favour.[20]

The stress upon the career value of the examination was echoed in the financial press. In the face of falling salaries, the bank clerk should not be downhearted: '. . . to improve himself, the bank clerk may now pass the examination held annually by The Institute of Bankers. The test opens up opportunities of bettering his position . . . and the man who masters all the intricacies may take rank as a great financier.' The same promise was held out in early examples of careers advice. The authors of a careers pamphlet in 1911, for example, explained that the Institute's examinations helped to ensure that the bank clerk's position 'is universally esteemed' as one of the 'aristocrats in the world of clerks'.[21]

This explanation of the Institute's role, combined with the widespread introduction of bonuses for examination success, was evidently accepted by the bank clerks. As a sign of their mounting confidence in the Institute, more and more clerks became members and sat for the certificate examinations. The upward trend in the number of members from 3,349 in 1898 to 7,248 in 1908 was maintained until 1914, when the total membership had reached 10,542 (see Appendix 3). In the same period an entry of 442 candidates for the examinations in 1895 and 644 candidates in 1898 had grown to 3,180 in 1908 and 4,366 by 1914. To contemporaries the rapid increase in membership and examinations appeared to mark a distinct shift in the Institute's priorities: '. . . the record increase reported in the number of candidates', *The Bankers' Magazine* reported in 1899, 'seems to indicate that the educational part of the Institute's work is gradually, and naturally, eclipsing the deliberative part'.[22]

These impressive results, although they depended upon bank officials' readiness to improve their chances of professional success, were facilitated by adjustments in the management and structure of the Institute. Some of these changes were simple modifications to the apparatus of membership. In 1898, as a matter of status and recognition, the Council agreed that successful candidates in the Institute's examinations could use the initials AIB (Associate of The Institute of Bankers) after their names.[23] In the tradition of many other professional associations, notably the Law Society and the British Medical Association, the Institute was also ready to expel or admonish members who were guilty of obvious professional misconduct. In the Institute's case, like the Chartered Insurance Institute and the Chartered Institute of Secretaries, but unlike the Institute of Chartered Accountants, there was no fixed code of conduct nor a regular disciplinary procedure.[24] The Institute's constitution allowed it to act against members who were convicted of criminal offences or larceny. These powers were used in 1907, for example, when a member was struck off the membership list after his implication in a treasurership fraud.[25]

If the Institute was to maintain and strengthen confidence in its work as an educational and advisory body, its syllabus, teaching methods, and publishing programme needed modifications. *Questions on Banking Practice*, first published in 1885, reached its fifth edition in 1898 and its sixth edition in 1909. It was regularly revised to serve as a standard work of reference both for practising bankers and examination candidates. In 1900 a companion reference work, *Legal Decisions Affecting Bankers*, was compiled and edited for the Institute by its Counsel, Sir John Paget, who had succeeded Leone Levi as the Gilbart Lecturer at King's College London after Levi's death in 1888. The new volume contained annotated reports of selected cases relevant to banking.[26]

The Institute's lecture programme, in the meantime, was not allowed to become too routine or settled, and efforts were made to choose topical themes. Courses on foreign bills of exchange (1897), the banks and company law (1898 and 1900), and papers on short loan funds (1902) and cheque endorsement practice (1903) reflected new or changing preoccupations in the world of practical banking.[27] The syllabus itself was under continuous review, and a standing examinations sub-committee of the Council was appointed in 1906 to strengthen the 'practical and technical' character of the examinations. (The original sub-committee comprised T. B. Moxon, Managing Director of the Lancashire and Yorkshire Bank; George Pownall, London Manager of Williams Deacon's Bank; and J. L. Whelen, Joint Manager of the National Bank.) From 1908, on the sub-committee's recommendation, the principal banks were invited to make suggestions for each year's paper on the practice of banking, and a new reading list was introduced for the practical banking syllabus, on the understanding that the list would be revised every year.[28] Appalled by the inability of candidates 'to write a simple business letter without unnecessary circumlocution on the one hand or slovenly curtness on the other', the Council was now persuaded to introduce a compulsory paper in English composition and banking correspondence, replacing commercial geography and algebra in the syllabus.[29]

The new sub-committee was also able to clarify the Institute's attitude to teaching courses for the Associateship examinations. By 1907 there were signs that private tutors, including correspondence tutors, were competing for the fees of Institute members. Offering rewards to successful canditates or prizewinners and reducing tuition fees themselves, many of the private tutors were clearly in danger of overstretching their resources.[30] In an effort to stabilize the position and encourage members to join recognized courses, the Council strengthened its links with City of London College and Birkbeck College. Special courses were held for Institute members and in 1908 the Council was invited to appoint representatives as governors of the two colleges. In Birmingham facilities for special tuition at the Faculty of Commerce of the University were made available in 1906, and a representative of the Institute was appointed to the Court of the University of Bristol in 1909. The Institute also encouraged its members to apply for diploma courses at the London School of Economics. Sir Felix Schuster, Governor of the Union of London and Smiths Bank, in a far-sighted review of banking education at his inauguration as President of the Institute in 1908, argued that

> the opportunities which [the London School of Economics] affords (probably unequalled in this country or in any other) for training in the higher branches of business administration are certainly worth the attention of our students, especially those whose ambition it is to rise to the higher grades and to take command of large administrative work of any kind, and for whom scientific as well as business capacity is essential.[31]

This close attention to the educational role of the Institute reflected the Council's growing determination to build up and defend the status of its members. At the same time the Institute was tackling the question of local participation in its affairs. Since the Institute's formation it had become increasingly obvious that centralized organization and control from London was not entirely satisfactory for serving a large and representative membership. The examinations, in particular, could not be staged effectively without a strong local base, and from 1880 onwards candidates had been permitted to sit the Associateship papers at local examination centres, usually at local colleges or on the premises of local banks, under the supervision of Fellows of the Institute. By 1884 examinations were being held at Liverpool, Manchester, Birmingham, Bradford, Norwich and Nottingham; in the early 1890s, when entries for the examinations were multiplying quickly, no less than 34 examination centres (excluding London) were in use, and the Council was urgently considering the possibility of

Figure 18 *Sir Felix Schuster was a leading figure in the London banking community between the 1880s and 1930s. Apart from his appointments as Governor of the Union of London and Smiths Bank between 1895 and 1918 and subsequently as a Director of the National Provincial Bank until his death in 1935, Schuster served as President of The Institute of Bankers between 1907 and 1909. He was also prominent in the Central Association of Bankers and the Committee of London Clearing Bankers.*

extending the lecture meetings to examination centres in order to consolidate membership outside London.[32] As a result the Institute's 1894 programme of lectures by A. K. Loyd, QC, was mounted in Manchester as well as London, and the Institute supported this experiment by publishing circulars recommending bank clerks in the provinces to join the Institute.[33]

These efforts, although warmly welcomed by the membership outside London, were soon overtaken by the organization of autonomous banking institutes at Liverpool in 1894 and Manchester in 1895. Both institutes were inaugurated with local programmes of meetings and lectures in mind; these activities were to be financed by members' subscriptions, and it was expected that support would be drawn mainly from officials of the major provincial banks based in Liverpool and Manchester. Although the two new institutes were self-governing, it was made clear that the links with The Institute of Bankers would remain close. Henry Billinghurst, chairing the Institute's annual general meeting in 1896, pointed out that the new local institutes were

> fellow-labourers in the same field, between whom and ourselves the most friendly feelings existed. A great number of the prominent members of these institutes belong to us, and the number of our adherents in their districts had in fact rather increased lately than otherwise. We had co-operated with them in giving lectures with great success, and they were reciprocating by preparing special classes of their members for our examinations.[34]

These initiatives soon bore fruit. The Manchester Institute saw the success rate of candidates sitting The Institute of Bankers' examinations in Manchester improve from 50 per cent in 1894 to 70 per cent in 1904. The news of these results, which were attributed to the Manchester Institute's lecture programme, helped to swell its total membership to about 950 by 1905.[35] The Council of The Institute of Bankers, recognizing the effectiveness of local lecture programmes, established its own course of lectures at Birmingham in 1896. About 250 bank officials attended the lectures, and the response encouraged the Council to mount lectures at a number of provincial centres on a regular basis.[36]

These developments were being closely watched by the banking community throughout Ireland, and in 1898 an independent Institute of Bankers in Ireland was established by F. L. Leet, a Dublin lawyer. Leet, who was subsequently appointed Secretary, planned that the Irish Institute should 'enable its members to acquire a knowledge of the theory and practice of banking', organize lectures on banking, open a library, and 'afford facilities for the cultivation of social relations among its members'. Like the Liverpool and Manchester institutes, the Irish Institute advised its members to sit for the examinations of The Institute of Bankers, but in contrast to the local English institutes and the Institute of Bankers in Scotland the prospectus also announced the publication of a quarterly institute journal; the first issue appeared in January 1899.[37] Funds for these activities were obtained from members' subscriptions and from special donations from the Irish banks. Leet and his colleagues recruited a membership of 725 from Dublin and the Irish provinces.[38] The first meeting of the Institute of Bankers in Ireland was held on 28 October 1898 when, emphasizing the close links with The Institute of Bankers, Sir John Lubbock gave the inaugural address.

The successful foundation and rapid growth of membership of the new banking institutes in England and Ireland in the late 1890s, paralleled by the formation of local insurance institutes in the same period, persuaded the Council of the Institute to persevere with its efforts to improve facilities for its own local members. The most straightforward of these tasks was the opening of new examination centres, both at home and overseas. By 1906 candidates were sitting the preliminary and final papers at no less than 326 local centres, and the importance of the examinations was widely acknowledged outside the British Isles; for example, Bombay, Cape Town, Hong Kong, and Yokohama already appeared on the list of examination centres.[39] In England and Wales, as part of this extension of its examining work, the Institute also deepened its commitment to provincial lecture programmes. T. B. Moxon and George Pownall, who had been prominent in the syllabus reforms in 1906, were especially determined to replace the general and topical lectures which had been presented since the late 1890s with lectures which were directly linked to the examination syllabus. Reporting to the Council in June 1908, Moxon and Pownall urged the Institute to appoint 'local committees' and 'honorary local secretaries' to supervise provincial centre lectures on commercial law and practical banking. The scheme was adopted by the Council, which agreed to spend up to £400 of the Institute's total annual income of about £5,500 on lecturers' fees over the next three years.[40] In the same way the Council was ready to contribute an annual subsidy of £50 to the costs of the Manchester Institute's busy programme of lectures and revision classes.[41]

These manoeuvres, good intentioned as they were, did not significantly alter the highly centralized structure of The Institute of Bankers. The membership and the government of its activities remained focused upon London, and many of the old doubts about the representativeness

Figure 19 *The City of London Sanatorium at Easthampstead, Berkshire, was under the management of the Institute between 1912 and 1919. The Sanatorium was maintained by contributions from the banks and finance houses, and places were reserved for bank employees undergoing treatment for tuberculosis.*

of the Institute had not been fully answered. Notwithstanding the sustained rise in the total membership since the 1890s, and despite a membership which was drawn from no less than 220 British and overseas banks by 1909, the Institute continued to represent only a minority of bank officials. The total number of bank employees in England and Wales, from the analysis given in the 1911 census returns, approached 41,000, whereas the Institute's membership had reached only 8,769 (about 21 per cent) by 1911.[42] Even in London banks with strong links with the Institute, the number of paid-up members probably did not exceed 25 per cent; in 1909, when Lloyds Bank's staff exceeded 2,880, its roll-call of Institute members amounted to only 28 Fellows, 212 Associates, and 451 ordinary members. Similarly, 437 of the London County and Westminster Bank's 2,032 employees, including 22 Fellows and 112 Associates, were members of the Institute. Amongst the officials of the private banks, membership was even more rare. Cox and Co., in the West End of London, employed only 11 Institute members, less than 10 per cent of its total work-force of over 150 in 1909.[43]

For bank officials the variation in the pattern of Institute membership between different banks and different regions had serious implications. In the years before the First World War, as the bank amalgamation movement again gathered pace, employees from banks or districts where Institute membership counted for little were bound to be at a disadvantage if and when they were transferred to the staff of a bank with a strong Institute tradition. With the banking industry increasingly dominated by a small number of large London-based banks, non-members and non-Associates were likely to suffer in the assessment of their salaries and promotion prospects. This inequality, as members of the Manchester and Liverpool institutes appreciated, could only be removed by widening the opportunities for participation in The Institute of Bankers' activities at local level and by ensuring that the voice of the provincial membership could be heard in the Council and at general meetings of the Institute.

The main initiative for finding and maintaining a more representative balance in the membership of the Institute came not from the officials of the banks but from the banks themselves. From the 1890s onwards, when the introduction of bonus schemes had helped to raise the status of the Institute examinations, the banks had been drawn into closer and more permanent contact with the Council's educational work. This involvement was particularly apparent after about 1899, when the Council itself began to fill vacancies in its own membership on the basis of bank nominations as well as by individual recommendation. Within another ten years the retirement or death of a Council member was often followed by the election of a senior representative from the same bank.[44] The banks were also drawn into the preparation of the examination papers on practical banking after the syllabus reforms of 1906–8.

As a rule the development of more formal links between the banks and the Council enabled the Institute to monitor the professional requirements of the banking industry more effectively. Yet the new contacts did not guarantee a unanimous or completely representative view of banking education and of the function of the Institute. The division of responsibility between the Institute and the banks for tuition and examination in practical banking subjects was especially contentious, and the idea that the individual banks were best equipped to organize the teaching of a banking syllabus was steadily gaining ground. Challenged on this question by Sir Edward Holden, a Vice-President of the Institute as well as Chairman and Managing Director of the London City and Midland Bank, the Council of the Institute decided to undertake a thorough review of the needs of its members throughout the United Kingdom.

In the banking world of the early twentieth century, few could ignore the achievements and influence of Sir Edward Holden. Holden had contributed significantly to the Midland Bank's sustained progress through amalgamations and branch extension in the 1880s and 1890s. In 1891 the Midland Bank, as a result of amalgamation with the Central Bank of London, transferred its headquarters from Birmingham to London, and with Holden as Managing Director from 1898 and Chairman from 1908 the company rapidly consolidated its position as a metropolitan and provincial branch bank. Holden, a hard-driving and ingenious negotiator, was one of the outstanding innovators in the banking business of his time. He took the Midland into important new ventures in foreign exchange business, correspondent links with overseas banks, and the development of trustee and executorship services.[45] On the other hand, the growth of the bank's branch network from only 27 offices in 1889 to 658 offices by 1909 made it essential for Holden to maintain minimum standards of experience and training in the appointment and recruitment of staff. The Midland's staff numbers increased from 1,640 in 1898 to 5,000 by 1914; in the interests of efficiency and uniformity of practice, the education of the bank's officials was of urgent importance. Apart from urging that his clerical staff became members of the Institute (Holden was himself a Vice-President of the Institute), Holden was also convinced that these standards could be controlled through internal bank tuition. In 1907, after the passage of a new Companies Act, he devised a voluntary examination 'of a most searching character' for the bank's officials on the technical aspects of the provisions of current company law. Ten £10 prizes were offered, and in response over 600 Midland Bank employees throughout England and Wales entered the competition.[46] Similarly Holden organized special classes and examinations in French, German and Spanish, and although only 80 clerks could be accommodated in the courses the demand for places exceeded 200 by 1911.[47]

As the Chairman and Managing Director of a leading British bank, Holden's views on banking education were determined by his requirements for a well-trained and efficient staff. Knowing that it was possible to organize internal bank courses for large numbers of his own staff, he had no qualms about questioning the value of the Institute as an educational body. In a comprehensive critique of the Institute, which was presented to the Council in May and June 1912, Holden asked whether the Institute's work was fully adjusted to the needs of the banks; would it not be more sensible to form

> an independent institute in connection with our own Bank [which would] direct the studies of our staff on lines more suitable to our own requirements? . . . No doubt the Institute is performing for its members a certain amount of useful educational work, but the work which it is now doing is not satisfactory to us, and I believe that if we had the education of our men under our own control, the benefits which they would receive would be much greater than they receive from the Institute at the present time.[48]

In Holden's view, this type of separation of control could be avoided if the Institute offered teaching courses in special skills relevant to banking. For example, there was an obvious need for classes in modern languages. Holden quoted the example of a young banker who had studied French, German, and Spanish: 'He has been sought after from South America, in London, and from the Continent, and he now occupies a very responsible and remunerative position abroad . . . just as this young gentleman is invaluable to his bank, so every other young British banker speaking three languages would also be invaluable.'

It was a forceful argument, buttressed by Holden's contention that the existing membership of the Institute was not being given value for its hard-earned subscriptions:

> Out of a total of 8,769 members, 6,329 members live in the country or abroad, and cannot make use of the offices; and further than that only an exceedingly small proportion of the

2,440 London members actually use them for the purpose of study. The usefulness of the offices is further curtailed by the fact that the library is only open generally from 10 till 5, the time during which members are engaged in their business.

The government of the Institute was similarly narrow as the constitution gave ordinary members 'no voice at all in the conduct of the Institute'. In practice, Holden reminded the Council, only about 30 Fellows and Associates exercised their right to vote at general meetings. He suggested that a system of voting by ballot by the whole membership was a preferable alternative: '. . . every member would then be in a position to say by means of his vote whether he considered he was receiving educational advantages commensurate with the fees paid, and greater enthusiasm would prevail throughout the Institute'. These reforms, he argued, would ensure that the whole of the membership would be drawn into the activities of the Institute; instead of losing interest after passing the Associateship examinations, members would begin to treat the Institute as a focus for continuing study.

The Council could not easily dismiss Sir Edward Holden's criticisms. With Holden's encouragement the Midland Bank contributed more members and a larger total subscription to The Institute of Bankers than any other bank.[49] If the idea of placing the education of its staff entirely under that bank's own control was put into practice, the loss of over 1,000 members or about 12 per cent of the total membership (including 257 Associates) would be a setback for the Institute. In July 1912 the Council took up Holden's challenge and appointed a committee to investigate his proposals. The committee comprised Frederick Huth Jackson, President of the Institute and a partner in Frederick Huth and Co.; George Pownall; Robert Holland-Martin, a partner in Martin and Co.; and R. T. Haines, an official of the National Provincial Bank.

Largely on the recommendation of George Pownall, who had come through the ranks of the banking profession to become London Manager of Williams Deacon's Bank, the committee agreed that the ordinary members should be given a voting interest in the Institute's affairs and improved access to its educational services. 'A complex society is demanding efficiency in all its parts', Pownall believed:

Figure 20 *Before 1913 the ordinary members of the Institute played relatively little part in its activities, and voting at general meetings was confined to Fellows and Associates. The suitability of this arrangement was questioned by Sir Edward Holden, a Vice-President of the Institute and Chairman of the Midland Bank between 1908 and 1919. In answer to his criticisms, the Institute gave voting rights to its ordinary members in 1913 and began to establish local centres as a focus for members' activities.*

The standard in all these cases is an increasingly high one, and the reward is not always apparently adequate to the effort, but that is because a great competition demands a greater average efficiency, and the average pay of an average clerk cannot be that of the few supremely gifted minds who direct the affairs of men and nations. All that can be done is by means of equality of professional training to give equality of opportunity.[50]

The committee's reforms were duly approved by the Council in April 1913.[51] On the special question of the Institute's facilities for teaching modern languages, the committee agreed with Holden, and from January 1913 classes in commercial French, German, and Spanish were held at the Institute's headquarters; a diploma was awarded to those who successfully completed the course.[52]

In the long term the most decisive of the committee's proposals was a plan to form local centres of the Institute in any area where at least 100 Fellows, Associates, and members were resident. The local centres would be empowered to raise separate subscriptions from their members, and to 'apply the money at their discretion in lectures, addresses, debates, tuition and such other methods of spreading technical education and information among members'. The Institute, for its part, would be responsible for making special grants to the local centres and providing the nucleus of a reference library at each centre. Finally, any local centre with more than 200 members would automatically have the right to nominate a member of the Council. This proposal was accepted in its entirety by the Council in April 1913, although in the event the local centres' powers to raise separate subscriptions were never used.[53]

The scheme for the formation of local centres fully answered Sir Edward Holden's requirements for a more broadly-based Institute. Alongside the changes in the constitution it allowed ordinary members throughout the country to take a more active role in the Institute's educational activities. Equally, the scheme was compatible with the members' own requirements for local representation. George Pownall, who had played a key role in the formation of the Manchester Institute in 1895, foresaw that existing or planned provincial associations could be assimilated within the new structure of the Institute. In Newcastle upon Tyne, for example, a group of bank accountants had been planning since 1911 to form a local committee. Initially, the committee members were to be nominated by the Newcastle bank managers, but when the Institute's proposals for local centres came to fruition in 1913, the plan was altered to include all Institute members within reach of the city.[54] The Manchester Institute itself was to remain independent of The Institute for Bankers for another 50 years, but the Liverpool and District Bankers Institute chose to join the Institute as a local centre. In addition to the Newcastle upon Tyne centre, other local centres were launched in 1913 at Birmingham, Bradford, Leicester, and Sheffield. An attempt to form a similar centre at Hull was unsuccessful, but new entries in Bristol and Leeds came into being during 1914. In each case the Institute provided grants towards local centre libraries, and by April 1914 the first local centre nominees were attending meetings of the Council.[55]

The Council of the Institute, as Lord Goschen made clear in his presidental address in November 1913, was well pleased with the innovations in the structure and Council of the Institute. Sir Edward Holden had warned that the organization of banking education in the United Kingdom would be fragmented if the ordinary membership was not given a voice, but that outcome had been avoided by a clear and imaginative commitment to the decentralization of the government and study programmes of the Institute. By making these 'concessions to more modern and more democratic methods of government', the Council was confident that a major expansion of the Institute's teaching and examining work was now possible.[56]

5

INTO

THE MELTING POT

1914–1927

*The progress of banking evolution has been widely
accelerated. . . . We allude in particular
to the coming of the routine work to the
banks. No one could have foreseen that
the problems would be solved by the method forced
upon the banks. The supernumerary male
clerk, and the already numerous battalions
of ladies have been enlisted, not from
motives of economy, but through
sheer necessity. . . . Banking education
must to some extent be thrown
into the melting pot and
recast in a different
form.*

The Bankers' Magazine (September 1915),
pp. 376–7

THE outbreak of the First World War in August 1914 introduced a
period of rapid but fundamental change in the banking industry and in
the British economy as a whole. The banks, in response to the gigantic
financial demands of the war effort, were immediately drawn into the
funding of the Government's war loans. By contributing almost one-
third of the £350 million War Loan of November 1914 and one-half
of the £400 million loan of July 1915, the British banks subscribed a
total equivalent to 30 per cent of their deposits. In 1917 these commitments were extended by large bank loans to customers subscribing to
the Victory Loan. Along with loans from the United States of America,

these facilities made it possible for the Government to raise approximately £6,500 million in loans between August 1914 and December 1919.[1] In spite of this massive switch in bank lending to the public sector, the banks also accommodated a sharp expansion in the level of advances to industry and trade. By the end of the war the bills and advances of the five largest clearing banks had risen from £403 million in 1914 to over £693 million in 1918. Total deposits of the five banks, reflecting the wartime extension of credit and the rise in the level of prices, more than doubled from £635 million to £1,307 million in the same period. Capacity was stretched even further during the post-war boom of 1919–20.[2]

Changes in the scale of banking business during the First World War could not fail to affect the structure of the financial system. The vital role of the banks in government borrowing made it necessary for the Treasury, the Bank of England, and the clearing banks to reinforce their lines of regular communication and to settle upon a coherent approach to the financial emergencies of the war. New levels of cooperation were achieved within the banking industry, as Walter Leaf, Chairman of the London County Westminster and Parr's Bank, and President of The Institute of Bankers between 1919 and 1921, recalled in 1920:

> In the first place we had conferences, for a time almost daily conferences, of all the banks when we could get them to send representatives. At these, a rough general agreement was reached from day to day on the main principles in which the banks could act together on the new problems of policy which were pouring in upon us in baffling complexity. These conferences . . . were of the utmost value; among other things they taught us to know one another; and moreover they were the first instance in history, I believe, of cooperation among English banks.[3]

These experiences were not easily forgotten, and soon after the war the banks agreed to form a single representative body by merging the Central Association of Bankers and the Association of English Country Bankers. Launched as the British Bankers' Association, the new organization was designed to 'perpetuate the lesson of mutual helpfulness which we learnt in the war'.[4]

From the customer's point of view, the most striking wartime development in the banking world was the concentration of clearing bank business under the roofs of a small number of commercial banks, popularly known as the 'Big Five': Barclays Bank, Lloyds Bank, the London Joint City and Midland Bank (renamed Midland Bank in 1923), the London County Westminster and Parr's Bank (renamed Westminster Bank in 1923), and the National Provincial and Union Bank of England (renamed National Provincial Bank in 1924). Although the bank amalgamations of the immediate pre-war period had reduced the number of major clearing banks in England and Wales to only thirteen by 1914, the growth in the volume of banking work in the war years persuaded senior bankers that larger units were essential for coping with the expanding demands of government agencies and industrial companies. This belief, justified during the war by the task of outstretching the 'konsortium' banking facilities available to the German and Austrian economies, was also based on the conviction that the enlarged scale of banking transactions would be maintained after the war. According to the Treasury Committee on Bank Amalgamations (the 'Colwyn Committee') in 1918, the representatives of the large London banks argued that

> large banks are better for traders, and particularly for large traders, than small banks because, with their large resources, they can safely make individual advances on a more generous scale. And it is argued that banks must grow now to keep pace with the growth in the size of business houses generally, and to enable them to deal with the demands of after-the-war trade both at home and abroad.[5]

Influenced by this type of argument, a series of decisive amalgamations was carried through in 1918: the National Provincial Bank acquired the Union of London and Smith's Bank, Parr's Bank was purchased by the London County and Westminster Bank, Lloyds Bank merged with the Capital and Counties Bank, Barclays Bank took over the business of the London Provincial and South-Western Bank, and the London City and Midland Bank absorbed the London Joint Stock Bank. The five enlarged banks held deposits of over £1,307 million by the end of 1918. Accounting for about 62 per cent of bank deposits in England and Wales, and with new affiliations with banks in Scotland and Ireland,[6] the emergence of this group of five clearing banks established a predominance which, as far as branch banking was concerned, was not significantly altered until the 1960s.

While the structure of the clearing banks was being recast in this way, far-reaching changes were overtaking the staffing and routine business of all types of banking offices. By the end of 1915 the pressing need for recruits for the armed forces depleted the pre-war staff of the banks by between 30 and 40 per cent. In 1918 it was estimated that 18,000 bank employees had joined the armed services. Most of the banks gave their encouragement to the recruiting campaign, ensuring that the appointments of their officials were kept open and paying them supplements to keep their incomes in line with current bank salaries. Support from the banks was also offered to the 'Bankers' Battalion',* which was raised by the Lord Mayor and the City of London in July 1915. Approximately 95 per cent of the battalion's full strength of 1,000 officers and men were recruited from the banks, and the battalion saw active service in France and Italy between May 1916 and the end of the war.[7]

The departure of the clerks of military age left enormous gaps in the staff establishments of the banks. At a time when the volume of work was expanding enormously, the pressures on routine banking work were obvious: '. . . the day's work in the average bank is at least one to two hours longer than before the war, with a prospect of indefinite extension as more and more men join the colours'.[8] In some measure the gaps could be filled by temporary junior clerks or by recalled pensioners, but as a rule the banks responded to the crisis with their first serious attempts to recruit female staff.

Before the First World War the banks appointed only small numbers of female clerks for typing and shorthand duties, and most of the secretarial work continued to be undertaken by male staff. As a proportion of the total banking work-force, women formed a tiny contingent: only 476 (or 1 per cent) of the 40,179 bank clerks enumerated in the 1911 census were female, in comparison with 26 per cent in the Civil Service and 37 per cent of the general category of 'commercial or business clerks'.[9] On the other hand, as *The Bankers'*

---

* The full title of the battalion was the 26th (Service) Battalion of the Royal Fusiliers (Bankers). The battalion was absorbed into the 53rd Battalion of the Royal Fusiliers in April 1919 and disbanded in March 1920.

Magazine had acknowledged in 1906, 'many employers speak highly of the interest shown in their duties by their women clerks', and at least one of the major joint stock banks was admitting women and girls to its permanent staff by 1911.[10] After the outbreak of war, however, women were recruited for war work in all branches of British commerce and industry, especially after the Treasury Agreement of 1915 whereby the trade unions agreed not to oppose the dilution of labour for the remainder of the war. As soon as the banks felt the strain imposed by the departure of volunteers for the army and navy, women and girls were recruited for clerical duties throughout the banking system. The London City and Midland Bank, for example, where 350 female clerks were at work by the beginning of 1915, reported that the experiment was 'highly successful'. As a measure of their value to the banks, the women and girls employed by Lloyds Bank comprised 29 per cent of the staff by 1918. This development was not confined to the clearing banks. At the Anglo-South American Bank the efficiency of female clerks persuaded the directors to appoint women to clerical posts in Buenos Aires and Valparaiso.[11] With these achievements to their credit, female clerks were an essential part of the new banking scene by the end of the war, and it was clear that many of the new recruits would be looking for permanent careers in banking as soon as the war ended.

The impact of these changes on the structure and work-force of the banking industry was profound. Almost before the work of the Institute's local centres could get under way, the number of examination entries and the frequency of Institute meetings declined as the younger members volunteered for military service. Only 2,262 candidates entered the 1915 examinations in comparison with the 4,366 entries recorded in 1914, and by 1917 the total had been reduced to 906 (see Appendix 3). By waiving or refunding the fees of members serving in the army or navy, and despite the death in action of at least 3,500 former banking men (from England and Wales alone), the Institute was able to hold the total membership at over 10,000 throughout the war. This level of membership was sustained only at the cost of disruption of the Institute's finances. Subscription income, which had stood at £6,012 in 1914, fell away to £3,405 when the number of members on active service reached over 5,200 at the end of 1917. As a result deficits were regularly recorded during the war

years, eating away at the Institute's reserve funds by as much as
£1,431 in 1918 alone. For the first time in its history, the Council of
the Institute now applied to the banks for a subscription subsidy. The
banks responded with lump sum donations during 1919 and 1920,
including a gift of £3,250 from the major clearing banks and another
£3,300 from the Governor and Court of the Bank of England. In
addition, in March 1920, the Council was forced to ask the banks for a
subsidy of 10s.0d. (50p) for each of their employees who were ordinary members or Associates; similar appeals were necessary throughout the immediate post-war years.[12]

In the war years the Institute, despite its financial predicament, was
not prepared to give up its existing responsibilities to the membership. The local centres continued to offer examination classes, and,
although candidates were in short supply and hard-pressed to find time
for study, examinations were held regularly throughout the country.
Conditions were not always ideal. In 1915, at the examination centres
at Blyth, North and South Shields, Hull, and York, for example, the
invigilators warned the examiners that candidates' answers on book-
keeping could be below standard: the examinations had been interrupted by a Zeppelin air raid over the north of England.[13] Further
afield, the Institute was providing facilities for British prisoners of
war. Supplied with books and material from the Institute, the 'Bankers'
Circle' at Mainz prison camp organized lectures and debates on the
theory and practice of banking. Courses were also organized at field
hospitals in France.[14]

The Institute now turned its attention to the eligibility of female
clerks for membership. The chief problem, the Editor of *The Bankers'
Magazine* contended, was to decide whether 'our fair colleagues' were
employed merely as temporary clerks carrying out routine duties in
'certain classes of work', or as candidates for a fully fledged career in
banking. At the beginning of the war it was widely assumed that
women and girls would be given mundane clerical work and 'not
taught banking in its wider sense':

> A line of demarcation must . . . be drawn at a point where lack
> of the necessary technical training and experience renders it
> impossible to carry the substitution of female for male labour
> any further. Whether ladies will . . . ever be considered eligible

Figure 21 *Although small numbers of women were working in the banks before the First World War, the recruitment of female staff accelerated rapidly after 1914. The new recruits quickly adapted to banking work. When the Gilbart Lecture examinations were opened to women in 1916, for example, the examination prize was won by Miss Rose Kingston of the London and South Western Bank. The Institute's own examinations were opened to women in 1917.*

for the higher posts is, for the time being, a question too revolutionary for present consideration.[15]

These distinctions were put aside during the First World War when more and more female clerks proved that they could carry out precisely the same duties as the male clerks whom they had replaced, and that many of the new recruits were efficient and successful in more specialist work. For instance, the legal departments of the banks,

[101]

recruiting from solicitors' offices, were particularly pleased with their new clerks and secretaries. Recognizing that the pattern of banking employment was undergoing long-term alteration, the Council of the Institute opened its examinations to women in September 1917 and admitted women to full membership in March 1919.

The Institute of Bankers could not claim to be an innovator in the admission of women. The Chartered Institute of Secretaries had elected its first woman Associate in 1917, and the Institute of Chartered Accountants took the same step in 1919.[16] On the other hand, few professional associations could claim such a large initial female membership as The Institute of Bankers. As soon as the examination and membership rules were changed, the women and girls already employed by the banks showed that they were determined to compete for professional status. Of the 1,218 entrants in 1918, 322 were women, and the local centres at Leeds and Manchester were able to organize preparation courses for female bank clerks.[17] Similarly the Gilbart Lectures were open to women in 1916 (when Miss Rose Kingston carried off the first prize in the lecture examinations), while *The Bankers' Magazine* published a series of special introductory articles on banking for the female clerks. By 1918 the Magazine was also ready to publish its 'first contribution from a lady writer'. The article, by 'One Who Knows', enthusiastically welcomed the Institute's decision: '. . . this is the herald of a great dawn in the future of women, and like the dawn it has come quietly . . . there has been no battering at the door of the Institute, no protracted pleading, no wordy warfare'.[18]

The admission of women members was welcomed by all the local centres of the Institute, and few individual members opposed the change. The Institute, as the *Journal of The Institute of Bankers* explained, was simply ensuring that female staff were 'given equal opportunities with the men of acquiring a technical education'.[19] None the less, this recognition was not a guarantee that women would be given wage parity or retained on the permanent staffs of the banks when servicemen returned to their secured appointments in the banks after the war. As soon as armistice was declared many women and girls already employed by the banks became uneasy about their prospects for pay and promotion, especially if they had been carrying out strictly routine work. As one of the women members pointed out to the Institute's debating society, 'they were quite capable of taking an interest in a business and wanted a fair field and no favour. Until they were offered posts of responsibility, they could not be judged incapable of holding such posts'.[20] These worries were inextricably entangled with the wider question of the division of banking staff into separate grades for administrative and routine work, on the lines of Civil Service grading. The successful employment of temporary male and female clerks during the war, some commentators believed, demonstrated that a two-tier system of recruitment was possible:

> One sometimes wonders whether the coming of the woman bank clerk will hasten . . . the differentiation of the staff into two classes. It may be that young men of superior education and qualifications will be admitted as 'first division clerks', . . . while the routine work will be performed by 'second division clerks, male and female'.[21]

If this type of classification was to be adopted by the banks after the war, then the value of banking education and qualifications to both men and women bank officials was bound to grow. Without an equal chance to obtain those qualifications, both male and female clerks could face a gloomy future in the 'second division'. As *The Bankers' Magazine* had forecast in 1915, this question of classification threw the future role of professional education 'into the melting pot'; The Institute of Bankers, with responsibilities to over 10,000 members at the end of the war, was faced with the daunting task of keeping open the opportunities for banking education.

For the staff of the banks, the immediate post-war period brought overcrowding and confusion in the employment market. The return of servicemen to their banking appointments, the banks' need to retain staff during the temporary post-war boom in industry and trade, and the duplication of branch offices as a result of the wartime banking amalgamations all helped to raise the numbers of bank employees from about 40,000 in 1914 to 65,000 by 1922.[22] Part of this growth, as Sir Edward Holden had warned in 1919, was purely a 'surplus of labour'.[23] As a result, the efficiency of the banking system was seriously threatened.

> Most of the large banks faced the post-war rush of business whilst still in the throes of one or more half-digested schemes

of amalgamation. Consequently, a part of the staff was engaged in routine work with which they were unfamiliar, and this difficulty was enormously aggravated by the return from active service of large numbers of men who had lost touch with their old work and with business habits. . . . The banks are, in fact, face to face with those difficulties inherent in institutions above a certain size.[24]

In these new conditions bank officials were justifiably concerned about their opportunities for promotion and the maintenance of their salaries. Amongst those members of staff who had returned from the war to find new names and faces in their banking offices, the sheer size of the post-war banks gave the impression that men with 'more than average ability' were being 'lost sight of'. Salary levels, which had been reduced in real terms by price inflation during and immediately after the war, were also creating anxiety among the banking employees, and the banks were earnestly advised 'to recognize more adequately the increased cost of living . . . the younger married men are feeling the pinch very acutely'.[25]

The strains of the immediate post-war period persuaded many bank officials that questions of pay and promotion could only be dealt with by setting up a trade union or 'guild' of bank employees. Pre-war attempts to form associations or unions had met with little success: the ambitious plans of the National Association of Bank Clerks, for example, launched in 1914, were abandoned at the outbreak of war.[26] By 1919 the employment position had markedly changed, and when the Bank Officers' Guild was formed in that year large numbers of bank clerks throughout England and Wales applied for membership. Impressed by the Guild's plans to act as a central negotiating body on pay and working conditions, over 26,000 officials had become members by 1920, and by 1922 the total membership was as high as 30,000.[27] Despite this success, the banks did not concede recognition to the Guild in pay negotiations, preferring to foster their own internally elected staff associations. Membership of the internal associations was available at nominal subscriptions, and the banks themselves supported their growth by discouraging their new recruits from joining any outside association. From 1919 onwards the Guild and the staff associations were in keen and often hostile competition

Figure 22 *The expansion of banking business during and immediately after the First World War led to a significant increase in the total numbers of bank employees. Large numbers of women, girls, and junior clerks, and more widespread use of office machinery, were required to keep pace with the volume of business. This photograph shows the staff of the Clearing Department of Cox and Co., Charing Cross, London, in about 1920 (Cox and Co. was absorbed by Lloyds Bank in 1923).*

for new members, but even *The Bankers' Magazine*, which was extremely cautious in its attitude to staff representation, admitted that both 'the outer and inner guilds' were inspiring bank officials with 'a greater pride in the banking profession . . . *pari passu* with the desire for higher salaries'. Moreover, the growth of representation in the banks of England and Wales did not coincide with the type of disruption which followed the launch of banking unions or staff associations in other parts of the world: short strikes of bank clerks brought business to a temporary halt in Egypt, Ireland, and the United States of America during 1920, and a strike called by the newly constituted Scottish Bankers' Association in June 1920 was

averted only after intervention by the Ministry of Labour.[28] In looking at the expectations of their members the Bank Officers' Guild and
the staff associations agreed that the education of bank officials was a
vital component in salary assessment and career prospects. From the
outset the Guild took a special interest in the educational opportunities
available to its members, believing that these opportunities should be
closely geared to the 'grading' of bank employment. In 1919, F. C.
Clegg, President of the Guild, recommended a system of three grades
for bank clerks: an apprenticeship grade entailing two years of pro-
bationary service; Grade 2, for clerks taken on to the permanent staff
after the two years, and after having passed the Part I Institute
examination; and Grade 1, for clerks who had served three years in
Grade 2 and passed the Part II Institute examination. After trans-
ferring into Grade 1, clerks could enter for a final degree-level
examination. Bank clerks passing this final examination could then
call themselves 'bankers', in the same spirit that 'accountants' or
'solicitors' were considered to be professionals regardless of whether
they were employers or employees. The purpose of the scheme,
coupled with a plan to obtain chartered status for bankers, was to give
a professional monopoly to qualified bankers. 'We should insist',
Clegg explained, 'that official posts be filled from the men holding the
title of "Banker".'[29]

   F. C. Clegg and his colleagues realized that the Bank Officers'
Guild policy on banking education, primarily designed to obtain
recognition for the status of bank officials and to protect their salary
levels, could achieve little without the support and services of the
Institute as an independent examining body. Rather than attempt to
bypass the Institute, the Guild now mounted a determined campaign to
win the Institute's cooperation. Early in 1920 Clegg approached the
Council of the Institute with a request for the appointment of a
representative of the Guild on the Council. The Secretary of the
Institute, placed in a difficult position, explained that 'members of
the Council do not represent any outside bodies', but conceded that
'if a suitable candidate approved by the Bank Officers' Guild were
nominated for election in accordance with the rules of the Institute
the Council would not oppose his election'. William Forrest, from
the Commercial Banking Company of Sydney, was duly nominated
to the Council in February 1920.[30] After Forrest's resignation (due to

pressure of work) eighteen months later, the Guild sought larger representation on the Council by contesting the Institute's own nominations at the 1922 annual general meeting. The Council, not surprisingly, objected to this change of approach and insisted that 'the Council represent the members and no one else', but in a postal ballot five of the Guild's nominees were elected to the Council. The Guild's successful candidates were J. W. H. Axtell and J. Barugh of the National Provincial and Union Bank of England; H. F. Frankl of the London Joint City and Midland Bank; W. J. Gray of the Standard Bank of South Africa; and R. B. Pughe-Morgan of Barclays Bank. Sir Charles Addis, the President of the Institute, accepted the vote with a good grace, recognizing that 'both old members and new members are animated by the common desire, namely the welfare of The Institute of Bankers'.[31]

The new Council members lost no time in asking for a review of the Institute's educational policy. J. W. H. Axtell and W. J. Gray, two of the Guild's nominees to the Council, spoke up at the 1922 annual general meeting in favour of a revision of the Institute's educational programme. They also urged the Council to apply for a Royal Charter for the Institute. In considering these resolutions, a sub-committee of the Council rejected the proposal to obtain a Royal Charter, echoing the Sheffield local centre's view that the grant of a charter 'would not improve the status or social position of the staffs of the banks'.[32] The educational work of the Institute, on the other hand, was considerably altered as a result of Axtell and Gray's suggestion when the Council's sub-committee initiated a series of changes in eligibility rules for the examinations and in the syllabus to be followed. The Council itself had already amended the syllabus in 1921 by replacing the arithmetic, commercial law, and book-keeping papers with examinations in economics, the practice and law of banking, English composition, commercial geography and foreign exchange, as well as optional papers in five foreign languages.[33] Now, in step with the Bank Officers' Guild's policy of 'grading', the sub-committee reviewing the 1922 resolutions recommended that all candidates for the Associateship examinations should be required either to pass a preliminary examination in English, arithmetic, and geography, or to furnish 'other satisfactory evidence of a good school education'. In addition, the Council was advised to impose a time limit of seven years between

Figure 23 *Dr Walter Leaf, like Sir John Lubbock and many of his other predecessors as presidents of The Institute of Bankers, was a distinguished scholar and educationalist, with a long list of publications to his credit. Dr Leaf was appointed Chairman of the London County and Westminster and Parr's Bank in 1918, and a year later he was elected President of the Institute.*

a candidate's first and final entries for Part I of the examinations. A more testing syllabus and reading list was recommended for the economics papers, and the sub-committee's report concluded that the banks should introduce a uniform system of bonus awards for successful candidates in the Institute examinations. The proposals were approved by the Council in March 1924 and implemented by the 'Big Five' in 1924–5.[34]

While the objectives and initiatives of the Bank Officers' Guild ensured that the Institute's basic examinations required a high standard from candidates, the Council of the Institute took an increasingly active role in promoting more advanced forms of education for bank officials. Many of the Institute's younger members, when they returned from war service, were critical of the existing procedures for selecting and training the future administrators of the British banks. In an anonymous article published in *The Bankers' Magazine* in 1920, for instance, three ex-soldiers suggested that the banks could learn from military life: '. . . the immediate problem of the banks is to re-classify their staffs . . . and after separating the men who by experience, enterprise and ability can reasonably claim to be placed in the professional section, spread them as far as possible throughout the whole service'. The argument, in contrast to the Bank Officers' Guild's proposal for a graded structure, favoured the selection and accelerated promotion of a small band of highly trained administrators. A first step in the programme would be the endowment of a faculty of banking or trade and finance at an appropriate university: '. . . then we should be able to train consciously the younger men for the administrative positions which should be filled in the future by men holding professional qualifications'.[35]

Walter Leaf, President of The Institute of Bankers between 1919 and 1921, was particularly impressed by their proposals. With his considerable academic achievements as a classical scholar and as a pioneer of adult education in the United Kingdom, Leaf sympathized with the notion of a 'special training for men who are to rise to the higher managerial posts' and advocated the recruitment of university graduates by direct entry, on the Civil Service pattern. The President envisaged the formation of a 'University Bureau' to provide guidance and to act as an employment agency for those studying as external students for the commerce degree at the University of London.[36] But Walter Leaf's case for graduate entry into the banks ran into strong opposition. Many Institute members, including Council members, could not accept that the selection of senior management should be slanted in favour of an 'élite' of university men. 'Practical bankers' who had come through the ranks of their profession would immediately be put at a disadvantage. The Institute's members agreed that promotion to higher administration should be open to all bank officials with the necessary experience and Institute qualifications. Frederick Hyde, for example, who had risen from the post of a junior clerk in the

Figure 24 *Local centres of the Institute were established in many cities and large towns in England and Wales by the end of the 1920s. The new centres enabled members based outside London, especially those in areas with a long tradition and important role in provincial banking, to take a more prominent part in the Institute's*

activities. The large staff establishment of the City Leeds Office of the Westminster Bank, formerly the head office of Beckett and Co. before its amalgamation with the Westminster Bank in 1921, was typical of principal branch offices in major banking centres outside London.

Derby Commercial Bank to an appointment as Joint Managing Director of the Midland Bank in 1919, replied to Walter Leaf by insisting
that 'the higher positions should be recruited almost entirely from the
rank and file . . . we should consistently aim at getting our bankers
from amongst those who had served us as junior clerks and whom we
ourselves have had the opportunity of training'.[37] This view was
given wide support both at the 1920 annual meeting of the Institute
and in the columns of the banking press.[38] Nevertheless, despite the
distrust of graduate entry schemes, some senior bankers favoured
increasing cooperation with the universities and colleges in the further
education of bank staff. In the post-war period the discussion of
qualifications for senior management drew attention to the advantages
of encouraging bank officials to register for external degree courses in
business-related subjects, supplementing the existing Associateship
examinations of the Institute. The banks themselves were instrumental in the formation of the external Bachelor of Commerce degree
at the University of London in 1919. Apart from helping to finance
the course and advising the University on the composition of the
syllabus, the banks also urged their employees to register for the
course.[39]

The Council of The Institute of Bankers, convinced that its examining role depended upon the support of external teaching bodies, was
similarly influenced by the call for closer cooperation between the
banking community and teachers in the further education colleges. In
the London area, these responsibilities were partly fulfilled by the
appointment of senior Institute members to the Bankers' Consultative
Committee which the London County Council had established after the
First World War. The duties of the Committee were 'to consider and
to advise the [London County Council] in regard to schemes for the
provision of education relating to banking'. Its members regularly
visited the colleges under the London County Council's control and
reported to the Committee on the standard of teaching in banking
subjects.[40] Valuable as this type of cooperation was, the Council of the
Institute believed that the availability of teaching facilities should be
more clearly explained to members throughout the country. During
the 1920s the cornerstone of this effort was the appointment of a
director of studies. In selecting Frank Steele for this post in 1923,
after his recent retirement from his appointment as Assistant General

Manager of the Westminster Bank, the Council made a shrewd choice. Steele was a long-standing and dedicated member of the Institute, and, as a measure of his interest in the extension of banking education, he had been the first contributor to the educational section of *The Bankers' Magazine* in 1905.[41]

The experiment soon justified the Council's confidence. Frank Steele visited the local centres, building up contacts with the local universities and colleges and persuading the Institute's members to make use of existing facilities for lectures and tutorial work on the syllabus. As part of this programme he arranged for the recognition of the examinations of certain 'approved' colleges for exemption from Part I of the Institute's Associateship examinations. An agreement with Leeds College of Commerce in October 1923 was followed by a similar exemption agreement with the City of Birmingham Commercial College in June 1924.[42]

This approach was in marked contrast to current methods of banking education in the United States of America. At the Harvard Business School, *The Bankers' Magazine* reported in 1924, courses in business administration were closely linked with the training requirements of the banks and large corporations; within the banking profession, the American Institute of Banking chose to rely almost entirely upon its own formal classes and courses of lectures in technical banking topics.[43] The Institute of Bankers, faced with these comparisons, saw its first priorities in drawing up a syllabus and examination papers, organizing the marking of papers, and scrutinizing methods and standards of assessment. The Council also stood by its preference for making tuition more accessible to members by cooperation with outside teaching bodies. 'It is the deliberate policy of the Council', Ernest Sykes, Secretary of the Institute, confirmed in 1926, 'to cooperate with other educational bodies rather than attempt to provide facilities for all of its scattered members to attend classes'.[44] Encouraged by the success of the exemption arrangements at Leeds and Birmingham, the Council announced in March 1927 that the Institute was preparing a list of approved teaching bodies. In this scheme, any university or college which was prepared to organize classes for Part I of the examination syllabus could apply for the Institute's recognition; if recognition was given, examinations held by the approved colleges would exempt successful candidates from Part I of the Associateship

[113]

Figure 25 *The growing volume of the Institute's administrative work in the 1920s made it necessary to move the offices and library from St Clements Lane to larger premises at 5 Bishopsgate, London, in 1923. In this photograph of the Institute's staff at Bishopsgate in the late 1920s, the batch of diploma certificates on the office counter is being prepared for delivery to new Associates of the Institute.*

examination. By 1929, fifteen colleges and institutes* had successfully applied for recognition under the scheme.[45]

The new scheme, by consolidating and classifying the Institute's arrangements for teaching, reflected the Council's continuing belief that the opportunities for study and examination should be available to banking staff throughout the industry. Yet although the Council's new plans for teaching settled many of the members' questions about the role of the Institute in the enlarged and reconstructed banking system of the post-war period, the success of the scheme relied heavily upon the effectiveness of the local centre network. The agree-

* The following London colleges were approved by the Institute by 1929: Balham Commercial Institute, Catford Commercial Institute, Hammersmith Commercial Institute, Highbury Commercial Institute, Kingston upon Thames Technical College, City of London College, The Polytechnic (Regent Street), Wandsworth Technical Institute, West Ham Municipal College. Outside London, the City oi Birmingham Commercial College, Bradford Technical College, Cardiff Technical College, Hull Municipal Technical College, Leeds College of Commerce, and Liverpool School of Commerce were given recognition.

ments with the teaching institutions could only be put to good use if
the local membership was both active and fully aware of the facilities
at the recognized colleges. In general, the picture was encouraging.
The revival of the local centre movement after the war was not long
delayed, and new centres were formed at Nottingham in 1922 and at
Derby, Swansea, and Cardiff in 1923.[46]

After the appointment of Frank Steele as Director of Studies in 1923,
with special responsibilities for liaison with local centres, this growth
accelerated markedly. Bankers at Bournemouth, Plymouth, Brighton,
Ipswich, Blackpool, Norwich, and in North Wales established new
local centres in 1924, and the Bristol centre was reconstituted.
Centres at Southampton, Middlesbrough, Exeter, Hull, Bath, Chatham, North Staffordshire, Northampton, Chester, Southend, Oxford,
Peterborough, Gloucester, Eastbourne, Cambridge, Reading, and
Bedford were added between 1925 and 1927.[47] In addition to visiting
each of the centres, Frank Steele supported these initiatives with
systematic publicity for the Institute and its work. His contributions
included lectures, articles in the local newspapers and in the specialist

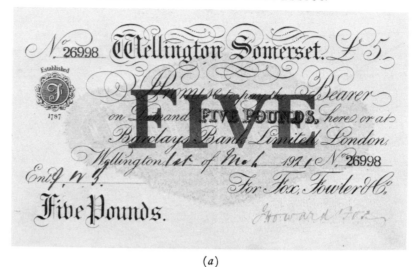

(a)

(b)

banking press, a prospectus for new recruits to the banks, and a pioneering broadcast on banking careers for BBC radio in March 1924.[48] Before his tragic death in a motoring accident in Wales in May 1927, Steele also persuaded the then President of the Institute, Sir John Ferguson, to visit many of the local centres during his term of office in 1926 and 1927. This innovation was a welcome point of contact between the Council and the local membership, and after 1927 the centre visits became a regular part of the presidential programme.

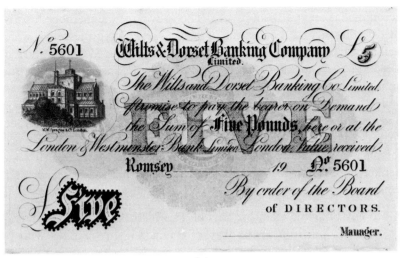

(c)

Figure 26 *The bank note collection of The Institute of Bankers is one of the largest and most comprehensive in the United Kingdom. Note (a) was issued by Fox, Fowler & Co. of Wellington, Somerset, which was the last private bank to issue its own notes until its absorption by Lloyds Bank in 1921. Note (b) was printed in the 1920s for Fox, Seymour & Gunner of Bishops Waltham, Hampshire, which was the last of the private country banks when it was acquired by Barclays Bank in 1953. The notes of the joint stock banks are also well represented in the collection; note (c) is an example of notes issued by the Wilts & Dorset Banking Company in the late nineteenth century. The Company was amalgamated with Lloyds Bank in 1914.*

By October 1926 Frank Steele had also organized the first conference of local centre secretaries, under Sir John Ferguson's chairmanship.[49]

Through the local centres, the Institute achieved rapid growth in the total number of its members in the post-war years. In a period when the total number of bank employees did not significantly change (levelling off at between 60,000 and 70,000 between 1921 and 1930),[50] Institute membership rose by about 170 per cent from 10,541 members in 1919 to 28,375 in 1927. The expansion in examination entries was even more remarkable. In comparison with a total of 1,500 candidates in 1919, no less than 12,395 candidates sat for the Institute examinations in 1927 (see Appendix 3). This rapid increase in the number of members markedly added to the volume of administrative work at the Institute, and in 1923 it became necessary to move the offices from St Clement's Lane (the Institute's address since 1891) to larger accommodation at 5 Bishopsgate. The growth of the membership also made an impact on the Institute's finances, removing the deficit which had appeared at the end of the war. Income exceeded expenditure by £560 in 1927, making it unnecessary for the Council to seek its usual subsidy from the banks.[51]

In the 1920s the encouraging increase in the numbers of members and candidates for the examinations offered the Council an assurance that the Institute's qualification was the main channel for the professional expectations of bank officials. The safest course for any banker, as Frank Steele had told listeners to his radio broadcast in 1924, was

> to enter for the examinations of The Institute of Bankers, for this will put him in the way of conducting his reading with method and with a definite end in view, while the possession of the certificates of the Institute, taken in conjunction with other qualifications, is one of the recognized stepping-stones to advancement.[52]

With confidence gained from an enlarged membership and financial solvency, combined with the more coherent approach to the organization and teaching of its syllabus, the Institute could look forward to a period of settled development and the consolidation of the status of the banking profession.

6

CONSOLIDATION
AND REFORM
1927–1945

Periods of great social and economic pressure on the members of professional groups in the United Kingdom were not always an obstacle to the expansion of representative institutes or associations. Although the initial growth of professional associations generally reflected a marked upswing or structural change in the relevant sectors of the economy, their subsequent progress was often maintained in the face of crisis or disappointment in the business life and expectations of their members. The institutes of professional engineers, for example, had continued to register huge increases in membership during the 1890s, at a time when economic uncertainties, reinforced by foreign competition and tighter profit margins, placed the British engineering industry under considerable strain.[1] When banking entered a similar period of stress between the late 1920s and the mid-1930s, bank officials continued to turn to the Institute and its qualifications. While the total number of employees of the clearing banks in England and Wales fluctuated between about 60,000 in 1929 and 64,000 in 1939,[2] the membership of the Institute increased from 31,413 to over 37,650 in the same period. This steady progress was matched by consistency in the numbers of examination candidates with over 14,000 entries each year between 1929 and 1939 (see Appendix 3).

The upward trend in the Institute's membership numbers was achieved in a period when serious challenges to the career prospects of bank officials were emerging. At the end of the 1920s, the widespread adoption of mechanized book-keeping systems began to alter the pattern of routine banking work. Adding machines had first been installed in the British banks before the First World War, but after the Midland Bank and the Westminster Bank introduced ledger-posting machines into their branch offices in 1927 and 1928, mechanized accounting rapidly became more familiar throughout the banking sector. The reduction in the routine work-load of the clerks was dramatic:

> . . . inventors have devised calculators for interest, tax, exchange, and other arithmetical computations, for the posting of ledgers, passbooks, security books, and all the interlocking records which go to make up the system whereby a bank keeps its books. The whole of the work can now be encompassed by fingering keys, pressing buttons, and manipulating switches, with infinite relief to the eyes and brains of the clerks.[3]

In the long term the progress of mechanization schemes was bound to alter the structure of the banking work-force, reducing the requirements for basic clerical work and increasing the demand for machine operators. The recruitment of junior male clerks was significantly reduced during the early 1930s, while large numbers of specially trained women and girls were employed as machine operators. In the period between 1929 and 1935, for example, when all the major clearing banks were committed to new mechanization plans, the number of men employed by the banks fell by about 4,000; in the same period, the number of women working in the banks rose by about 2,000. As a result of these developments the total number of female bank officials in the clearing banks of England and Wales rose to over 13,000 by 1939. Although the banks were not recruiting female staff for the higher clerical and managerial duties, the changes brought about by mechanization raised serious questions about the job-security and grading of banking appointments. The Bank Officers' Guild, echoing the fears of many of its members, hoped that the coming of mechanization would not lead to the displacement of staff or the slowing down of recruitment.[4]

By the early 1930s worries about the effects of mechanization in banking offices were eclipsed by the strains imposed by the major depression in the British economy. Following the crisis in the American economy in 1929, the slump in world trade and the effects of the British Government's monetary policy contributed to the rising level of unemployment and bankruptcies in many sectors of British industry by 1931. The collapse in business confidence and drastic economies in the management of large industrial companies soon affected the level of banking business. Total bank deposits in the United Kingdom, which had exceeded £2,500 million through the boom of 1920–1, had fallen to £2,362 million by 1931. In the aftermath of the slump, although the volume of deposits began to recover, lending business remained stagnant until the mid-1930s; advances of the London clearing banks had fallen from £991 million in 1929 to £753 million by 1934.[5]

Leading bankers, in their public statements, were able to steady the nerves of their depositors and shareholders and a major financial panic was averted. Behind the scenes, on the other hand, the directors and general managers of the clearing banks were alarmed by the heavy accumulation of bad debts which were incurred as a result of business failures during and immediately after the slump. The financial implications of collapse in the textile industry and shipping industry were especially serious. In the cotton industry, for example, the burden of debt brought one major provincial bank close to ruin. These setbacks were soon evident in the profit returns of the clearing banks. Williams Deacon's Bank and the Manchester and County Bank dropped their dividend payments altogether in the mid-1930s, and Lloyds Bank followed suit on dividend payments for its 'A' shares in 1931.[6] For banking staff the implications of the turndown in profits were all too clear. With salaries accounting for about 75 per cent of the running expenses of the banks, levels of pay were reviewed and promotion prospects were restricted as the banks sought to reduce costs for the task of recovering the momentum of their domestic and international business. The Bank Officers' Guild, more determined than ever to defend the position of its members, pointed out in the early 1930s that at least one of the 'Big Five' clearing banks was cancelling its bonus payments to staff by up to £150 per head and trimming its salary scales. Similarly, the Midland Bank Staff Association agreed to limits on the amounts of annual increments and to the suspension of overtime payments during the crisis period. For the first time, banking staff were also required to meet their own income tax liabilities. The

Figure 27 *Throughout its history the Institute has relied heavily upon its secretariat for the administration of membership registration, examinations, and other services. Ernest Sykes, seen here in his office at Bishopsgate in the late 1920s, was appointed Secretary in 1905, and he subsequently took on the secretaryships of the British Bankers' Association, the Committee of London Clearing Bankers, the Bank Clerks' Orphanage, and the City of London Sanatorium Association. Ernest Sykes retired from the Institute in 1935, and after his death in 1958 the Institute's spring lectures were named in his honour.*

banks had previously taken on the whole of these liabilities, but when an additional income tax was introduced as a crisis measure in 1931 members of staff were required to pay the new tax themselves. Although the banks had been devoting a much greater proportion of their earnings to staff pension, orphanage and benevolent funds and to luncheon clubs and sports facilities since the First World War, these benefits could not hide the unease over the level of net salaries.[7] Equally there were worries about the security of banking appointments. In 1935 the Banking Unemployment Insurance Board, for the first time since its formation in 1924, reported that the cost of unemployment benefits exceeded the agreed contributions from the banks; a total of £29,318 was paid to unemployed bank officials eligible under the scheme in 1932–3.[8]

In these conditions the outlook for recruitment and promotion in banking was discouraging. One of *The Banker*'s correspondents felt

that the coming of mechanization and the effects of the depression had transformed career structures in the banks by the mid-1930s:

> Where a bank would formerly have taken on ten boys it now only wants five. It was in the nature of things nearly impossible that more than two of the ten boys previously taken on *would* attain to the dignity of a branch manager. . . . The position is now different. With the bulk of the monotonous work done by female labour on machines, a far higher standard of intelligence is required . . . three out of each present batch of five [must] possess the necessary qualifications for becoming a branch manager eventually.[9]

Influenced by this slowing down in recruitment, the banks and the banking press advised young clerks to prepare for a long period when opportunities would be few and far between. Even the most promising employee 'may have to wait several years for promotion to a responsible post, and this is a very trying period for a young man who is confident that he is capable of better things'.[10] At the same time the banks exercised a much tighter control over the educational standard of their recruits, progressively raising their own entrance requirements. All candidates were expected to have reached school matriculation standard, but additional internal qualifying examinations were now in use throughout the banking system. As Francis Bland, President of the Institute between 1933 and 1935 and a director of Barclays Bank, explained to the National Conference on Commercial Education in June 1936, 'quite good school records are frequently belied by our simple tests and experience indicates that we tempt providence if we disregard the results of the latter in making an appointment, as we occasionally do under pressure of one kind and another'.[11] This attitude was shared by most of the major clearing banks in the late 1920s and early 1930s, and from 1930 onwards Lloyds, Martins, Midland, the National Bank, and the Yorkshire Penny Bank recognized a 'common entrance' banking examination supervised by the City of London College. The examinations, comprising papers in arithmetic, English composition, and commercial geography, had attracted 1,056 entrants by February 1932.[12] These developments, by ensuring a higher standard of basic education for recruits, made it less necessary for the Institute to impose its own preliminary tests on new members, and in January 1935 the Council of the Institute announced the abolition of the qualifying examination. Over 12,000 candidates had sat for the qualifying examination since its inception in 1925, but the Council recognized that the improvement in the banks' own methods of recruitment had made the test superfluous.[13]

With the prospect of a long-term restriction of opportunities in the banking industry the continuing expansion of the membership and entry for the examinations of The Institute of Bankers demonstrated that professional status, tied to gratuities from the banks, was the main channel for the expectations of bank officials. Growing confidence in the Institute was obvious, not only in its numerical strength during a difficult phase in banking business, but also in the sustained interest in local centre activities. After the spate of new local centres in the early 1920s the Institute's countrywide representation was consolidated by the formation of centres at Richmond and Kingston upon

Thames, East Kent, and Jersey in 1930, followed by Cornwall, Mid-Lancashire, York, Grimsby, Portsmouth, and Tunbridge Wells in 1931.[14] Members in the Greater London area were also keen to build up local Institute activities. In 1934–5, for example, a group of members in the Catford area formed a 'Banking Students Society' for lectures and study programmes. Similar experiments, with the full backing of the Council, were launched in 1936. Programmes of lectures were organized at Clapham, Croydon, East London (Stratford), Golders Green, Hammersmith, and North London (Wood Green), and 'large audiences' attended each series of lectures.[15]

The development of new facilities for members of the Institute during the 1930s relied heavily upon the coordination and advice offered by the Institute's Council and secretariat. Impressed by Frank Steele's work as Director of Studies in the mid-1920s, the Council appointed Wilfred Hinton as Director of Studies for the local centres in March 1929.* Under the guidance of Ernest Sykes (the Institute's Secretary) and Wilfred Hinton, the annual conferences of local centre secretaries became an appreciable influence on the work of the Institute; from 1933 onwards, the conferences' recommendations formed the basis of the annual reports of the Director of Studies.[16] Hinton's appointment also allowed the Council to strengthen the Institute's control over examinations and teaching. A useful conference of examiners had already been held in 1928, but Hinton assiduously reinforced the Institute's links with the recognized Institutions during the early 1930s; 46 colleges were recognized by 1938, and Hinton also organized courses for teachers of banking studies.

As a distinctive contribution to this work, the Director of Studies began to offer tutorial help and advice to the Institute's examination candidates from 1932 onwards. While reluctant to convert this service into an Institute-sponsored correspondence course, the Council encouraged the members to consult Hinton about their special difficulties with the examination syllabus. Candidates who failed in any subject three times, for example, were permitted to apply to the Director for

---

* Wilfred Hinton, a graduate of the University of North Wales, had lectured on economics at the universities of Sheffield and Belfast before his appointment as Professor of Political Economy at the University of Hong Kong between 1926 and 1929.

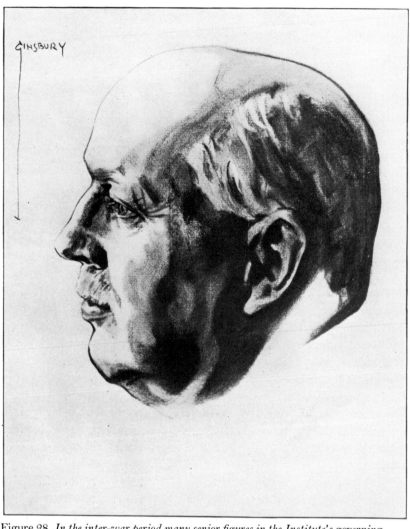

Figure 28 *In the inter-war period many senior figures in the Institute's governing Council were men who had obtained the Institute's qualification at an early stage of their careers. Frederick Hyde, Managing Director of the Midland Bank between 1919 and 1938, began his career in 1885 as a junior clerk in the Derby Commercial Bank and subsequently passed the Associateship examinations of the Institute. Frederick Hyde served as President of the Institute between 1927 and 1929; a prize, for aggregate examination results in practice of banking and finance of foreign trade, was named in his honour in 1952.*

an examiner's report. By 1934 the success of the scheme gave the Director of Studies a large volume of advisory work, and, to simplify the task, Hinton began a series of 'surgery' interviews with new entrants to the banks. Announcing a busy itinerary for the 1934–5 session, when he interviewed nearly 1,500 young bank officials, Hinton explained that

> these young men, in many cases, are not quite fully adapted to the change from school to business and find their first year a difficult one. Each is eager to make a success of his career, but generally anxious about the examinations and often ignorant of the methods of preparation available to him. The Director of Studies will see these men with the approval of the head office of their bank, help them to set about their studies and try to save them from wasting their energy and leisure in failure.[17]

Throughout the 1930s these extensions to services for members were backed up by efforts to persuade examination candidates to make more use of the recognized teaching colleges. It is probable that the majority of students relied upon correspondence courses for the Associateship examinations, but in 1938 and 1939 the Institute issued circulars to the local centres and the banks urging members to take advantage of 'class tuition' at the recognized institutions.[18]

While the work of the Director of Studies was designed to improve the distribution of the Institute's services, the Council believed that the Associateship qualification needed regular modification: an up-to-date and flexible syllabus was needed to win the confidence of the growing numbers of bankers who were turning to the Institute for help in their careers during the 1930s. In particular, the addition to the syllabus in 1934 of a diploma in executor and trustee work was a response to the rapid growth of trustee business since the First World War. Many of the banks and insurance companies had undertaken this type of business since the early twentieth century, but after the amalgamations of 1917–18 the 'Big Five' clearing banks began to offer executor and trustee services throughout their branch networks. Special qualifications and training, particularly in the intricacies of legal title, were needed for the staff of the departments or companies dealing with trustee business. In its content, the Institute's new diploma syllabus shared papers in English composition, book-keeping, and the practice and law of banking with Part I of the existing Associateship examination, but substituted papers on the general principles of law and on death duties and probate practice for the economics and commercial geography papers. The Part II requirements for the new diploma were entirely distinct from the Associateship, however, testing candidates in the theory and practice of investment, the law relating to wills, trust accounting, and the law of real property and practical trust administration. The Institute's new diploma was quickly recognized by all the major banks, and by 1937 1,500 candidates were entering for the executor and trustee examinations.[19]

The decision to offer a diploma in executor and trustee work helped to ensure that the Institute's qualification was open to bankers with specialist interests as well as bankers who were looking forward to careers in branch banking. In the same way the Council acknowledged that specialists in foreign banking business needed improved facilities for acquiring qualifications in commercial languages. The Institute itself had provided tuition classes for its optional language diplomas in French, German, and Spanish since 1913, and Italian and Portuguese lessons had been offered since 1920.[20] The marked rise in the volume of foreign banking business in the United Kingdom after the First World War and in the 1920s, especially in correspondent business between London and overseas banks, made it difficult for the Institute to keep pace with the numbers of applicants for the language diploma courses. An entry of over 150 members by 1928, although small in comparison with the numbers studying at local colleges or correspondence colleges, was a considerable strain on the Institute's teaching and accommodation resources; the classes were also run at a loss of about £150 per annum. Consequently, in 1931 the Council of the Institute transferred the teaching of its language diploma syllabuses to the City of London College. The College offered a 'wider range of classes' than those offered by the Institute, and by 1937 some 200 members of the Institute were studying for the language examinations under the new scheme. The transfer of this teaching work brought the Institute's language qualification in line with the existing system of tuition in local authority colleges. When a diploma in the Welsh language was introduced in 1938 after long negotiations between the Institute and the Board of Education, the teaching of the syllabus was allocated to the recognized colleges in Wales.[21]

The work of the Director of Studies and the transfer of the language diploma courses brought The Institute of Bankers into closer and more productive association with the recognized teaching institutions during the 1930s. For members of the Institute, especially examination candidates, this progress both improved facilities for study and began to give the Institute's qualification comparability with the diploma or certificates of other professional organizations. It was a crucial phase in business education. As more and more professional bodies turned to colleges and other institutions for the teaching of their syllabuses, real opportunities emerged for the organization of courses which could serve as common denominators for several professions and business occupations. Under the auspices of the Association for Education in Industry and Commerce and the British Association for Commercial Education,* for example, senior representatives of all sectors of British business were debating their common requirements for management education from the 1920s onwards. By the mid-1930s the leading figures in the movement were looking forward to a more coherent approach to the examination and post-graduate education of new recruits to industrial companies and business houses. The Council and secretariat of The Institute of Bankers, which had joined the British Association for Commercial Education in 1930, shared these ambitions. Addressing the National Conference on Commercial Education at Bournemouth in June 1936, Francis Bland explained that bankers 'welcome all the help we can get from the teaching bodies in such technical training as our young officers will need if they are to fill adequately the senior posts . . . the more need, therefore, to learn from the experience of others'. [22] Yet there was room for a positive commitment to the principle of cooperation between the main business professions, and in 1938 the Council of the Institute favoured the introduction of a common syllabus. The rationale of this policy was summarized by Reginald Wilson, in his address as President of the Institute in November 1938:

* The Association for Education in Industry and Commerce was established under the presidency of Lord Leverhulme in 1919. The British Association for Commercial Education was organized in 1930 and acted as the host to the International Congress on Commercial Education in London in 1932. The two associations were merged to form the British Association for Commercial and Industrial Education (BACIE) in 1934.

Each professional body has had its own ideas about what was the best course of study in any particular subject and has been inclined to regard its own syllabus as sacrosanct. The result has been that the colleges have been faced with a bewildering variety of syllabuses and regulations which have gravely hampered them in their efforts . . . in provincial towns throughout the country there may be groups of ten or twenty young men all reading for examinations in a certain elementary subject and although the teachers are there, a class cannot be formed because only a few are reading for any one examination. It is greatly to be hoped that examining bodies will show a less unbending attitude in regard to their requirements and make further unification feasible. It will then be possible to form classes where they are now impracticable, and candidates will not only have the advantage of oral teaching which has been denied them, but will also gain a breadth of outlook from different viewpoints by associating in the same classes with candidates for other professions.[23]

In fulfilment of these hopes, in 1938 the Council of the Institute negotiated an agreement with the Institute of Chartered Secretaries for the use of a common syllabus in the respective Part I examinations in English composition, book-keeping, and economics. Without significantly disturbing the existing syllabuses of the two institutes, the agreement made it possible for classes to be combined where there was a risk of failure through lack of support. The joint scheme subsequently won the support of the Building Societies Institute, which adopted the common syllabus for the Part I book-keeping and economics papers in August 1939.[24]

Keeping pace with the increasing numbers of bank officials seeking professional qualifications, the organization of teaching and examinations was the main focus of the Institute's work in the 1930s. At the Institute's headquarters, however, the members were also offered much improved facilities for study and research. The library, after playing a relatively small part in the Institute's activities since the formation of the local centre libraries during and after the First World War, was given a higher priority after the appointment of Miss Irene Shrigley as Librarian in November 1930. The rate of new accessions rose steadily during the 1930s, reaching a total stock of 15,000 volumes by 1937. This expansion made it necessary to extend and refurbish the library and reading rooms in 1933 and to publish a supplement to the catalogue in 1935. By 1937, when the Institute's offices were moved to leased premises in the new Glyn, Mills building in Birchin Lane, the library had become a more important ingredient in the Institute's facilities for members. Similarly, the Secretary and Librarian were responsible for dealing with a growing volume of enquiries, especially from members in search of economic information.[25]

The Institute's own publications programme was not neglected. A new edition of *Questions on Banking Practice* was published in 1930. In the editorial work for the new edition, the Institute's team of regular lecturers (notably R. W. Jones and Ernest Spicer)* gave expert help to the secretariat. In contrast to this tradition of publishing works of reference, the Council also envisaged the Institute acting as an initiator of research work. This role was emphasized by the foundation of 'The Institute Prize' to commemorate the fiftieth anniversary of the Institute in 1929. With an award of £50 for each year's winning entry, the competition invited members of the Institute to submit theses on 'some topic of a banking, financial or economic character'. There was to be no limitation on the length of theses, and the Council stressed that 'the adjudicators will be asked to give special consideration to original work'.[26] The innovation attracted a series of impressive entries throughout the 1930s, including a study entitled *The Imperial Banks* by A. S. J. Baster in 1930 (the first year of the prize award), a thesis on central banking by J. F. Church in 1932, Oscar Hasan's paper on 'Advances by Bankers' in 1933, and Dr H. C. F. Holgate's study of Scandinavian banking in 1939. The use of prize awards as a proving ground for research work was subsequently endorsed by the Bank of England's gift of an annual prize of £30 for the best essay on a central banking topic.[27]

The expansion of the Institute's study facilities in the early 1930s

* R. W. Jones, a popular lecturer on the list of local centre speakers, also served as Gilbart Lecturer in 1931–2 and subsequently as editor of the educational section of *The Bankers' Magazine*. Ernest Spicer, a chartered accountant, gave Institute lectures on accountancy and book-keeping, and was an external examiner for the Associateship examinations (including the executor and trusteeship syllabus).

Figure 29 *The Institute's library at Bishopsgate was greatly extended during the 1920s and 1930s. By 1937 the total stock exceeded 15,000 volumes.*

mirrored a long-term alteration in the role of the Institute within the banking world. Under the secretaryship of Ernest Sykes since 1905, the Institute was identified and often confused with the several inter-bank responsibilities which Sykes took on in addition to his work for the Institute. These duties included the secretaryships of the Commit-tee of London Clearing Bankers, the British Bankers' Association, and the Bank Clerks' Orphanage Fund. He also served as Secretary of the City of London Sanatorium Association, which had been formed in 1919 to administer the income and make grants from the proceeds of the sale of the Sanatorium at Easthampstead. Under the management of Ernest Sykes, the Association received free clerical assistance from The Institute of Bankers. Moreover, the Institute's offices had been used for meetings of the Bankers Health Insurance Society (formed in 1913) and the Bankers Beneficent Society (formed in 1923) through-out the 1920s and early 1930s.[28] This type of cooperation inevitably linked the Institute with the major bank-sponsored representative associations and charitable foundations. When Sykes retired from the

Institute in September 1935, he kept his appointments with the Committee of London Clearing Bankers, the British Bankers' Association, and the Orphanage Fund for another five years. By not inheriting Sykes's additional duties, the secretariat of the Institute could give full-time attention to its educational, technical and information work. The opportunity was recognized by the *Financial News* in November 1935 in a perceptive forecast of the Institute's future work:

> The Institute has a good library and the skeleton of what could be a really extensive statistical and legal service. A small proportion of senior bank officials do, in fact, call upon the Institute for this type of assistance, and they have good cause to appreciate it. But the majority of Institute members lose touch with it as soon as they receive its certificate. . . . There are many ways in which the Institute—by providing a large-scale financial and economic statistical service, by conducting expert surveys of current banking problems, by publishing authentic accounts of conditions in foreign markets and the like—could be of inestimable assistance. . . .[29]

In the first two or three years after the retirement of Ernest Sykes, there was a prospect that some of these ambitions would be fulfilled. Maurice Megrah, who had joined the Institute from the Westminster Bank to become Assistant Secretary in 1929, and had been appointed to succeed Ernest Sykes as Secretary in 1935, was already familiar with the local centre apparatus of the Institute and the crucial role of the Director of Studies in organizing examinations and teaching facilities. Megrah, who was called to the Bar in 1937, was also sympathetic to the Institute's growing commitment in providing advisory services and developing a research tradition.

The change in outlook was soon evident in the Institute's efforts to build up links with overseas bankers. Acting as hosts to visiting groups of bankers from Norway and Germany between 1934 and 1939, the Institute also arranged a guest lecture on the problems of international finance by Dr Viktor Kienbock, President of the Austrian National Bank, in November 1937. In return, representatives of the Institute were invited to discuss common problems of staff training at meetings of professional bankers in Berlin in 1934, Frankfurt in 1937, and Brussels in 1938. The growing importance of these international visits persuaded the Council, in 1937, to offer visiting students from overseas banks a short course of lectures on British banking. About 200 foreign bankers from 25 different countries attended the opening course in December 1937, but the approach of war in Europe led to the cancellation of the series after the completion of similar courses in 1938 and 1939.[30]

By the end of the 1930s many senior members of the Institute were also reappraising the possibility of some form of 'third stage' of qualification for bankers. The structure of the banking work-force had altered markedly since the debates on postgraduate education for bankers after the First World War. Although the number of bank employees in England and Wales had remained at between 60,000 and 65,000 throughout the 1930s, the total included an increasing number of machine operators and typists who were not seeking any professional banking qualifications. At the same time the continuing rise in the membership returns of the Institute indicated that clerical staff were more than ever anxious to obtain the Institute's certificate. Consequently, by the end of the 1930s, well over half of the clerical staff in the banks were members of the Institute, and a total of nearly 15,000 bankers had qualified as Associates. Concerned by the possibility that banking was becoming saturated with professional men, some members of the Institute envisaged the need for an additional qualification which would mark out the men of special promise early in their careers. Reginald Wilson, as President of the Institute in 1937–8, had no doubt that 'men who are to rise to managerial and high executive posts must be specially trained in theory as well as in practice if our banks are to continue to keep pace with the times and to function efficiently'.[31] This view had the influential support of A. V. Barber of Glyn, Mills & Co., who was the then Chairman of the Bankers' Consultative Committee to the London County Council. Barber, realizing that virtually all new recruits to clerical appointments began their careers after leaving school by entering for the Institute examinations, foresaw 'more specialized training' for selected recruits.

Figure 30 *The Institute's administrative and library work continued to expand in the 1930s, and larger premises were again required. In 1937, pending completion of purpose-built offices at Lombard Street, the Institute's headquarters were transferred to the new Glyn, Mills building in Birchin Lane.*

Designed to secure the succession to 'the high administrative positions of the banking world', this type of training could be based upon a diploma award on completion of a tailor-made university examination:

> With the necessity ever present for maintaining the highest possible educational standards, a greater reliance upon university education than hitherto, supplementary to that which is provided by the public institutions, may well prove in the end to be the best means of meeting the growing demand for specialized training.[32]

The Council of the Institute, through its examinations sub-committee, investigated the alternative means of introducing a third stage of qualification during 1938. In contrast to A. V. Barber's arguments for linking the third stage with a university examination course, however, the Council contended that any higher level of qualification should be integrated and controlled as part of the Institute's own examination system. By the autumn of 1938 the Council had agreed to offer a diploma examination which would be open to certificated Associates; candidates were to obtain tutorial guidance from the Institute itself. Announcing the launch of the Diploma in Higher Banking in November 1938, Reginald Wilson explained that the new qualification would 'furnish a welcome guide and incentive to the studies of those who are reluctant to lay aside their reading'. Frederick Hyde, on his retirement as Managing Director of the Midland Bank in October 1938, offered to endow a prize for the best candidate in each year's diploma examinations (this endowment was subsequently the foundation for a prize awarded on the basis of Associateship examination results and personal interviews: see Appendix 5).[33]

Before a syllabus for the new examination was ready, the development of the Institute's higher diploma scheme was interrupted by the outbreak of the Second World War in September 1939. It was soon obvious that most of the Institute's activities would be suspended for a long period. By November the Council of the Institute had authorized emergency arrangements which would ensure that members on active service were not put at any disadvantage. The subscriptions of members in the armed services were waived (following the practice adopted during the First World War), and temporary clerks taken on

Figure 31 *As part of the broadening of its activities in the 1930s, the Institute was keen to build up links with overseas bankers through exchange visits and lectures. In 1937, for example, the Institute organized a guest lecture by Dr Viktor Kienbock, President of the Austrian National Bank. Those in the welcoming party included, from left to right, R. A. Wilson, President of the Institute; the Right Hon. Montagu Norman, Governor of the Bank of England; Baron Georg Franckenstein, the Austrian Minister in London; Dr Kienbock; Dr Neumayer, the Austrian Finance Minister; and Sir Josiah Stamp, a Director of the Bank of England.*

by the banks were permitted to become temporary members of the Institute. To meet the loss of subscription income the Council agreed to suspend the essay competitions and lectures, to reduce publication of the *Journal* from six issues to four issues each year, and to cancel the optional language examinations for the remainder of the war. The secondment of Wilfred Hinton to the Ministry of Information and the departure of Henry Eason, the newly appointed Assistant Secretary, to join the Royal Air Force, left much of the administrative burden on the shoulders of Maurice Megrah and Charles Lidbury, who had begun his term as President in June 1939. Charles Lidbury retained the President's chair throughout the war, in addition to his duties as Chief General Manager of the Westminster Bank, and in 1944 he was knighted in recognition of his services to banking. Recalling Lidbury's achievements in this period, Anthony Tuke (then General Manager and subsequently Chairman of Barclays Bank), said that he had 'no hesitation in saying that in the whole of my career I have never met a man with such ability and with as quick a mind as Charles Lidbury'.[34]

During Lidbury's presidency the Institute was able to prepare wartime contingency plans for the use of the Chartered Insurance Institute or Law Society offices in the event of the destruction of the Institute's headquarters by enemy bombing; in return the Institute agreed to house the Chartered Insurance Institute and the Institute of Chartered Accountants if their buildings were destroyed. Fortunately these arrangements were not needed, but in May 1941 the Council learned that the Liverpool and District Bankers' Institute (the oldest of the Institute's local centres) had suffered badly: '. . . the library and reading rooms, together with almost all the Institute's records, were destroyed by fire in a recent raid on the city'.[35]

As in the First World War the reduction of the Institute's activities reflected the absence of many thousands of bank employees on active service. By early 1942 nearly 50 per cent of the pre-war staff of the banks and large numbers of women and girls had volunteered or been called up. In all, by 1942 23,000 employees of the clearing banks of England and Wales had joined the armed forces, including 400 in civil defence work; 525 members were killed in action, reported missing, or held as prisoners of war. The Kennet Committee, investigating the manpower resources of banking and insurance in 1942, recognized that the release of bank officials for war service had led to the closure of 1,745 of the 8,469 branch offices open in the United Kingdom before the war.[36] By 1945 the bank staffs included few fit men under the age of 41, and the departure of many women and girls for war service had made it necessary to dilute the clerical work-force with large numbers of temporary junior clerks, married women, and recalled pensioners. The net result of these measures was an overall increase in the number of female employees to over 20,000.

At The Institute of Bankers, after the waiving of the subscriptions of members in the services, the total membership was not significantly altered. A new record enrolment of 41,000 was achieved in 1945, but, with two-thirds of this membership having served in the forces, the impact of the wartime changes in banking staff on the examination work and finances of the Institute was serious. Entries for the Associateship examinations were more than halved in the first year of the war, and by 1943 only 4,558 candidates for the Associateship and 237 entrants for the Executor and Trustee Diploma were recorded (see Appendix 3). On the other hand there was little interruption of tuition classes at colleges in the United Kingdom, and members who were serving with the forces in South Africa and in distant theatres of the war were able to attend classes or enter examinations by using reciprocal facilities of overseas institutes.[37] From 1942 onwards examinations were also held in prisoner-of-war camps in Germany, and 169 members had sat the examinations in the camps by the end of 1944.* The success rate was high, with 28 members achieving distinctions and all 18 candidates for the executor and trustee papers obtaining the Diploma. Another 300 prisoners of war from the United Kingdom, Australia, Canada, and South Africa were studying for the examinations when the war ended in 1945.[38]

The waiving of membership fees and the reduction in examination entries hit hard at the Institute's finances. In the seven years of the war the subscription income of £58,200 was lost and total expenditure exceeded income by £16,384. An additional deficit for the first three years after the war was forecast. In these circumstances the Institute was given the unstinting financial support of the banks. The response to an appeal by the Council at the end of 1945 was a total of £32,392 in *ex gratia* donations by the banks, including £28,000 from the 'Big Five' clearing banks and the Bank of England. These contributions allowed the Institute to restore its reserve fund to £32,500 and to form a post-war contingency account to cover projected deficits in 1946, 1947, and 1948.[39]

If there was little that the Council and the secretariat could do to avoid the reduction in educational work and the exhaustion of the Institute's financial reserves, the latter part of the war gave them the opportunity to plan for the peace-time recovery and development of

* The examinations excluded the commercial geography paper, as the German authorities forbade the use of any books or publications which featured maps or map-reading information.

Figure 32 *In addition to his heavy responsibilities as Chief General Manager of the Westminster Bank, Sir Charles Lidbury served as President of The Institute of Bankers throughout the Second World War. His other wartime duties included the chairmanship of the Committee of London Clearing Bankers and the British Bankers' Association. Despite these arduous tasks, Lidbury and Maurice Megrah (Secretary of the Institute) successfully carried through far-reaching changes to the Institute's qualification system at the end of the war.*

the Institute after the war. At the administrative level Sir Charles Lidbury and Maurice Megrah set to work to ensure that the local centres of the Institute were ready to resume their regular programme of lectures and meetings. The *per capita* grants to the local centres, for example, were resumed in May 1945. In response, a number of the centres were keen to present occasional lectures even before demobilization was complete.[40]

Vital as the rebuilding of the local centres was, the Institute's main wartime achievement was the planning of reforms in the examination system. From 1942 onwards, as the tide of the war in Europe began to turn, the British banks began to project their likely staff requirements in the post-war world. The banks, mindful of post-war depression in the 1920s, were reluctant to accept the type of manpower surplus which they had faced at the end of the First World War, yet they sought to honour their commitments to the returning servicemen. One of *The Banker*'s correspondents recognized the problem as early as August 1943:

> The standard of ability of recruits has shown a progressive decline. . . . The retention in the service of many of these juniors can only create problems for the future, necessitating a larger staff with a lower standard of efficiency. . . . In deciding which temporary members [of staff] shall be retained, efficiency and merit must be the deciding factors.[41]

With 'efficiency and merit' as their yardsticks, the banks were committed to continued recognition of the Institute's qualification as an essential part of the process of selection for appointment and promotion. This situation, as many members recognized, placed a responsibility on the Institute for maintaining and improving the standard of its qualifications. If the Institute was to play a useful role in banking education, banks and their employees needed to be sure that the qualification was up-to-date in content and that the Institute was strict in the application of its standards. In a lively debate on the Institute's educational policy in *The Bankers' Magazine* early in 1944, Leonard Mather (later to become President of the Institute) recalled that the pre-war banking industry had been oversupplied with fully qualified bankers. The time limits for the Institute's examinations had been too generous: '. . . by dint of patience rather than effort and self-organization every member eventually passed'. Mather argued that after the war he 'would like to see a much higher standard set for the Associate certificate, and the abolition of the one subject per year system'.[42]

The Council and secretariat broadly sympathized with these

objectives, and during 1943 and 1944 Sir Charles Lidbury and
Maurice Megrah reviewed the rules and syllabus for the Associateship
examinations. After consulting the banks about 'the needs of members
and the legitimate requirements of the employing banks', the results
of the investigation were published in a statement by the President
in April 1945. A series of wide-ranging reforms was recommended,
with three main principles for the future educational policy of the
Institute. First, influenced by the concept of guiding the members'
studies as well as testing their banking knowledge, the Council
recommended a complete reform of the syllabus for both the banking
and executor and trustee qualifications. Now renamed the Banking
Diploma and the Trustee Diploma, the two qualifications shared a
common set of Part I examinations in English, economics, book-
keeping, and the law and practice relating to negotiable instruments.
Part I candidates for the Banking Diploma were to sit a separate
commercial geography paper, while the Trustee Diploma candidates
entered for a test in the general principles of law. In Part II, the
requirement for the Banking Diploma omitted the English paper and
reconstructed the syllabus in two sections. Section I comprised three
subjects: commercial law; accountancy; and currency, money market,
and public finance. Section II was devoted to the finance of foreign
trade and the practice of banking. On the trustee side, Section I
contained papers in the law relating to wills, the law of real property,
and the theory and practice of investment, and Section II was matched
to the old papers in trust accounting and practical trust administration. Optional papers in taxation, elementary statistics, and English
economic history were offered in the Part I syllabus of both diplomas;
these options gave candidates 'a means of acquiring distinction'. The
Council also proposed optional language papers in French, German,
Italian and Spanish.

Closely linked with the recommended reforms in the syllabus, the
policy statement urged that the time limits for taking the examinations
should be more closely controlled. In line with other professional
examinations, including the accountancy and company secretary
qualifications, the proposed scheme would not permit candidates to sit
any of the Part II papers before completing Part I. Equally important,
success in Part I was not to be achieved 'in penny instalments'.
Candidates were expected to pass three papers at one sitting, or, in the

event of failure, to begin the examination again. In Part II, all three papers in Section I were to be taken at one sitting, and passes in specified papers were needed before a candidate could move on to the Section II papers. For instance, no candidate would be permitted to sit the practice of banking paper in Section II before passing the Section I commercial law examination. The entire qualification, Lidbury anticipated, would take between three and five years to complete. These rules imposed a new degree of control over the time allowed for qualification, and eliminated the opportunities for candidates to choose 'an almost fantastic number of combinations of subjects and timing, most of them unsuitable'.

Finally, keeping faith with the pre-war plan to introduce the Diploma in Higher Banking, the President's statement held the door open for a third stage of qualification by asking for a review of the existing plan in 1948. Although the Council and secretariat expected that the new syllabus provisions would raise the educational standard and public status of the Institute's examination, the notion of an advanced qualification was not abandoned. Wilfred Hinton, who had returned from war duties in February 1945, explained that 'in any case it would seem desirable to associate any such high qualification with a university in some way, though not to exclude the exceptional man whose qualifications are not a bachelor's degree but some professional diplomas, combined with special experience'.[43]

This major programme of reform in the Institute's examinations was duly approved by the Council in March 1945 and implemented (with the exception of the deferred decision on the Diploma in Higher Banking) between 1946 and 1947. The initial reaction from members, the banks, and the banking press was favourable, as *The Banker* acknowledged in May 1945:

The members must be both pleased and astonished at the speed and vigour with which their governing body has acted during the past months, months punctuated by serious air-raids and burdened with the anxieties of constant staffing difficulties . . . there can be few who will not approve of the main body of the Council's policy as likely considerably to raise the standing of the Institute's examinations; while those bank officials whose task it is to select promising juniors for promotion will also rejoice at the setting up of a test whose passing will tell something specific about the successful candidate.[44]

Equipped with the reformed syllabus, The Institute of Bankers could anticipate increasing professional recognition for its members during the post-war years. In the longer term, moreover, the planning of the revised qualification was not simply the outcome of the pressures of wartime banking. It emphasized that the profession had made great strides towards a coherent system of business education since the recognition of approved teaching institutions in 1927. Throughout the 1930s and the Second World War, in a period of tremendous pressures on the banking work-force, the Institute had offered a qualification which was open to most new entrants to the banks. This progress, which converted the Institute into one of the largest qualifying associations in the world at the end of the war, was now combined with a welcome and thorough overhaul of professional education for bankers.

7

OUTWARD BOUND

1945–1960

ALTHOUGH many senior bankers thought that the end of the Second World War would create the type of manpower surplus which had affected the banks immediately after the First World War, these fears were largely unfounded. Paradoxically, the banks' staff managers faced the likelihood of a long-term shortage of suitably qualified new entrants to the banks. In the post-war period there were repeated complaints that promising school leavers were being 'creamed off' as a result of new opportunities in higher education and in industry. In particular, the Education Acts of 1944–5 were widely expected to reduce the 'supply of first-grade material' to the banks; 'most of the "bright" boys will stay longer at school, with the probability that the best will proceed to higher education'. This trend, one of *The Banker*'s correspondents expected, would divert large numbers of school leavers and graduates to the enlarging education system, the Civil Service, and to industry, leaving the banks with a diminishing supply of above-average new entrants.[1] *The Bankers' Magazine* agreed that this alteration in the pattern of recruitment was already obvious by 1948:

> The difficulty of replacing juniors is one [symptom], and perhaps another is the difference in contemporary salary scales—200 per cent increase or more on 1939 levels for new entrants, as against something like 25 per cent at the 15-year mark. The 1930 vintage, remembering a laborious three or

four years' climb from £50 to £80 per annum, looks with some envy at their successor of 1948 who, starting in the neighbourhood of £150, is not always even of the moderate educational standard considered essential in the far-off other-world days.[2]

This concern over future developments in recruitment was shared by other employers of clerical labour, including the insurance companies, shipping companies, and merchant houses. Even the accountancy firms, which had relied upon a plentiful supply of school leavers in the inter-war period, were alarmed that the increased facilities for sixth-form and university education would undermine the system of training under articles.[3] Facing the challenge that 'dilution has begun, and standards are dropping', the major British banks began to alter their approach to recruitment. 'Today there is no normality in recruitment', one commentator explained; '. . . there is almost a scramble to obtain suitable young men and women. The banks have been driven to advertise in their own names in the "situations vacant" column'.[4] In the place of the long-established practice of waiting for applications from school leavers, staff departments of the banks now sought recruits through the careers advisory services of the schools. The Midland Bank, for example, broke fresh ground in 1948 by publishing careers booklets which set out the entrance qualifications, promotion prospects and training facilities for new recruits. By the early 1950s, using careers publications and liaison arrangements with the schools themselves, the 'Big Five' banks had accepted that they were recruiting new staff in a large and competitive market.[5]

The clearest expression of the banks' anxiety about the educational standard of their new entrants in the post-war years was the opening of internal staff training colleges. Anticipated by the formation of training schools for machine operators in the 1930s and training branches for temporary junior clerks during the Second World War (complete with model branches, replica documents, and instructional films),[6] the concept of internal instruction was not fully developed until the banks began to retrain members of staff returning from the armed forces immediately after the war. Closely following the establishment of the Westminster Bank's residential junior training centre at Oaken Holt in October 1945, all but one of the clearing banks opened training colleges between 1945 and 1948. Similar training schools were established by the Scottish banks between 1946 and 1948.[7] The exact purpose of the colleges varied from bank to bank, depending upon each bank's analysis of its recruitment and career patterns. *The Banker* summarized the position in 1948:

> One bank . . . has no training establishment; another bank concentrates its efforts on juvenile training in a residential school, but also gives some attention to the training of women; a third has considered it essential to train staff at all levels—and this policy is now to be adopted by another of the Big Five; the remaining one of the Five considers high level training necessary but pre-entry training of little importance.[8]

In spite of these differences of approach, the staff managers of the banks were in close consultation over the content and structure of their training courses. Once the colleges were open, cooperation was maintained at meetings of the college principals and tutors, including an influential conference under the auspices of the Institute of Bankers in Scotland at St Andrews in 1950. The conference, which examined the relationship between the 1944–5 Education Acts and the planning of education and training in the banks, gave an opportunity to compare and criticize the new internal training schemes.* Henry Eason, who attended the conference on behalf of The Institute of Bankers, reported that the discussion of internal training schemes showed that 'banking is, in this respect at least, in the van of progress'.[9]

Although the training schools quickly became an established and successful part of the British banking scene, the banks did not pretend that they could answer all their staffing problems through internal teaching. The Government's efforts to multiply the opportunities for university education convinced many of those at the top of the banking profession that the banks should make more room for graduates. Lord Balfour of Burleigh, Chairman of Lloyds Bank, at the end of his presidential term at The Institute of Bankers in 1950, expressed the view

---

* The conference was attended by delegates from the Ministry of Education, the Scottish Education Department, the Bank of England, 13 English joint stock banks, 7 Scottish, 3 Irish, and 13 foreign and colonial banks, 3 accepting houses, the Scottish, English, and Irish Institutes of Bankers, and the Savings Banks Institute, which had been formed in 1948.

that staff departments would be forced to recruit more entrants from the universities if they were to maintain the same type and average standard of staff which they had come to expect before the Second World War: '. . . from this aspect, it would be the quality that we were after, not the university education *per se*'. Lord Balfour of Burleigh was especially impressed by the views of the Carr-Saunders Committee on university and technical education for commerce. Reporting to the Government in 1949, under the experienced chairmanship of Sir Alexander Carr-Saunders, Director of the London School of Economics, the Committee advised that 'young people with ability and enterprise are able to go in larger numbers to universities, and the result may be that any occupation which neglects the graduate will recruit largely from among those who are below the average in these qualities'.[10] This pragmatic approach to recruitment slowly gained ground during the 1950s; although the banks were not ready to introduce any form of 'streaming' for university entrants, the intake of graduates (particularly for specialist work in economics, law, or trusteeship) rose significantly after the appearance of the Carr-Saunders report. This shift in recruitment, small as it was in the staff pattern as a whole, was backed up by a new willingness to enter selected staff for post-experience management courses. By 1950, two of the major clearing banks were regularly sending members of their staff to the Administrative Staff College at Henley, which had been opened in 1948 to provide advanced management education for both the public and the private sectors.[11]

In their efforts to improve and maintain the standard of training for their staffs the British banks could not relax their use of professional qualifications as a test of calibre. The Associateship of The Institute of Bankers, especially after the examination reforms of 1945, offered an assessment of a banker's basic professional training at a time when competition in the employment market threatened a deterioration in the educational standard of the banking work-force. The diploma became an indispensable part of the framework of staff selection and recruitment. Reporting the Institute's seventy-fifth anniversary in 1954, *The Banker* claimed that 'not for many years, if ever, has the work of the Institute been so important to the banking community as it has become in recent times . . . it is the main educating force within the banking system'.[12]

As a measure of this confidence in the Institute's services, the banks were increasingly willing to underwrite its heavy running costs in the post-war years. After rebuilding the Institute's reserves at the end of the war, the banks reasoned that the contribution of the Institute to the education and training of their staff deserved some form of permanent subsidy. From 1947, for the first time in over sixty years, the Council of the Institute had been forced to raise its membership fees. Ordinary members and certificated Associates were asked for subscriptions of £1.1s.0d. (£1.05p) instead of 10s.6d. (52½p), and the subscriptions of Fellows were increased from £2.2s.0d. (£2.10p) to £3.3s.0d. (£3.15p). Examination fees were altered to 5s.0d. (25p) for each Part I subject, and 10s.0d. (50p) for all Part II and optional subjects.[13] In 1948, as a means of ensuring that the income from these increases was guaranteed, the clearing banks decided to contribute to the Institute's funds at the rate of 10s.0d. (50p) for every member of their staffs who belonged to the Institute in 1948 and 1949. Including donations of £4,000 from the Bank of England in 1948 and 1949, this subsidy of some £20,000 per annum gave the Institute 'a fresh breathing space'; '. . . the principle has been accepted, in effect, that so long as the Institute continues to work efficiently in the best interests of banking and the people engaged in it, it may rightly look to the banks as well as their staffs for financial support'.[14] This agreement, which was largely the result of negotiations between Sir Clarence Sadd, President of the Institute between 1946 and 1948, and the chief executives of the 'Big Five' clearing banks and the Bank of England, was renewed in 1950. The banks' *per capita* contribution was subsequently increased to 15s.0d. (75p) for the five years from 1952. Apart from this subsidy, the Committee of London Clearing Bankers agreed to provide and furnish purpose-built premises at Post Office Court, 10 Lombard Street, as the Institute's modern London headquarters. The opening of the new premises in October 1951 was, as Sir Cecil Ellerton pointed out in his presidential address six months later, a landmark in the development of the Institute: '. . . for the first time in our history we find ourselves permanently housed and amply equipped . . . we should like to see an increasing demand for [the new library] as a lecture hall and meeting place for those interested in banking and kindred subjects'.[15]

In return for the banks' new offers of support the Institute was

Figure 33 *The choice of lecturers has always been important to the success of the Institute's programme of activities. R. W. Jones, Deputy Chairman of the Institute in 1950–1 and an Assistant General Manager of the Westminster Bank, was widely regarded as one of the Institute's most effective lecturers in the 1930s and 1940s. R. W. Jones was also a Gilbart lecturer and author of* Studies in Practical Banking.

keenly aware that its financial stability and future expansion depended upon the secretariat and members proving to the banks 'that their confidence in the Institute is not misplaced'.[16] In the late 1940s and during the 1950s, influenced by the changing relationship with the banks, the secretariat and local centre representatives set about the task of making the services of the Institute more widely understood throughout the banking industry. It was a task which required an outward-looking approach, strengthening the lines of communication both in the Institute's existing education work and in providing new services for members.

Reinforced by the formation of 23 new centres between 1947 and 1959 (see Appendix 4), the local centre network was an ideal channel for discussing and publicizing the Institute's work. In the recognition of approved teaching institutions for the diploma examinations, for example, the Institute's local centres were well placed to encourage young bankers to use the available teaching programmes. This local representation was invaluable in a period when more and more colleges were applying for the Institute's recognition: by the 1954–5 session, 94 colleges had been given recognition, and the total rose to 108 by 1959.[17] The value of these links was also evident in tutorial experiments at Liverpool, where the Liverpool Education Authority, the Liverpool City College of Commerce, and the Liverpool and District Bankers' Institute combined to offer personal instruction and correspondence tuition to diploma candidates, and in Devon and Cornwall, where candidates were able to visit tutors at the South Devon Technical College at fortnightly intervals.[18]

Welcoming these developments, the Council of the Institute looked forward in 1954 to the setting up of study groups for diploma entrants at the local centres. At that stage, study groups were already in operation at the Bristol and Leicester centres and at the Liverpool and District Bankers' Institute.[19] The success of these experiments amongst the younger members now convinced the Council that local centre 'forums', attended by a member of the Institute's secretariat, could become a regular part of each centre's programme. Designed 'to enable members to ask questions about the Institute and to give perspective to their work for the banking diploma', the first of the 'forum' sessions were held at nine selected local centres during 1955. Henry Eason, Assistant Secretary of the Institute, who was responsible for the 'forum' tour, reported a 'keen and lively' response and recommended an extension of the scheme to include forum meetings in the initial training courses run by the banks. In the first two years of the scheme, over 3,000 young bankers attended 53 forum meetings at local centres and bank staff colleges throughout England and Wales; for the Council and secretariat, it was a welcome opportunity to explain the role of the professional association to new members.[20]

Figure 34 *The Institute's coat of arms and the motto* Probus et Fidelis *were awarded by the College of Heralds at the time of the Institute's seventy-fifth anniversary in 1954. The crest and motto are one of Lombard Street's most familiar street signs.*

By the later 1950s, the forum scheme was one of a series of campaigns to raise the level of participation in the Institute's work. A particularly imaginative scheme was the organization of short residential courses, under the auspices of the Yorkshire local centres and the West Riding County Council Education Committee, at Grantley Hall, near Ripon, in 1957 and 1958. Over the country as a whole, none the less, the Council was worried by the evidence that many young bankers in the first five to ten years of their careers were unwilling to be drawn into the educational and local centre activities of the Institute. Maurice Megrah, Secretary of the Institute, recognized six basic reasons for this lack of balance:

(i) The much heavier turnover in bank staffs
(ii) The declining ratio of male to total bank staffs, particularly in the younger grades
(iii) The unsettling effects of military service
(iv) The demands of preparation for the new Banking Diploma
(v) Social or, rather, anti-social developments, especially television . . .
(vi) The dominating quest for light entertainment rather than for broader educational development.

To meet these challenges, the Secretary argued, 'the Institute should be brought to the young men'. Forum meetings were an important step in this direction, but it was *vital* [that] this campaign is supplemented by constant internal support from the managers of the banks'. The Council, accepting Maurice Megrah's analysis, asked the general managers of the clearing banks to encourage their branch managers to take a more active role in the guidance of young bankers; the value of Institute membership in a new entrant's career would only be taken seriously if local managers gave a positive lead to their members of staff.[21] In answer to the appeal, the local centres were able to draw an increasing number of senior bank managers into the planning and implementation of their activities in the mid-1950s. This trend, which helped to raise the status of local centre work within the profession, was especially obvious at meetings of the Institute's Council in London. In contrast to the relatively small attendance at the Council's pre-war monthly meetings, the minutes of meetings in the 1950s record a strong local centre representation. At meetings under the presidency of Tom Bland, who like his father had been particularly active in the Institute's local centre affairs, the regular attendance in 1956 and 1957 exceeded 60 members of Council, mostly from the centres.[22]

Parallel to its objective of increasing the awareness of the Institute's services amongst the membership, the Council gave close attention to public relations work during the 1950s. In the view of the Council and the secretariat, publicity for the aims and activities of the Institute was part of its responsibility 'to maintain and, over the years, to improve the standards of banking in this country'.[23] It was a duty which was relevant to recruitment as much as to questions of professional status.

In 1959 The Institute of Bankers joined the clearing banks in a promotional display at the National Education and Careers Exhibition at Olympia. A year later the Institute acted as host to a careers convention for head teachers and representatives of the clearing banks. This initiative was followed by the Institute's decision to publish two new booklets for school leavers, *Professional Education: An Introduction*, and *Women in Banking*, in 1960. The Council was also considering the production of a recruiting booklet for the banking profession as a whole, but this plan was eventually abandoned.[24] At the other end of the public relations spectrum, the need to promote the Institute's image was not underestimated. Although a ballot of the membership in 1951 turned down a renewed proposal for obtaining a Royal Charter, the Institute obtained its own grant of arms on the occasion of its seventy-fifth anniversary in 1954. The new crest and motto, *Probus et Fidelis*, were soon brought into use in the presentation and design of the Institute's publications.[25] The Council also augmented the Institute's social calendar in 1959, when, during the presidency of Lord Monckton of Brenchley, the first 'President's Dinner' was organized in the belief that occasional meetings with government ministers, the heads of other professions, and the leading figures in British industry would help to promote the interests and maintain the prestige of the banking profession. The dinners, held at Goldsmiths' Hall, London, at two-yearly intervals, subsequently became a regular part of each presidential term during the 1960s and 1970s.[26]

The use of the local centres in explaining the Institute's position and responsibilities within the banking system, together with the evolution of a more positive approach to public relations, reflected the large gains in cooperation between the banks and The Institute of Bankers since 1945. The banks, as Tom Bland implied in his speech as President in 1958, were rewarded for their support by the Institute's attention to 'the quality of British banking':

> The Institute aims not only to provide an efficient technical service to its members and to the banks, but, more important, to help those of our members who are willing to help themselves to equip themselves as bankers better qualified and fitted to occupy progressively senior positions within their profession.[27]

[154]

Recognition of these objectives did not inhibit the banks from asking for modifications to the Institute's educational reforms of 1945. The proposals for a 'third stage' qualification for selected bankers, which had been due for consideration in 1948, were not revived. Likewise, the 'three subject rule' for the Part I diploma examinations was eventually relaxed in 1957 in favour of the more generous requirement that candidates should pass two Part I subjects at one sitting; similar concessions were made in the Part II, Section I syllabus of the diploma in 1959.[28] In each of these decisions, the Council was influenced by the banks' uneasiness at the prospect of lengthening the periods of study leave for their officials. Since 1936 the banks had given their employees half-day leave on days when they were to sit the Institute's evening examinations, but, when proposals for daytime examinations were put forward in 1947, the 'Big Five' clearing banks were unwilling to accept any further inroad into normal working hours.[29] Subsequently, as the Institute drew into much closer contact with the staff departments and training schools of the banks, the banks began to modify their attitude to examination and study-leave facilities. In 1960, for example, the Midland Bank announced a study-leave programme which provided release for one day or two half-days a week (excluding the summer months) for employees in their final year of preparation for the Institute's Part II examinations.[30]

Despite this progress the question of study leave was to remain a sensitive issue in the relationship between the Institute and the banks in the 1960s and 1970s. Yet the post-war years saw the Institute and the banks moving steadily towards agreement on a system of exemptions from sections of the diploma examination, partly as a simplification of the examination rules, and partly as a means of maintaining or improving the standard of recruits to the profession. Both the Institute and the Chartered Institute of Secretaries had agreed to recognize the National Certificate in Commerce on its first, and abortive, introduction in 1939; in 1951, after the Carr-Saunders Committee of 1946–9 spoke up in favour of a common syllabus and certificate for commercial education, the banks and the Institute were willing to give recognition to the National Certificates of Commerce, if these were now to be revived. In principle these certificates were the business equivalent of the Ordinary and Higher National Certificates which had been offered through the technical colleges since 1921.[31] When the scheme again

Figure 35 *The Institute's modern headquarters at Post Office Court, 10 Lombard Street, London, which were acquired and furnished through the generosity of the clearing banks, were opened in 1951. The new library premises quickly proved their value as a lecture hall and meeting place as well as a purpose-built library for members.*

failed to obtain general support, the Institute was ready to accept alternative qualifications for exemptions from its Part I examinations. In 1951, for example, the Council agreed to offer exemptions from the diploma papers in English, economics, and book-keeping to incoming members who had passed the equivalent examinations of the Savings Banks Institute or the Corporation of Certified Secretaries. A much more ambitious scheme to exempt all university graduates from Part I, whatever their degree subjects, was turned down in 1956 on the grounds that it put school leavers at a significant disadvantage, but in 1958 the Council of the Institute approved exemption from Part I papers for all candidates who had obtained the 'A' level General Certificate of Education in the appropriate subjects.[32] It was a logical step both for the Institute and for the banks, as it reduced the wasted effort of bank employees in duplicating their GCE studies, and added to the incentives offered to above-average school leavers who were considering banking as a career.

Perhaps the most important of the exemption arrangements was the

Institute's recognition of the Ordinary and Higher National Certificates in Business Studies. When the introduction of the certificates was made known in 1960, with courses commencing at the technical colleges in the autumn of 1961, the Institute was one of the first professional associations to give its recognition.* The Institute offered subject-for-subject exemption from Part I examinations and appointed a representative to serve on the Joint Committee for Business Studies (the governing body for the Certificate scheme).[33] This network of exemptions, and recognition of the Certificates in Business Studies in particular, laid the foundations of the Institute's modern links with public sector teaching and examinations.

Financial subsidies for the Institute after the Second World War,

---

* On the announcement of the scheme, the other associations giving exemption were the Association of Certified and Corporate Accountants, Chartered Institute of Secretaries, Corporation of Secretaries, Chartered Insurance Institute, Institute of Cost and Works Accountants, Institute of Export, Institute of Transport, and the Advertising Joint Examination Board.

coupled with a closer working partnership with the banks in the education of young bank officials, enabled the Council and secretariat to
develop their ideas for the Institute as an information and research
centre and as an international meeting place for the banking profession. These ambitions, which had been hinted at before the war, were
specified by Sir Clarence Sadd at his inauguration as President of the
Institute in 1946:

> The functions proper to the Institute are much wider and
> greater than those of an examining body. . . . I look forward to
> the time when we may reach out to a more extensive library
> and information service, to the promotion of individual and
> collective research on the banking and financial problems of the
> day, and to the provision of a forum for free and lively discus-
> sion of matters of banking and finance.

Side by side with this type of development, Sir Clarence argued that
the Institute should build up its contacts with professional banking
institutes in the British Isles, the British Dominions, and the United
States:

> It is my earnest desire that these relations should be broadened
> and deepened as between bank men throughout the English-
> speaking world. . . . I find it difficult to believe that bankers
> have no part to play in this general process of world-wide
> collaboration in the development of understanding and trust at
> all levels and along lines of common interest.[34]

The President's views were evidently shared by the Institute's
secretariat, which stressed the potential value of research work and
international cooperation. In 1947 Maurice Megrah, when explaining
the Institute's need for stability of income, called for new initiatives in
teaching, research, and the opening or revival of overseas contacts.
The Institute had the choice of either allowing 'its wider qualities and
opportunities to wither' or of functioning 'through positive education
in the wider sense' and offering 'an information and research service
of equal rank with that of the highest educational institutions of its
kind in the world'.[35]

The pursuit of these aims brought distinct changes to the balance of
the Institute's work in the late 1940s and throughout the 1950s. On
the information and research side of its activities, the Institute's

library underwent a tremendous growth after the war. Irene Shrigley, the Librarian, greatly expanded the work of collecting and collating business information and replacing a large backlog of out-of-date textbooks. Total stock, which had comprised only 7,000 books in 1929, had climbed to 45,000 books by 1954, making the Institute's library perhaps the largest of its kind in the United Kingdom. By the time of Miss Shrigley's retirement in 1957, the library had become a major source of information for bankers and academics alike.[36] W. J. Thorne, with his experience both as a bank economist and as a contributor to the banking press, paid tribute to the Institute's 'wise eclecticism' in its expansion of the library's facilities: '. . . for many years now the Council has been ready to find room for works whose utility is best described as "cultural", and it is not unlikely that the attraction exerted by these has drawn more than a few clerks onwards to the literature bearing directly on their means of livelihood'.[37]

While the library and its information services were improving the quality of life for students of banking, the Institute was authorizing an increasing number of its own publications. Its two principal works of reference, *Questions on Banking Practice* and *Legal Decisions Affecting Bankers*, were updated in revised editions, but the Institute also produced a series of books and pamphlets on current banking topics. Prepared in most cases by prominent members of the Institute, including Leonard Mather (later to become President of the Institute, 1969–70, and Chief General Manager of the Midland Bank), these publications included studies of the sterling area, the finance of foreign trade, the capital market, stock exchanges, unsecured advances, and the European Economic Community.[38] Many of the new titles were revised versions of lectures which had featured in the Institute's lecture programme in the immediate post-war years. In 1946, the Council negotiated a joint lecture programme with the University of London whereby an autumn series on a general, financial or economic topic alternated with a spring series on a technical banking topic.* Lectures in the early years of the scheme included Henry Lawson (Principal of Lloyds Bank's Legal Department) and W. F. Crick (General Manager for Research and Statistics at the Midland Bank,

---

* When Ernest Sykes died in 1958, the spring lectures at the Institute were named the Ernest Sykes Memorial Lectures in honour of the former Secretary of the Institute.

and Deputy Chairman of the Institute in 1953–5), and audiences at some of the lectures in the joint programme reached 500 in the late 1940s.[39] Meanwhile, at King's College London, the Gilbart Lectures enjoyed a welcome post-war revival during the tenure of R. W. Jones, Manager of the Westminster Bank's Trustee Department, one of the Institute's best-known lecturers, and Deputy Chairman in 1950–1.[40]

True to Sir Clarence Sadd's promise the post-war Institute gave much greater attention to its regular contacts with other professional banking institutes both in the United Kingdom and overseas. His inaugural address was warmly welcomed by the institutes in Scotland, Ireland, Australasia, Canada, India, South Africa, and the American Bankers' Association. In practical terms the Institute was able to give full backing to the Scottish Institute's conference on banking education in 1950.[41] In 1952 and 1953 members of the Institute's secretariat visited Pakistan (where Henry Eason, Assistant Secretary of the Institute, advised the Government of Pakistan on the administration of that country's newly formed bankers' institute) and the United States of America, where the Secretary, Maurice Megrah, prepared a detailed comparative report on the American Institute of Banking, the American Bankers' Association, and the Graduate School of Banking at Rutgers University, New Jersey. He found it especially helpful to compare the American Institute's teaching methods and system of local 'chapters' with the practice of the British institutes, but the main value of the visit was an agreement for 'the closest cooperation' with the American banking institutions.[42]

By the late 1940s, while contacts with overseas bankers' associations were being reinforced, the Council and secretariat of the Institute realized that international contacts between professional bankers could be significantly improved by regular meetings or seminars. Continuity of the pre-war experiments in cooperation was not the sole factor in the Council's willingness to provide a forum for international bankers. Wilfred Hinton, as Director of Studies, had been highly impressed with the aims and teaching reputation of the Graduate School of Banking at Rutgers University during his frequent visits to the United States of America before and immediately after the Second World War. The School, sponsored and managed by the American Bankers' Association, required its students to attend an intensive two-week period of study each year in a three-year course of tuition.

Maurice Megrah, who visited the School during his American tour in 1953, reported that the yearly courses were designed 'to improve [a banker's] technical efficiency beyond an accepted minimum and to broaden his outlook'. The School's courses were also intended to contribute to the common identity and status of the banking profession in America: '. . . it is my impression that the real purpose of the Graduate School of Banking is the development of a banking tradition. . . . The Graduate School certainly gives a great sense of corporate interest and has established itself as a most desirable development in American banking'.[43]

When international cooperation became a firm commitment of The Institute of Bankers after the Second World War, the lessons of the pre-war courses for overseas bankers and the example of the Graduate School of Banking led the Council to investigate the opportunities for regular programmes of short courses for qualified bankers. By July 1947 the Council was envisaging a two-week summer course at either Oxford or Cambridge for between 50 and 100 young bankers visiting the United Kingdom. Enthusiastic and efficient groundwork by the secretariat and by the Oxford local centre of the Institute enabled the Council to announce the launch of its first International Banking Summer School at Christ Church, Oxford, in September 1948. A number of prominent speakers were invited to present papers on current banking topics, ensuring that the first school would set high standards and encourage a high level of participation by delegates.* Group discussions in syndicates were also arranged to supplement the lecture programme. Nominations for places were requested from the banking institutes in Scotland, Ireland, Australasia, Canada, and India. Banks throughout western and eastern Europe, the Middle East, and the Americas were invited to send representatives, and the eventual registration comprised 108 overseas bankers from 31 countries.

---

* Speakers included W. F. Crick (on British monetary policy) and R. W. Jones (on trustee work) from the Institute's current list of lecturers. The universities were represented by Roy (later Sir Roy) Harrod of Christ Church College, Oxford, Professor R. S. Sayers, University of London (on central banking questions) and Sir Henry Clay, Warden of Nuffield College, Oxford (on the problems of sterling). Contributors from the financial press included Paul Bareau of the *News Chronicle*, later a regular contributor to the Institute's *Journal* (on international banking organizations), and W. T. C. King, Editor of *The Banker* (on the London discount market).

Under the direction of Wilfred Hinton, the School was a striking success. From the outset, 'formality was out of the question', and the delegates were able to debate major national and international banking issues 'in a friendly yet critical atmosphere'. The secretariat of the Institute, which had borne the administrative burden of organizing the School and publishing promptly the School's lectures in book form, was sufficiently confident of the benefits of the innovation to recommend holding International Banking Summer Schools on an annual basis. The Secretary recommended that after a return visit to Christ Church in 1949, future schools should perhaps be held abroad, in major foreign financial centres, with the school returning to England again in some years. [44]

The promising reports of the first Summer School from both the secretariat and from the School's lecturers and students drew a positive response from the international banking community. The Council of The Institute of Bankers organized a second school at Christ Church in the summer of 1949. Despite the death of Wilfred Hinton, who had given such distinguished service to the cause of banking education over the previous twenty years, the School maintained the high standards of the first meeting. Subsequent schools were organized at Saltsjobaden, Sweden (1950), Paris (1951), Knokke, Belgium (1953), Granada, Spain (1954), New Jersey, USA (organized for the Americans by Maurice Megrah, with the assistance of other Institute officials in 1956), Garmisch, Germany (1957), St Andrews, Scotland (1958) and Burgenstock, Switzerland (1959), with return visits to Oxford in 1952 and 1955. By the end of the 1950s nearly 3,000 bankers had participated in the International Banking Summer Schools, whose growing reputation created a heavy demand for places each year. Much of the credit for this success belonged to the Institute itself, as the instigator and principal host for the schools. The Secretary, on his visit to the United States of America in 1953, found that American bankers were 'loud and unstinting' in the praise of the Institute's initiative. [45]

For the Council, perhaps the most encouraging proof of the enhanced international standing of the Institute was the discernible increase in the numbers of overseas bankers applying for membership, especially after about 1954. The Institute's membership register had always included small numbers of bankers from foreign banks and

British bankers resident overseas, quite apart from the employees of foreign banks in London. Before the Second World War, for example, notwithstanding the dominant position of the 'Big Five' clearing banks, the membership of the Institute was drawn from no less than 329 domestic and international banks; the list included banks in Europe and the Far East as well as British-owned international banks in English-speaking countries and the sterling area. The total number of overseas members hovered at around 1,500 in the years after the Second World War, but by the end of the 1950s the pattern was altering rapidly. Some 4,000 members, or nearly 10 per cent of the Institute's membership, were resident overseas by 1960.[46] Yet there remained an important difference between a dispersed and unco-ordinated overseas membership and the more highly organized local centre system in the United Kingdom. This difference, in the view of many overseas members, could be narrowed by adapting the concept of local centres to their own needs. While retaining all the advantages of Institute membership, some of the burden of leadership and organization could sensibly be transferred to bankers in major overseas financial centres. A proposal to open a local centre in Nigeria in 1954 came too early to win strong local support, but in 1960 the Council heard that members in Singapore and Nairobi were ready to form their own local centres. Both centres, each with over 100 members, were formally constituted in 1960; the Council of the Institute offered its full backing to the new ventures, with the promise of a *per capita* subsidy on the same basis as the finance of the United Kingdom centres. It was a landmark in the Institute's career, as Sir Eric Carpenter acknowledged in his presidential address to the Institute in May 1961:

The spontaneous formation during the past twelve months of two overseas centres . . . is a development which reminds us that the Institute has no territorial limitations either constitutionally or in fact . . . we have 4,000 members overseas in 94 territories throughout the world. Some of these countries have old-established and deeply rooted banking systems, others are of newly independent status. It is not without significance that many of their young bankers—and some not so young—look to our Institute . . . as an intellectual power-house of the profession.[47]

Boldly optimistic as this interpretation was, it was characteristic of the change in the public face of The Institute of Bankers since the war. In contrast to its relatively passive and discreet role in the 1920s and 1930s, the Institute now offered a positive approach to the organization of banking education and international cooperation between bankers. The shift in emphasis was bound to affect the Institute's responsibilities to its members; by 1960, while the new overseas centres were putting together their first programmes, the Institute prepared to accept the heavy load of leading and coordinating the activities of a worldwide membership.

8

THE TESTS
OF MODERN BANKING
1960–1979

EVEN when compared with the rate of new enrolments in the inter-war period, the membership of The Institute of Bankers expanded at an impressive pace in the 1960s and the 1970s. Over 82,000 bankers were members by the end of 1970, almost doubling the total since 1960; the strong upward trend was sustained in the late 1970s and over 113,000 members were enrolled by 1977. Examination statistics were equally encouraging, showing that more than 46,000 candidates sat for the diplomas in 1970, with over 60,000 entrants annually after 1975 (see Appendix 3). At the Institute this massive increase in membership and examination work transformed the responsibilities of the Council and secretariat. By the 1970s, as well as the greater size and complexity of its administrative duties, the Institute faced the task of devising or extending services to keep pace with innovations in banking business.

This acceleration in the membership and examination work of the Institute was achieved in a period of major adjustments in the United Kingdom's banking system. In 1977 the London clearing banks, in a review of banking developments since 1957 as part of their evidence for the Wilson Committee's enquiry into the functioning of the financial system, described a period of long-term alteration in the structure and business of the banks:

> It is hard to exaggerate the extent of the changes that have
> occurred in the twenty years since [1957] both in the banks
> themselves and in the financial system within which they
> operate. The number of clearing banks has been reduced from
> eleven to six through mergers, while the total number of
> commercial banks (domestic and foreign) operating in the
> United Kingdom has expanded from under 125 to over 300.
> The total resources at the clearing bank's disposal have in-
> creased from some £7,000 million to some £50,000 million.
> . . . There has been a vast increase in the numbers of payment
> items handled by the banks and wholly new systems, heavily
> dependent upon computer technology, have been introduced
> to cope with them. . . .[1]

Branch banking, at the traditional centre of the clearing banks'
business, had been progressively strengthened during the 1950s and
early 1960s, raising the total representation from 8,469 branch
offices before the Second World War to 11,250 offices in the United
Kingdom in 1962. The merger between Barclays Bank and Martins
Bank in 1968, and the completion of the union of the National
Provincial Bank (which had acquired the District Bank in 1962) and
Westminster Bank in 1970, led to the closure of branches in areas
where the enlarged banks were represented by several offices. These
closures and the further 'streamlining' of branch networks checked
the rise in the number of offices during the 1970s. Even so, the
search for comprehensive coverage brought the total number of the
clearing banks' outlets to over 11,600 in 1976. Between 1962 and
1976, as the money supply expanded and inflation dominated the
economic scene, the value of sterling deposits in the branch system was
lifted from £7,066 million to £17,737 million. In addition to these
changes in the volume and distribution of banking business, those
working in the branch offices of the clearing banks were adapting to
fundamental changes in the industry's ways of conducting its business.
In 1971 the Bank of England's introduction of the system of 'Competition and Credit Control', which was designed to broaden the
opportunities for competition in banking, required the clearing banks
to adopt new reserve asset ratios and remove the quantitative ceilings
imposed upon bank lending. As a result the banks dismantled most of

their standard tariffs and interest rate agreements. Although there were important departures from the new system in the late 1970s, professional bankers found themselves learning new techniques in a more competitive environment.[2]

In the 1960s and 1970s, while deposit banking in the home market remained the staple of their business, the British banks were increasingly committed to the extension of their international activities and to diversification into financial services which were not previously associated with the banking sector. Some of these changes were already becoming obvious in the early 1960s, as Sir Eric Carpenter, President of the Institute, acknowledged in 1961 : 'The field of banking operations has broadened and has become infinitely more complicated than it was, say, thirty years ago'.[3] In 1958 each of the 'Big Five' clearing banks had entered the instalment finance market by taking shareholdings in or purchasing the ownership of existing hire purchase finance companies. On the international side of their business, the decline in the role of sterling in the world economy was forcing the major British banks to look for alternative sources of income, including the new Eurocurrency market, special schemes for export credit, and foreign exchange business. It was not until the late 1960s and early 1970s, however, that the twin processes of diversification and the development of international business brought far-reaching changes in the structure of British banking. In contrast to the relatively narrow corporate base of the clearing banks between the wars and in the 1940s and 1950s, the banks now emerged as 'groups' of companies offering banking and non-banking services in the United Kingdom and overseas. Subsidiary and associated companies for international business, merchant banking, instalment finance and related services, unit trusts, and investment advisory work were operated by most of the clearing bank groups in the 1970s, together with the forging of links with the travel business, insurance broking, and export finance. By the late 1970s, subsidiary companies (especially the international banking units) were contributing as much as 40 per cent of the gross profits of some of the clearing bank groups.[4]

These striking alterations in the framework and business of the British banks could not be completed without an expansion in the number of bank employees. Despite the manpower savings achieved by the transfer of routine book-keeping and processing work from

Figure 36 *The success of the Institute's first International Banking Summer School at Christ Church, Oxford, in 1948 was followed by a regular series of similar schools at Oxford and overseas. The School, with its mixture of lectures and group discussions for young bank executives, attracted applications from banks throughout the world. Speakers at the 1961 School at Christ Church, Oxford, included W. F. Crick, a former Deputy Chairman of the Institute (at the lectern), and, to his left, Henry Eason, Secretary of the Institute and Director of the School.*

mechanized systems to computer-based procedures, the number of employees of clearing banks almost doubled from nearly 106,000 in December 1959 to over 203,000 in 1976. Another 25,000 employees were working for subsidiary companies of the banks by 1976, with a further 50,000 employed wholly or mainly outside the United Kingdom. As a measure of the structural shift in banking, only 155,000 bank officials, or 56 per cent of the staff establishments of the clearing banks in 1976, were directly employed in branch bank offices; apart from those working for subsidiaries or in overseas countries, the remaining 48,000 employees were employed in head office services, international services, trust companies, instalment finance, merchant banking, and other group activities. A further change in the overall picture had been brought about by the intake of women for clerical and cashiers' duties. The proportion of women in the staff of the banks had risen from 40 per cent in 1959 to 55 per cent in 1976, but less than 2 per cent of the banks' management appointments and only 10 per cent of 'appointed' posts were occupied by women in the late 1970s.[5]

The sharp rise in the membership of The Institute of Bankers owed much to these developments. With so many new recruits to the banks, it was especially important that the banks should begin to reinforce their support for the Institute and to make it easier for their young members of staff to participate in the Institute's affairs. The financial position of the Institute, for example, was regularized in 1962 when the banks agreed to provide a subsidy of up to 25 per cent of the Institute's annual expenditure, the remaining 75 per cent to come from members' subscriptions.[6] For incoming recruits the banks' support was made more meaningful by the widespread introduction of study leave for Institute examinations. Following the announcement of the Midland Bank's scheme for study leave in 1960, all the major banks were offering part-time day release for diploma candidates by the mid-1960s. These allowances were supplemented in the 1970s by the introduction of the banks' own revision courses for the main diploma subjects.[7]

Not all the Institute's new members entered as a result of the expansion of the domestic banking system. Although the numbers of women employees in the clearing banks had risen from 42,801 in 1959 to 112,100 in 1976, the increase in the Institute's female membership

Figure 37 *In the 1960s and 1970s The Institute of Bankers continued to act as the principal host and organizer for the International Banking Summer School. The School made return visits to Christ Church, Oxford, in 1961, 1964, 1970, and 1973.*

from 2.9 to 8.7 per cent of the United Kingdom membership scarcely reflected their contribution to the change in the staffing structure. Disappointingly, women bankers comprised less than 2 per cent of the Associates of the Institute in 1976.[8]

In response to the Institute's efforts to develop an international role in the post-war years, strong support from overseas bankers was now building up. The focus of this confidence was the network of overseas centres, each constructed along the lines of the centres set up at Singapore and Nairobi in 1960. Relying upon the initiative of local bankers, and depending upon the signatures of at least 100 Institute members before they could obtain recognition from the Council, new centres were launched in Malta in 1961, Hong Kong, Accra and Lagos in 1963, Kampala in 1967, Lusaka in 1969, and Cyprus in 1970. Each centre was regularly visited by members of the Institute's Council or secretariat both to maintain communications and to ensure that the centre's activities matched the objectives of the Institute.[9] The progress of the overseas centres was not always straightforward, and on more than one occasion the Institute found itself lobbying senior bank executives for their active support to ensure the success of a centre. On balance, none the less, the overseas centres were responsible for generating sustained local support for the Institute and its professional qualifications, and in 1966 the Council arranged that representatives of the overseas centres should be admitted to the Council on the same basis as the local centre representatives.[10] Like the local centres in the United Kingdom, the new overseas organizations offered programmes of meetings and study facilities for diploma candidates, and these services helped to introduce many thousands of overseas bankers to membership of The Institute of Bankers. Of its 13,000 overseas members in 1970, 4,000 were registered with the new centres. When overseas membership reached about 30,000 in the late 1970s, at least 12,000 members belonged to the overseas local centres, including some 6,000 in Hong Kong alone.[11] These returns were maintained even after the formation of an independent Nigerian Institute of Bankers in 1976, based upon the 5,000-strong membership of the Lagos centre of The Institute of Bankers. Although the Lagos centre was wound up as soon as the Nigerian Institute had been launched, The Institute of Bankers was able to offer cooperation in the management of the Nigerian examinations. The Institute also provided advice and support for the formation and organization of independent institutes in Jamaica and Malaysia in 1977.[12]

If the new centres were the main channel for the growth in the overseas presence of the Institute, it was important that the post-war reputation for international cooperation in banking studies should be maintained. The International Banking Summer School for young bank executives, which the Institute had initiated in 1948, was the type of venture which added to this reputation. As in the late 1940s and 1950s, The Institute of Bankers continued to act as the principal organizer and host for the School, with further two-week sessions at Christ Church, Oxford, in 1961, 1964, 1970, and 1973. The Institute also retained its traditional role as adviser for the summer schools, and similar courses were held at Noordwijk, Netherlands in 1960, Moscow (1962), Semmering, Austria (1963), Melbourne (1965 and 1976), Bergen, Norway (1966), Kingston, Canada (1967), Dublin (1968), and Aarhus, Denmark (1969). In the 1970s, locations for the Summer School also included Chianciano, Italy (1971), Brown University, USA (1972), Aulanko, Finland (1974), La Baule, France (1975), Ronneby, Sweden (1977), and Liège, Belgium (1978). By acting as a forum for representatives from all quarters of the banking world, in addition to its purely educational function, the concept of the International Banking Summer School drew attention to the Institute's services for overseas members. Likewise, the Council and secretariat of the Institute were confident that the selective introduction of international exchange visits for young members would contribute to improved understanding and cooperation between professional bankers in different parts of the world.

As a major contribution to these international activities, the Institute sponsored a Transatlantic Banking Scholarship in 1963. The scholarship was first suggested in a Stonier Memorial address by Henry Eason, Secretary of the Institute, to the Graduate School of Banking of the American Bankers' Association, at Rutgers University, New Jersey, in June 1963:

> Do you not think an adequate fund could be raised by voluntary annual subscriptions from banks in both countries, to be partially administered in each, with the object of encouraging and facilitating banking exchanges between young domestic

banking executives. . . . It would be a vital part of the scheme that each subscribing bank should agree to take a successful candidate from the other country into their organization for, say, three months and generally to facilitate his education.[13]

The American banks declined to offer a reciprocal scholarship but agreed to accept winners of the Institute's scholarship competition. The Council was not discouraged, and a scholarship scheme for study visits to the United States of America was successfully launched in 1965; each year's scholarship was open for competition among members who had qualified in the top 50 places of the diploma examinations.[14] This imaginative scheme, primarily for the benefit of the successful candidates but also as a means of improving the Institute's international standing, was supplemented by the Bank of England's sponsorship of the Institute's European Banking Scholarship in 1970. The Bank of England's award was intended to encourage members of the Institute to study the principles and practice of central banking and the scholarship gave the winning candidates the opportunity to visit European central banks. International exchange projects also included reciprocal study-tours for young bankers, organized in conjunction with the Carl Duisberg-Gesellschaft, Germany. A similar study-tour scheme was arranged with the help of the Association Belge des Banques and the Nederlands Instituut voor het Bank-en Effectenbedrijf in 1976.

This emphasis upon the Institute's international projects and the rising importance of the overseas centres helped to raise the number of overseas members from 4,000 in 1960 to some 30,000 in the late 1970s. While recognizing that the doubling of the United Kingdom membership from 42,000 in 1960 to approximately 80,000 by 1977 was largely the result of the absolute growth in staff numbers, the Institute could attribute part of this expansion to the solid progress of the local centre network in England and Wales. By 1977, 98 local centres (including the Berwick-upon-Tweed centre, which was formed as a joint centre of the Institute and the Scottish Institute in 1952) were in operation in the United Kingdom, each acting as a home base for new members and for members whose careers involved repeated transfers to different parts of the country. The roll-call of local centres included, from 1965 onwards, the Manchester and District Bankers'

Institute. Originally formed in 1895, the Manchester Institute was affiliated to The Institute of Bankers when it became clear that the banks' day-release schemes reduced the demand for the Manchester Institute's evening classes. After the affiliation in 1965 the Manchester Institute took its place as one of the largest of the local centres, with a membership of over 2,500 in 1978.[15] In the local centre system as a whole, membership figures were also boosted by the merger of the Savings Banks Institute with The Institute of Bankers in 1977. The Savings Banks Institute had been launched as a qualifying association for employees of the British savings banks in 1948, but, as the savings banks increasingly extended their business to personal lending and other mainstream banking services in the 1970s, the professional requirements for officials of the savings banks drew closer to the curriculum for employees of the clearing banks. When the merger was completed in 1977, 6,000 members of the former Savings Banks Institute were transferred to the membership register of The Institute of Bankers. The new members were soon participating in the Institute's local centre programmes, especially in areas where the savings banks movement had deep roots. The Manchester centre, for example, has a strong savings banks presence amongst its local membership.[16]

The continuing progress of the local centre network in the 1960s and 1970s was reflected in the wider range of activities and opportunities offered to members.[17] In the late 1970s most of the local centre programmes combined formal lectures with audience-participation meetings, quizzes, industrial visits and, in some cases, short seminars and overseas study-tours. In 1977, as a measure of this activity, the total number of meetings organized by the 106 local and overseas centres of the Institute climbed to 850, including 28 seminar courses. Although this level of participation could only be obtained on the initiative of local members, the contribution of the Institute in London could not be underestimated. The local centre conferences, which had been part of the Institute's liaison arrangements since the 1930s, were an effective means of exchanging views on the management of the centres and keeping the honorary officials of the centres in close contact with the Council and secretariat of the Institute. In an attempt to ensure that more young members were drawn into the Institute's non-examination activities, the Council took new steps 'to explain itself to new entrants'.[18] This objective was partly fulfilled by the publication of a new series of booklets outlining the work of the Institute. The Institute's *Journal* was also extensively remodelled and redesigned to give more space to topics of special interest to young members. Another successful project was the compilation of the audio-visual package *Presenting the Institute* in 1976. The package was supplied to local centres throughout the United Kingdom for presentation at special meetings of school leavers and new recruits; over 80 meetings were held in 1976 and again in 1977, with a total attendance in each year of over 4,000. Apart from stepping up these efforts to draw attention to the modern role of The Institute of Bankers, the launch of the Institute's 'Banking Game' in 1973–4 was a popular addition to the local centre programmes. Initially sponsored by the Swiss Bank Corporation, the Banking Game was planned as an inter-centre competition on the solution of problems in modern branch banking. Most of the Institute's centres, including the overseas centres, entered teams for the annual competition, and by the late 1970s the Banking Game was fully established in the local centre calendar; the winning teams in the first four years were Southampton (1974), Worcester (1975), Hong Kong (1976), and Bristol (1977).

While the production of publicity material and the launch of the Banking Game were intended to encourage young members to participate more fully in the non-examination activities of the Institute, the upkeep of facilities for qualified men and women in middle management was not forgotten. Working from their experience as organizers of the International Banking Summer School, the Council and secretariat of the Institute felt that yearly seminars for selected members, preferably between 30 and 40 years of age, would provide an incentive to those who had completed their diploma examinations but looked for the additional experience of advanced study courses. As a result, the Institute organized the first of its 'Cambridge Seminars' for young British banking executives in 1968. These courses, held each year, at Christ's College, Cambridge, gave delegates the opportunity to undertake syndicate work and case studies in some of the major issues of modern banking. By 1978 approximately 1,000 students had attended the Cambridge Seminars, and topics in the 1970s included 'Banking for Profit' (1972), 'The Banks and Society' (1974), 'The Banks and Industry' (1976), and 'Banks and the British Exporter' (1977) and 'The Banks and Small Businesses' (1978).

[175]

(a)

△ (b)   (c) ▽

(d)

(e)

Figure 38 *The residential training and management colleges of the major banks have played a key role in banking education since the late 1940s. The colleges include (a) Barclays Bank Group Management Training Centre, Ashdown Park, Sussex; (b) Lloyds Bank Staff College, Eyhurst Court, Kingswood, Surrey; (c) Midland Bank Residential College, Oxted, Surrey; (d) National Westminster Bank Staff College, Heythrop Park, Oxfordshire; and (e) Williams & Glyn's Bank Management Training Centre, Cheadle, Cheshire.*

The Council and secretariat of the Institute, attributing the impressive intake of new members to the combined influence of the expansion of bank staff numbers and the success of its own network of local and overseas centres, believed that the quality and relevance of the Institute's educational work was itsgr eatest responsibility in the 1960s and 1970s. This duty was at its most obvious in the sheer size of the administrative burden of the diploma examinations. When the number of candidates began its sharp rise in the early 1960s, the Council was evidently worried by the 'growing problem of finding examination accommodation for so many students'.[19] Registration of many thousands of students, each at a different stage in the diploma examinations, also created difficulties. The administrative load was lightened when the Institute transferred its membership records to a computerized system in 1967, and the continuing shortage of accommodation for members' services was eased when the Institute's Registrar's Department was moved to new premises at Canterbury, Kent, in December 1975.[20]

In attempting to cope with the growth in the number of diploma candidates and their need for up-to-date study aids, much could be achieved by taking on greater responsibility for the commissioning and publishing of textbooks. The Institute significantly extended its publication list in the 1960s and 1970s. In addition to new versions of *Questions on Banking Practice*, *Leading Cases in the Law of Banking* (a consolidated digest of cases replacing *Legal Decisions Affecting Bankers*) and the published proceedings of the Cambridge Seminars and the International Banking Summer Schools, the Institute's range of textbooks now included L. S. Dyer's *Practical Approach to Bank Lending*, F. E. Perry's *Elements of Banking*, James Dandy's *Branch Banker*, B. S. Wheble's *Uniform Customs and Practice for Documentary Credits*, A. J. W. Watson's *The Finance of International Trade*, and H. H. Hutchinson's *Interpretation of Balance Sheets*.[21] These publications were well received in a period when commercial publishers were competing to offer a wide range of textbooks on similar subjects. By 1977 total sales of Institute publications (excluding the *Journal*) were running at over £96,000 per annum, largely as the result of the sale of textbooks to Institute members at special prices.

A more fundamental problem for the Institute, in common with the educational work of the other major business professions, was the need to ensure that existing tuition facilities had the capacity to cope with the growth in the number of examination candidates. In the Council's view, this responsibility could best be met by strengthening the procedures for liaison with the further education colleges. The appointment of Frank Steele and Wilfred Hinton as directors of studies between the 1920s and 1940s was a helpful precedent for this type of commitment, as their regular contacts with the colleges had ensured that the teaching of the Institute's syllabus reached a common standard as nearly as possible. These duties had fallen upon the secretariat with the help of assessors from the Ministry of Education after Hinton's death in 1949, but during the 1960s the time and resources needed for the supervision of tuition facilities made it essential that this work was placed on a more systematic basis. In 1969 the Council responded by reintroducing the post of Director of Studies. Eric Glover, who had joined the staff of the Institute in 1963, was now redesignated Under-Secretary (Director of Studies) with special responsibility for tuition arrangements.

The announcement of a recognition scheme for correspondence colleges in 1969 was typical of the Council's growing awareness of its tuition responsibilities at this time. Traditionally, relationships between the Institute and the correspondence colleges had been poorly defined. Partly out of caution about the advertised claims of the colleges and partly through its anxiety to ensure that teaching-aids were fully up-to-date, the Institute had been reluctant to draw the tuition colleges into the regular discussion of syllabus problems. In the late 1960s, as a survey of 'home study' by the Adult Education Department at the University of Manchester confirmed in 1971, it was still true that more than half the candidates for Part II of the Institute's diploma examinations were studying by correspondence courses.[22] There was obviously room for an improvement in communications, and in 1968 an investigation of the workings and educational standards of the principal correspondence colleges was authorized. As a result the Council agreed to introduce a recognition scheme for the colleges from 1969 onwards. The scheme brought the advantages of greater coordination in the preparation of correspondence study material, emphasis upon the use of approved textbooks, and the monitoring of advertisements for courses for the Institute's examinations.[23] The scheme formed the basis for regular contact between the Institute and the tuition colleges in the 1970s, making it possible for the Institute and the colleges to collaborate in the updating of students' course material.

Alongside these initiatives, contact with the teaching colleges was extended to cope with the remarkable influx of diploma candidates throughout the 1960s and 1970s. The colleges looked to the Institute for advice on the teaching of the syllabus and those setting Internal Part I examinations received guidance on attendance requirements. A major step forward in this area of responsibility was the introduction of study courses for teachers of banking in 1970; three-day courses were held at Huddersfield and Garnett College, Roehampton, where teachers of banking subjects could discuss tuition problems with teacher training experts, the Institute's examiners, and the secretariat. Additional courses were arranged for full-time teachers of banking from 1975, and other services included the compilation of a register of banking teachers in the United Kingdom, with each teacher receiving educational news and copies of the latest tuition aids.

Worthwhile as these links were to prove during the 1970s, it was crucial that the Institute should maintain regular communications with the teaching colleges throughout England and Wales. The local centres were ideally placed to share the work of maintaining contact with the colleges, and in 1970 the centres were urged to appoint education officers to coordinate tuition facilities in their own areas. The experiment greatly simplified the task of representing the Institute's interests, notably at the regional advisory councils concerned with the allocation of National Certificate courses in business studies. From 1973 education officers met at an annual conference to review syllabus changes and to discuss means of improving the performance of students at examinations. A useful result of these education conferences was the launch of a campaign to bring students into closer touch with the examiners' requirements, and in 1976 the chief examiner in practice of banking travelled to a number of local centres in the United Kingdom and held discussion meetings for candidates.[24]

These adjustments in tuition arrangements soon proved their worth during the introduction of the Institute's new qualifying requirements in the 1970s. By 1970–1, while coping with the increase in the numbers of home and overseas members, the Council of the Institute were keenly aware that the recruitment and training pattern in the major banks was undergoing far-reaching changes. These changes were likely to affect the organization and content of banking education throughout the 1970s and into the 1980s. Clearly the diversification of banking services and the greater emphasis upon international business in the 1960s and early 1970s demanded a broadly based education for bank staff. The professional bankers of the next two decades would need to understand the intricacies of invest-ment and taxation advice, and leasing and factoring services as well as mainstream banking roles. Expansion in the world of higher educa-tion, however, was also bound to influence the recruitment and training of new entrants. The number of students in full- or part-time higher education had more than doubled from 192,000 to 463,000 be-tween 1962 and 1972, and because the expansion seemed likely to continue the banks reckoned to recruit a growing number of graduates for non-managerial positions. At the same time the growth of busi-ness studies courses at polytechnics and technical colleges appeared to offer an opportunity for the professional associations to integrate their qualifications with public sector awards, particularly the certificates and degrees awarded at polytechnics and other colleges approved by the Council for National Academic Awards. Degree courses in busi-ness studies at CNAA-approved colleges were attracting over 6,000 students each year in the late 1970s. As an undercurrent to these trends, the banks and other business employers sensed a distinct change in staff attitudes to employment. At the beginning of the 1970s the turnover of personnel was strikingly higher than at any time since the Second World War. If they were to compete successfully in the recruitment market, the banks recognized that in the years ahead their professional qualifications would need much greater flexibility in entry conditions and wider recognition outside banking.[25]

Geoffrey Dix, taking over as Secretary-General in 1971, suggested that the time had come for a full consideration of the Institute's role as a qualifying association, to ensure that it continued to offer to its members an up-to-date professional qualification which would also continue to meet the changing needs of the banks as employers. In April 1972, the Council agreed to 'set up a fully representative work-ing party to undertake a comprehensive study of the Institute's future

Figure 39 *The publication of the* Journal of The Institute of Bankers *remains one of the Institute's principal services to its members throughout the world, and its uninterrupted appearance since 1879 is a significant contribution to the literature of banking. Since January 1976 the* Journal *has appeared in a new and larger format.*

role as a qualifying association'. Under the chairmanship of Derek Wilde, a member of Council and then Vice-Chairman Designate of Barclays Bank,* the working party agreed to consider the Institute's qualifying role in its widest sense, including the formal examination and tuition work and 'career-long post-graduate activities'. In the knowledge that the review would be the most comprehensive investigation of the Institute's educational responsibilities in its history, the Wilde Committee approached its task by asking 'if we were starting from scratch today, what sort of qualification would we recommend?'[26]

Between April 1972 and July 1973 the Wilde Committee undertook a detailed survey of the recruitment and training policies of 29 United Kingdom and overseas banks. The Committee also compared the Institute's existing qualifications with the educational programmes offered by other banking institutes and by other professional associations. On questions of tuition, the Committee consulted the teaching colleges and the Department of Education and Science, and drew upon the advice of J. R. Deans, an H.M. Inspector of Education and the Institute's assessor of the college banking courses. Working from this evidence, the Committee adopted five main objectives in framing its recommendations: flexibility (providing more than one level of qualification), variety of course content (including management skills), public recognition (giving the Institute's qualification a 'market value' outside the banking world), links with public sector qualifications (closer integration with existing business studies courses), and a suitable allowance of study leave. The Committee's commitment to these principles was reflected in its detailed recommendations to the Council in July 1973. Three tiers of qualification were proposed. Stage 1, for clerical staff below supervisory level, specified an Ordinary National Certificate or Diploma in Business Studies, including papers in English, economics, law, accountancy, and elements of banking. Tuition would be provided mainly through the

---

* Other members of the working party were Malcolm Wilcox, then Assistant Chief General Manager of the Midland Bank, as Deputy Chairman; Philip Chappell, Director, Morgan Grenfell & Co.; J. G. W. Davies, Executive Director, Bank of England; D. M. Duncan, General Manager (Staff), Standard Bank; N. W. Jones, General Manager (Group Coordination), Lloyds Bank; T. P. Lyons, Executive Director (Personnel), Williams & Glyn's Bank; and P. H. Spencer, Assistant Regional Director, National Westminster Bank.

300 colleges teaching these courses, each requiring about 35 days of study leave per annum. In Stage 2—designed for senior clerical staff and junior management, and open to those who had passed through Stage 1 or could offer two GCE 'A' levels (together with a one-year conversion course in law, accountancy, economics, and elements of banking)—the syllabus was again linked closely to the public sector awards in business studies. Candidates for Stage 2 would be expected to obtain a Higher National Certificate or Diploma in Business Studies after a three-year course available at 90 further education colleges, but the course would also include two special papers on the practice of banking, set and marked by the Institute. The banks would be asked to allow some 30 days of study leave each year for Stage 2 candidates. For those who were not within reach of a teaching college, the Committee envisaged an 'Institute route' whereby candidates would be required to take examinations set by the Institute. Finally, beyond Stage 2, the Committee planned a third stage of qualification for the majority of staff of management potential. Breaking new ground in banking education, the emphasis in the proposed Stage 3 qualification fell squarely upon advanced banking and financial studies. The Stage 3 level would be open to holders of the Stage 2 qualification, graduates or qualified members of other appropriate professions, and holders of the existing Associateship of the Institute. The Committee envisaged that this third stage would provide a degree-level qualification based on the Institute's own two-year syllabus. The Stage 3 qualification, with papers on the practice of banking, human aspects of management, business planning, and the marketing of financial services, would clearly need the teaching support of the polytechnics and business schools, with an allowance from the banks of eight weeks' full-time study leave each year. To lend weight to the proposals the Committee devised an outline syllabus for each stage in the qualification.

In the view of the Wilde Committee, these recommendations needed to be placed in the context of an expanded range of post-qualifying activities. In a second report, published in September 1974,* the Committee investigated the Institute's role in management

* The members of the original working party were now joined by T. F. H. Cullum, Assistant General Manager, Lloyds Bank, and R. J. Mortimer, Assistant General Manager (Personnel), Standard and Chartered Banking Group, replacing N. W. Jones and D. M. Duncan. Another new member was T. J. W. Ivey, the Council representative of the Chatham and Maidstone local centre.

education for banking, the provision of information services and the work of the local centres. The Committee was impressed with the Institute's facilities for information and library study and satisfied with the direction of the local centres, but it was keen that The Institute of Bankers should take a lead in the organization of short post-experience courses for qualified bankers at home and overseas. The report recommended a series of experimental short courses to test the level of support from the various banking sectors, envisaging that the courses could be organized in collaboration with the universities and business schools. As a rule, these experiments should give priority to qualified Institute members in the junior management category, but the Committee foresaw that banking staff with other academic qualifications and a limited number of students from other business professions could benefit from an expanded post-qualifying programme.[27]

The two reports, which gave 'the most radical examination of the Institute's role as a qualifying association . . . since its formation in 1879', deserved full and wide-ranging consultation throughout the membership. The Committee's proposals were circulated to members and widely discussed at local centre meetings during the summer of 1973. Although many members were worried that the Stage 3 qualification could jeopardize the status of the existing Associateship, the new Stage 1 and Stage 2 schemes won praise and support. In the meantime the banks were asked for a response to the Committee's proposals for study leave for their members of staff, and in 1973 six of the major banks gave the Institute a 'declaration of intent' to provide the recommended day release for Stage 1 courses from September 1975 onwards. This encouraging answer allowed the Institute's Council to accept the Committee's recommendations in principle, and to announce the inauguration of the Stage 1 scheme in 1975 and the gradual phasing-out of the old Part I examinations by 1978.

The implementation of the Stage 2 and Stage 3 schemes was a much more complex task, partly because time was needed to design the Institute's contribution to the syllabus, and partly because the status of the Stage 3 qualification needed clarification. On the question of the rating of Stage 3 *vis-à-vis* the Associateship of the Institute, the Council understood that the main problem was the designation of the new qualification. The Wilde Committee's proposed designation of 'MIB' (Management Diploma of The Institute of Bankers) had been opposed by many Associate members, and as a result the Council appointed a committee to review possible alternatives. This committee, under the chairmanship of W. G. License (the Council representative of the Leeds local centre), suggested that the uneasiness of many Associates could be dispelled by allowing them to qualify for the Stage 3 designation by *performance* either in their banking careers or through a further academic test (possibly a 'management' thesis).[28] In the event the Council decided to retain the examination route to Stage 3, and to redesignate successful candidates 'AIB (M)' to bring the new qualification into closer parallel with the existing AIB designation. On this basis, the Council was able to obtain a further 'declaration of intent' from the banks, which undertook to provide the recommended study leave for candidates in Stages 2 and 3 by September 1978. This interval allowed the Institute to coordinate tuition for the new qualifications, to commission appropriate textbooks, and to plan pilot Stage 3 courses. The regulations for Stages 2 and 3 were duly published in May 1975, together with 'exposure draft' syllabuses, and pilot courses for about 100 direct entrants at four selected polytechnics were planned for the academic year 1976–7.[29]

The Institute now made impressive progress towards the introduction of the other parts of the Wilde Committee's scheme. In 1975–6, the first year of the Stage 1 programme, about 8,000 young members in the United Kingdom enrolled for the Ordinary National Certificate courses or for the 'A' level conversion courses. Three hundred and thirty teaching institutions cooperated in this major reorganization. For overseas members of the Institute, equivalent Stage 1 courses (organized largely by the overseas centres) were brought into operation in 1976. At the other end of the educational spectrum, the Wilde Committee's confidence in the future role of post-experience work was fully vindicated by the late 1970s. Early experiments included a short course at the Graduate Business Centre of The City University, London, in November 1974, a one-week course at Warwick University's Business School in March 1975, and courses at Bradford University and Ashridge Management College in 1975 and 1976. Good attendance at each of these pilot courses encouraged the Council to develop more permanent links with post-experience business colleges from 1976 onwards, notably through seminar courses at the Administrative Staff College, Henley, and the organization of further short courses at Ashridge Management College, Bradford University and Warwick University. In 1976 and 1978 the Institute also organized International Banking Seminars at Deauville, France, as joint ventures with the International Chamber of Commerce.

In the meantime, in 1975 and 1976 the Institute was confronted with evidence that some of its members harboured doubts about the value of the Stage 3 qualification. Echoing a theme that had been heard at many points in the Institute's history, it was argued that a third stage would 'devalue' their own Associateship status. The use of the AIB(M) designation was not reckoned to be sufficiently separate from the Associateship. Although the Wilde Committee had explicitly stated that its third stage of qualification was intended for the majority of potential managers (with perhaps several thousand candidates for each year's examinations), some members interpreted the rules as a divisive measure. The entry regulations for graduates, in particular, were criticized on the grounds that they would create 'an élite who would have direct access to a qualification with a "management" label'.[30] Clearly, the Council had underestimated the extent of the suspicion of a multi-tier system of qualification. Parallel to this concern in the mid-1970s, a number of members doubted whether the direct entrants to Stage 3 would have sufficient grounding in the basic banking subjects of accountancy and the law relating to banking. More serious than any of these criticisms, however, was the news that certain banks were not ready to meet the terms of the 'declaration of intent' to provide the required study leave for Stage 3. This development could quickly upset the plans for a third stage of qualification. Without study leave, a candidate would be faced with the huge task of completing in his or her own time over 500 hours of study (including lectures and tutorials) in each year of the two-year course.

These doubts emerged in a period when the recruitment and staffing policies of the major British banks were markedly affected by the downturn in the economy and the troubles in some sectors of the financial system. In these new conditions, the narrowing of promotion prospects was bound to influence the morale of many banking men and women and to increase their suspicion of higher level qualifications. Eric Glover, the Institute's Director of Studies, pinpointed some of the factors which led to this change of stance in the three years after the publication of the Wilde Committee's report:

Recruitment . . . had become a lot easier at all levels, and staff turnover figures had declined dramatically in most areas. On the training side, the failure of many of the secondary banks had the effect of turning attention once again to the virtues of instilling into rising managers the classical banking principles. . . . For the same reason, all the banks grew rapidly more cost-conscious, as they found themselves making ever-increasing provision for doubtful lending. At such times, extra expenditure on education, whose benefits, at least in the short term, are so hard to assess, was not likely to be a welcome commitment.[31]

These changes in attitude became obvious only shortly before the pilot Stage 3 courses were due to begin in 1976, but the seriousness of the criticisms forced the Institute to call off the courses while the Council reviewed the position. Similar pilot courses for the Stage 3 trustee qualifications were also abandoned. Although determined to retain a third stage of qualification, the Council was anxious to remove the suspicion that the existing Associateship was being devalued. This emphasis was reflected in the Council's announcement of a revised scheme in October 1976. The principal alterations were the restriction of direct entry to Stage 3 to those with *appropriate* degrees, the introduction of a larger accountancy element in the Stage 2 syllabus, and the redesignation of the third stage as the 'Financial Studies Diploma', with no designatory letters attaching to it. It was hoped that the change of title would reduce any interference with the public status and recognition of the Institute's Associateship but satisfy the aspirations of members who had previously studied beyond their Associateship for part-time degrees or other professional qualifications. As far as the study leave problem was concerned, however, a compromise with the banks was urgently needed. After lengthy negotiations in 1976 and 1977, it was agreed that candidates for the new Stage 3 Financial Studies Diploma would be allowed five instead of two years to complete the course, thus removing the earlier requirement for study leave for Stage 3 candidates.[32]

The resolution of these difficulties by the end of 1976 made it practicable for the Institute to announce that the Stage 2 and 3 courses would commence under the revised rules in September 1978. By mid-

1978 it was clear that most of the recognized colleges would be offering courses leading to the Institute's Stage 2 examinations. In preparation for the new Stage 3 scheme, about 20 colleges and polytechnics in the United Kingdom agreed to provide evening classes for the Financial Studies Diploma, and three of the large correspondence colleges were willing to supply tuition courses for the Stage 3 candidates. In addition, many of the organizational and teaching aspects of the new Financial Studies Diploma were tested in a pilot course for some 30 candidates organized by the Hong Kong local centre and the University and Polytechnic in Hong Kong in 1977–8. In its revised form, the Financial Studies Diploma won encouraging support from the Institute's members. In June 1977, for example, 2,000 Associates indicated their intention to take the diploma course, and over 1,000 members had been supplied with details of the Stage 3 syllabus by June 1978.

The completion of the first full two-year cycle for the Institute's Stage 1 qualification in 1977, the winding-up of the old Part I examinations in 1978, and the launch of the Stage 2 and Stage 3 courses in 1978 entirely altered the structure and content of the Institute's professional qualification. In the six years since the appointment of the Wilde Committee, it had been possible to reconstruct and extend the examination syllabus and tuition facilities of one of the largest professional associations in the world. With the Institute's total membership at home and overseas increasing from about 42,000 in 1960 to over 110,000 in the late 1970s, these adjustments emphasized relevance, accessibility, and high educational standards to meet the needs of a rapidly changing banking community. For the members themselves, although the initial recommendations of the Wilde Committee had been revised to accommodate the practical requirements of both the banks and the Institute's Associates, the groundwork and principles of its reforms (including the emphasis upon study leave) offered a long-term response to the problems of banking education. At the end of the 1970s, quite apart from the Institute's increased range of post-qualifying activities, those beginning a career in banking could turn to the Institute for a set of qualifications with flexibility in their entrance requirements, variety in the content of their syllabuses, and links with public sector awards.

9

CONCLUSION:
NEW DIRECTIONS IN
BANKING EDUCATION

THE Institute of Bankers, no less than any organization which undergoes a fundamental reform of its range of services, could not carry through major changes in its educational work in the 1970s without taking a long view of the future role of professional institutes. A key factor in the development of the profession in the late twentieth century, in the view of many members, was likely to be the relationship between banking qualifications and public sector awards in business studies. For tuition purposes the Institute had recognized colleges in the public sector as early as 1927, and in 1960 it had been one of the first professional associations to give its recognition, for exemption purposes, to the new Ordinary and Higher National Certificates in Business Studies. In the view of the Wilde Committee, however, the integration of banking qualifications with national awards needed to be significantly strengthened. The Committee recognized that in the study of commerce, law, and accountancy, the framework needed for banking was basically the same as the requirements for insurance, corporate finance, or investment management. A single course of study would create a qualification with 'marketability' in the business world but with less waste of teaching resources: '. . . it seems desirable to use the public sector as far as possible to provide a background in general business studies, whilst the Institute concentrates on its specialist subjects of banking practice and management'.[1]

NEW DIRECTIONS IN BANKING EDUCATION

The problems of planning the Institute's future responsibilities for banking qualifications were highlighted in the late 1970s by important alterations in the administration of the Ordinary and Higher National Certificates and Diplomas in Business Studies. Since 1961, when these awards had been introduced, teaching and examinations in business studies had been under the supervision of the Joint Committee for National Awards in Business Studies and Public Administration, representing the Ministry of Education and the associations which recognized the awards for qualification purposes. At local level the work of the joint committee was coordinated by regional advisory committees and the appropriate governing bodies of technical colleges and other institutions. The Wilde Committee, meeting between 1972 and 1974, had worked on the assumption that this type of administration, so far as it affected the Institute's new Stage 1 and Stage 2 qualifications, could continue for the foreseeable future. In 1975, however, the supervision of all non-degree courses in business studies was brought within the scope of the newly established Business Education Council (BEC). The formation of BEC in 1974 fulfilled a recommendation of the Haslegrave Committee on Technical Courses and Examinations, whose report in 1969 had favoured the setting-up of a unified national system of courses in business studies. Unlike the joint committee, BEC's Chairman and members were appointed by the Secretary of State for Education and Science in their personal capacity, and the membership of BEC's boards and committees was widely drawn from the worlds of education, business, and the professions. By 1976, to carry out its role in the introduction of an integrated system of business studies, it was clear that BEC was planning to devise and to supervise its own series of public sector awards. These awards, to be known as General, National, and Higher Level Awards, were designed to replace the existing system of National Certificates and Diplomas during the late 1970s (September 1978 was provisionally chosen as the starting date for courses under the new scheme). In line with modern practice in business studies at graduate and post-graduate level, BEC proposed new awards on the basis of an inter-disciplinary 'modular' approach to tuition and assessment. This emphasis, replacing the traditional subject-by-subject approach in further education, cut across the traditional boundaries of the banking subjects of pure accountancy, economics, or business law, and called

[191]

for the application of a wide range of knowledge and skills in studying different aspects of business life. For example, in place of the existing subject options for Higher Certificates or Diplomas, the BEC Higher Level award in financial studies was expected to offer 'core modules' for the study of the nature of business activity, the role of financial institutions, analytical techniques used in the measurement of business activity, and the problems of corporate organizations. BEC's officials proposed that its own boards would be responsible for validating the courses offered by colleges and other institutions. For assessment purposes BEC planned to appoint its own moderators to ensure that standards of examination and course-work assessment were maintained.

The announcement of BEC's objectives was bound to make professional institutes question whether the new awards would meet their requirements in the late 1970s and 1980s. By the end of 1976, before BEC had produced detailed syllabuses for each of its awards in business studies, there were signs of unease amongst the employers and professional institutes which then used public sector awards as part of their entrance or qualification structure. At a conference organized by the Inner London Education Authority in December 1976, representatives of the professional bodies and the employers pointed out that 'the present system of public sector awards worked well during its fifteen years of life in its present form; it had taken a long time for employers to familiarise themselves with what was offered'.[2]

At The Institute of Bankers, because the formation of BEC had coincided with the restructuring of its own examination requirements, it was acknowledged that there was room for cooperation between the two organizations. In May 1975, for instance, the Institute's 'exposure draft' syllabuses for Stage 2 of its new qualification was approved by BEC for inclusion in the existing courses for Higher National Certificates and Diplomas.[3] As soon as it became clear that BEC was preparing a replacement set of public sector awards, the Institute was again one of the first of the professional bodies to enter discussions over the content and administration of the new awards. The Institute, together with all the other professional bodies, was not represented on the BEC main council. Nevertheless, there was no danger that the views of the banking community would not be heard at BEC. Philip Chappell, a member of the Wilde Committee, was appointed to the main BEC council in 1974, and S. C. Prior (a Fellow of the Institute) served as Chairman of the Financial Studies Board of BEC, both in their personal capacities. The Council and secretariat of the Institute, while conscious that the Institute's own Stage 2 examinations would be retained for the foreseeable future for those at home and overseas who preferred this route to the AIB qualifications, knew that the Institute was and would remain one of the largest 'customers' for public sector awards in business studies. It was therefore essential that the Institute's voice should be heard in the settlement of any new scheme of awards.

By mid-1978 this new factor in banking education was already influencing the content of the Institute's qualification. BEC's proposals for the introduction of its National Level Awards were published in November 1977, and with its own Stage 1 level in mind The Institute of Bankers was able to offer detailed comment on the course specification. Although this made it possible for some colleges to start courses leading to the National Level Award as early as September 1978, the Institute expressed its preference that banking students should not be entered for the new courses until September 1979. This postponement would allow both the Institute and the teaching colleges the breathing space 'to deal with the problem of converting teachers from their traditional subject-based approach to the "modular" treatment which is part of the Business Education Council's philosophy'.[4] In the interval before September 1979, it was expected that most candidates would continue to enter for Ordinary National Certificate courses.

The Institute's Stage 2 qualification, which had already created problems in the transition from the old Part II Associateship requirements, was less easily matched to the proposed new range of public sector awards.[5] Questions about the supervision of the awards and the timing of their introduction emerged as the main obstacles to progress, and members of the Institute were clearly anxious that the Institute should maintain control of technical standards in the Stage 2 qualification. Delays in the publication of the full BEC syllabus and course specification made it unlikely that colleges would be able to offer the BEC courses for Higher National Awards before September 1979. The complexity of the arrangements for the moderation of the new awards also made it difficult for the Institute to give a commitment to use the proposed Higher Level courses.

In an attempt to clarify the arrangements for the introduction of the new Stage 2 course in September 1978, the Institute's Council and secretariat asked for detailed consultations between local centres, colleges, and other interested parties in late 1977 and early 1978. Writing to members of the Council in January 1978, the President of the Institute, Malcolm Wilcox, explained that the overwhelming need was to simplify the arrangements and give clear guidance to the Institute's members in the selection of the route which they should follow towards the new Stage 2 qualifications. In the short term, the President suggested, the most practical policy appeared to be to concentrate on the Institute's own Stage 2 examinations (modelled on the Wilde Committee's recommendations) rather than to embark on the new public sector awards at that level. In the longer term this solution did not rule out a link with public sector courses at the higher level for exemption purposes. The President emphasized that the Institute's examination structure could only be a proper measurement of knowledge in banking subjects by maintaining the Institute's own educational standards and by ensuring that its qualification was compatible with the best practices in modern business education. 'From my conversations with Mr John Bruce Lockhart, the Chairman of the Business Education Council, and those of his colleagues most concerned with our affairs, it is evident that they understand and support our ambitions. Our joint task is to find an acceptable solution to our needs in the longer term future.'[6]

In answer to the President's letter and as a result of discussions at local centre meetings, the Council of the Institute agreed to concentrate attention on the Institute's own Stage 2 examinations for all papers set up to and including September 1980. The Council also decided to continue to work with BEC on plans for the Higher Level Awards to ensure that they would be suitable for exemption purposes. The Council, to prevent misunderstandings, also stressed that the Institute would continue to offer a full range of examinations for the Stage 2 subjects for the foreseeable future. The Council explained that this commitment would continue to be necessary in view of the Institute's large number of overseas members. There were also significant numbers of members in the United Kingdom who would not be able to follow the route through the system of public sector awards, mainly because they were not eligible for study leave or because they were not within easy reach of an appropriate college.

By the late 1970s The Institute of Bankers had emerged as an important influence on the planning of further education in business studies; by its adoption of public sector courses for Stage 1 of its qualification, the Institute had become the largest single 'customer' for the new National Level Awards. This contribution made certain that the banking profession held a strategically useful share in the future development of business education in the United Kingdom. At the same time the weight of the Institute's experience in initiating and supervising its own system of education allowed it to offer well-defined qualifications of its own. In comparison with the relatively narrow base of banking education in the late nineteenth and early twentieth centuries, these qualifications could now cover the ground between basic professional training (at Stage 2 of the AIB qualification) through to the degree-level Diploma in Financial Studies and a wide range of post-qualifying facilities, including short courses and seminars. In contrast to the somewhat inflexible syllabuses provided by the Institute in its earlier years (especially before 1945), this mix of education services was more easily adapted to meet the rapid and continuing changes in banking techniques and banking employment.

As The Institute of Bankers approached its centenary in 1979 the changes in the examination structure after the publication of the Wilde Committee's report were a striking reminder of the Institute's contribution to business education. Traditionally, the demand from the banks and their employees for an industry-wide criterion of professional knowledge and competence had always remained at the heart of the Institute's objectives. George Rae, in the discussion which led to the formation of the short-lived Banking Institute in 1851, had argued that the award of 'a testimonial . . . to the range and accuracy' of a bank official's practical knowledge was a sure means of winning recognition for a professional institute.[7] The failure to take this advice made it unlikely that the 1851 Institute could ever attract widespread support from the many thousands of officials already working in the banks. The founders of The Institute of Bankers in 1879, on the other hand, were deeply influenced by the search for a banking qualification. 'The proposed institute', Richard Martin had argued in 1878, 'would enable those who pass such examinations to be known by their more or less distinguished abilities, and would at once give them a position within the circle of the profession'.[8] The task of devising an examination system and organizing the assessment of large numbers of candidates could not be underestimated, but as soon as the Institute's examinations were put on a regular and carefully monitored basis, the support of the banks and their employees quickly followed.

Confidence in the Institute's qualification, especially from those who saw the career value of a tailor-made banking diploma, brought a massive expansion of the total membership of the Institute in the 1920s and 1930s. Yet this support, and the continuing growth of the Institute after the Second World War, was only sustained by the Institute's readiness to adapt its qualification system to meet the changing needs of banking. This task was simplified by the greater cohesion of the banking industry in the United Kingdom; whereas the Institute's membership was drawn from over 200 banks in the late nineteenth century, amalgamations and alliances between the banks in the first quarter of this century transformed the distribution of banking staff. From the 1920s onwards the banking scene was dominated by a relatively small number of clearing banks, and, although The Institute of Bankers has always had the support of bank officials from the merchant banks and from overseas banks, the majority of the Institute's members were now working for large banks with a much greater range of banking services. This concentration in the banking system simplified and speeded-up the process of harmonizing the Institute's qualification with modern banking requirements, and enabled the Institute to look forward to long-term expansion of its membership and examination facilities. In response to this closer communication between the Institute and the banks, the adaptation and extension of the Associateship qualification reflected significant developments in the banking sector: language qualifications were offered shortly before the First World War to meet the demand for linguists in the rapidly expanding overseas business of the British banks; preliminary examinations were provided when the banks were worried by the standard of new recruits' education in the 1920s and 1930s; and a diploma in executorship and trustee work was launched when this type of business grew in importance in the 1930s. Similarly, the tightening-up of the Institute's examination rules after the Second World War was governed by changing staff requirements in the banks as well as by the need to update and improve the technical context of the examinations. This same concern for flexibility in matching the educational needs of the banks to the maintenance of high standards of professional qualification was a key factor in the 1970s, influencing the Wilde Committee in many of its recommendations:

> In the last few years, however, the pace of change has been so rapid, both in banking and in the educational system which provides its recruits, that the Council decided that a fundamental reappraisal of the Institute's role had become necessary . . . we believe that the scheme we recommend would offer a great many advantages over the present system through its flexibility, wider scope and links with other business qualifications—which should all have a very beneficial effect on the quality of recruitment into banking.[9]

By the late 1970s The Institute of Bankers, through its commitment to its own distinctive range of qualifications and its willingness to adapt its examination structure, was drawing most of its membership support from those in search of a professional banking qualification. Each year, from a total membership of over 110,000 more than 60,000 members were candidates for the Institute's examinations. Entrants for the examinations were certainly encouraged by their employers, but in an industry where professional qualifications were not fully compulsory the high numbers of candidates were a mark of widespread confidence in the Institute's qualifications. This confidence was not simply based upon 'the sense of belonging' to a professional institute. It was also the outcome of thorough evaluation of the content and relevance of the Institute's awards both by members and by their employees. Although the development of the Institute's third-stage qualification, the Financial Studies Diploma, was only in its earliest stages in 1978 and 1979, the promising initial response was a measure of the high value put upon the Institute's awards in the careers of young members.

The emphasis upon adjusting qualifications to the needs of modern banking, especially in the 1960s and 1970s, gave the Institute a role which was both larger and more coherent than its founders had ever envisaged. In the years after its formation in 1879 the Institute had attempted to combine the work of a qualifying association with watching over the interests of banking as a whole; in the first fifty years of its existence the Institute also took on responsibilities for banking charities and other duties outside the usual scope of professional institutes. These additional duties had been gradually transferred to more appropriate organizations. After 1895, for example, the Central Association of Bankers (subsequently the British Bankers' Association) took on the responsibility for monitoring legislation which affected banks in the United Kingdom.[10] This redistribution of responsibilities within the banking community was substantially complete by the late 1920s, leaving the Institute to give closer and more exclusive attention to issues in the education of professional bankers.

Although there were periods in the modern history of the Institute when the standards and content of its examination syllabuses seemed to dominate its affairs, the educational work of the Institute has always extended beyond the administration of its qualification. The library, the *Journal*, and the issue of publications had emerged as important contributions to banking studies from the outset of the Institute's career. From the late 1940s onwards these services were imaginatively augmented by the Institute's initiation and administration of international summer schools, close involvement with the educational work of overseas banking institutes and the Institute's own overseas centres, and more intensive use of prize awards and exchange visits for young qualified bankers. By the 1970s, however, it was clear that the Institute's educational services for qualified bankers could be usefully widened and improved. The membership of the Institute included many thousands of qualified Associates who were keen to participate in post-qualifying activities as a means of refreshing their technical knowledge or as a means of broadening their knowledge of modern banking. In many cases, it was this type of member who was ensuring that the activities of the local and overseas centres of the Institute were sustained.

The importance of post-qualifying educational work was fully acknowledged by the Wilde Committee in its second report of 1974: 'Clearly no qualification or set of qualifications taken at the beginning of one's career can provide the necessary professional knowledge without constant updating . . . provision for continued professional education is vital to the careers of the Institute's qualified members and the future of banking'.[11] A similar approach was described by Geoffrey Dix, Secretary-General of the Institute, in a discussion paper at an international meeting of the secretaries of banking institutes in 1975. This meeting, arranged by the Institute of Bankers in Scotland as part of its centenary year programme, reviewed some of the long-term trends in banking education. Arguing that 'people with breadth of mind' were needed for management in banking, Geoffrey Dix suggested that the professional banking institutes should provide better facilities for the qualified banker to update and refresh his professional knowledge at short post-experience courses, seminars, and conferences:

> It seems to me that the most important part of a banker's career development takes place . . . between the ages of 25 and 65, a span of some forty years. . . . If the world continues to change at its present rate, it is going to be more and more necessary to provide career-long facilities for the banker to update and refresh his professional knowledge . . . giving short courses of probably no longer than a week's duration, organizing seminars, two- or three-day conferences, and so forth.[12]

Many of these suggestions were being followed up in the late 1970s, and the Institute quickly built up experience in devising and organizing short courses, seminars, and conferences for qualified bankers, often in conjunction with universities and business schools. While recognizing that the three levels of the Institute's qualification would continue to be the main focus of its membership services, the Institute was clearly preparing to provide a much larger range of educational facilities for the qualified banker of the 1980s.

When Francis Bacon suggested that 'every man [is] a debtor to his profession', he was urging the lawyers, doctors, and clergymen of seventeenth-century England to be 'a help and ornament' to their chosen profession in repayment for the skills and status which they had acquired.[13] In Bacon's view, professional men should attempt to add to the body of knowledge in the relevant discipline long after they had reached the basic level of competence which would bring them 'countenance and profit'. This notion of the career-long responsibilities of professional men is a recognizable theme in the history of qualifying associations, learned societies, and study groups. The founders of The

[199]

Institute of Bankers, for example, by stressing the importance of library study and specialist publications, foresaw that its members would wish to contribute to the study of banking and maintain and refresh their professional knowledge throughout their careers. By the 1970s the linkage between the Institute and its qualified members was being reinforced. The Institute's modern range of qualifications and activities emphasized that the professional banker is a member of his profession not just at the moment of qualification but throughout his career. In response, members both at home and overseas could identify the Institute as the main channel for the study and discussion of important issues in banking business. This approach was closely adjusted to the technical and managerial needs of modern banking. If, as the Wilde Committee expected, the pace of change in the contemporary banking industry would be maintained into the 1980s and 1990s, it was essential that there were recognized facilities for the professional banker to revise, update, or enlarge his knowledge in response to new developments in banking. The Institute of Bankers, through its new examination structure and the extension of post-qualifying activities, ensured that it was well placed to fill this role.

REFERENCES

Abbreviations

BM   *The Bankers' Magazine*
IBAR   The Institute of Bankers, Annual Reports
IBCM   The Institute of Bankers, Council Minutes
JIB   *Journal of The Institute of Bankers*

INTRODUCTION

1 W. PETTY, *Quantulumcunque Concerning Money* (1682), quoted in P. L. COTTRELL and B. L. ANDERSON, *Money and Banking in England: The Development of the Banking System 1694–1914* (David and Charles, 1974), p. 109.

2 L. S. PRESSNELL, *Country Banking in the Industrial Revolution* (Oxford University Press, 1956), pp. 4–7.

3 W. F. CRICK and J. E. WADSWORTH, *A Hundred Years of Joint Stock Banking* (Hodder and Stoughton, 1936), pp. 16–18.

4 ibid., pp. 21, 207.

5 W. J. READER, *Professional Men* (Weidenfeld and Nicolson, 1966), p. 148.

6 G. RAE, *The Country Banker: His Clients, Cares and Work* (Murray, 1885).

7 G. ANDERSON, *Victorian Clerks* (Manchester University Press, 1976), pp. 22–5.

1 PROLOGUE: THE BANKING INSTITUTE 1851–1853

1 G. MILLERSON, *The Qualifying Associations. A Study in Professionalization* (Routledge & Kegan Paul, 1964), pp. 51, 57–61.

2 PRESSNELL, op. cit., Chapter 4.

3 COTTRELL and ANDERSON, op. cit., p. 40.

4 CRICK and WADSWORTH, op. cit., pp. 281–2, 289.

5 COTTRELL and ANDERSON, op. cit., p. 244.

6 *BM* (November 1846), p. 68.

7 [Anon.], *The City, or the Physiology of London Business, with Sketches on*

Change, and at the Coffee Houses
(1852), quoted in *BM* (January
1852), pp. 15–21.

8 R. C. SIMMONDS, *The Institute of
Actuaries, 1848–1948* (Institute of
Actuaries, 1948), pp. 40, 108.

9 MILLERSON, op. cit., p. 255.

10 *BM* (February 1851), p. 71.

11 ANDERSON, op. cit., p. 14.

12 *The City, or the Physiology of London Business,* quoted in *BM* (January 1852), pp. 15–21.

13 J. W. GILBART, *Practical Treatise
on Banking* (1852); J. S. DALTON,
The Banker's Clerk (1843).

14 ANDERSON, op. cit., p. 91.

15 *BM* (November 1846), p. 69;
(April 1850), p. 193.

16 *BM* (November 1846), p. 70;
(June 1847), p. 184.

17 A. M. CARR-SAUNDERS and
P. A. WILSON, *The Professions*
(Oxford, 1933), pp. 300–4.

18 MILLERSON, op. cit., pp. 23,
39–41.

19 *BM* (November 1850), p. 633.

20 ANDERSON, op. cit., pp. 20–2;
BM (November 1850), p. 633.

21 *BM* (February 1854), p. 257.

22 ANDERSON, op. cit., p. 24.

23 *BM* (June 1851), p. 308.

24 *BM* (November 1844), p. 144.

25 *BM* (September 1845), p. 330.

26 London Joint Stock Bank, shareholders' minutes (1845): Midland
Bank archives, Q53.

27 *BM* (August 1845), pp. 287–8.

28 ibid., pp. 325–30.

29 R. S. SAYERS, *Lloyds Bank in the
History of English Banking* (Oxford, 1957), p. 82.

30 *Banking Almanac and Directory*
(1849), p. 171.

31 Guarantee Society, general meeting minutes (10 November 1842):
Guarantee Society archives.

32 e.g. *BM* (February 1847), pp.
309–10.

33 London Joint Stock Bank, board

minutes (4 February 1847): Midland Bank archives, Q5.

34 *Great Exhibition 1851: Official
Description and Illustrated Catalogue,* 3 vols (London, 1851).

35 Liverpool Union Bank, board
minutes (16 June 1851): Lloyds
Bank archives, 93.

36 e.g. Huddersfield Banking Company, board minutes (8 August
1851): Midland Bank archives, H7.

37 *BM* (December 1850), p. 749.

38 *BM* (January 1851), pp. 1, 181–2,
239–40.

39 G. SHARP, *The Gilbart Prize Essay
on the Adaptation of Recent Discoveries and Inventions in Science and
Art to the Purposes of Practical
Banking* (1854).

40 *BM* (February 1851), p. 72.

41 ibid., pp. 240–2.

42 *BM* (August 1851), pp. 453–7.

43 *BM* (September 1851), p. 517.

44 ibid., pp. 516–22; see also *BM*
(June 1852), p. 314.

45 *BM* (November 1851), pp. 625–6.

46 ibid., pp. 624–31.

47 ibid., p. 627.

48 ibid., pp. 628–9, 631; MILLER-
SON, op. cit., p. 121.

49 *BM* (December 1851), pp. 632,
684–8; see also *BM* (May 1850),
pp. 340–1.

50 *BM* (April 1852), p. 161.

51 G. J. SHAW, 'On the law and practice with reference to crossed
cheques', *BM* (February 1852),
pp. 66–70; W. NEWMARCH, 'On
the application of the principles of
assurance to guarantees for the
fidelity of bank officers', *BM* (April
1852), pp. 161–2; J. S. DALTON,
'The probable effects upon the currency of the recent discoveries of
gold in California and Australia',
BM (March 1852), pp. 108–16.

52 *BM* (May 1852), p. 232.

53 *BM* (August 1851), p. 456.

54 *BM* (May 1852), p. 234.

55 MILLERSON, op. cit., p. 51.

56 *BM* (November 1852), p. 556.

57 L. LEVI, 'On the state of the mercantile, maritime, and bankruptcy laws of the United Kingdom', *BM* (February 1853), pp. 68–77; H. STEPHENS, 'On the frauds that the banking and commercial interests are liable to from the chemical decomposition of writing inks', *BM* (April 1853), pp. 262–8.

58 *BM* (June 1853), p. 484; *BM* (April 1853), p. 246.

59 e.g. *BM* (February 1852), p. 65; *BM* (January 1853), p. 5.

60 MILLERSON, op. cit., pp. 121–2.

2   PLANNING FOR A PROFESSIONAL INSTITUTE 1853–1879

1 'Cantab', *BM* (January 1863), p. 13.

2 COTTRELL and ANDERSON, op. cit., p. 248; Joint Stock Banking Companies Act (1857): 20 and 21 Vict., c.49; Joint Stock Banks Act (1858): 21 and 22 Vict., c.91; COTTRELL, *The Finance of British Industry 1850–1918* (Methuen, forthcoming).

3 J. DUN, *British Banking Statistics* (Edward Stanford, 1876), p. 74.

4 ibid., p. 74.

5 COTTRELL, op. cit.; S. NISHIMURA, *The Decline of Inland Bills of Exchange in the London Money Market 1855–1913* (Cambridge, 1971), pp. 6–9; CRICK and WADSWORTH, op. cit., p. 37.

6 e.g. RAE, op. cit., Chapter 4.

7 *BM* (April 1860), p. 225; National Westminster Bank archives.

8 CRICK and WADSWORTH, op. cit., p. 35.

9 DUN, op. cit., p. 78; COTTRELL and ANDERSON, op. cit., pp. 330–4.

10 CRICK and WADSWORTH, op. cit., pp. 34–6, 39.

11 W. NEWMARCH, 'The increase in the number of banks and branches . . . 1858–1879', *BM* (October 1879), p. 853.

12 RAE, op. cit., p. 195.

13 *BM* (April 1846), p. 27.

14 *BM* (September 1857), p. 776; *BM* (October 1857), pp. 830–1; *BM* (November 1857), pp. 930–1; *BM* (December 1857), p. 1017.

15 *Banking Almanac* (1850–80).

16 *BM* (February 1853), pp. 140–3.

17 W. M. ACRES, *The Bank of England from Within* (Oxford, 1931), Vol. 2, p. 554; *BM* (November 1876), p. 914.

18 *BM* (March 1855), pp. 207–8; Provident Mutual Life Assurance Association archives, Guildhall Library (uncatalogued).

19 Guarantee Society, results book (1848–70); general meeting minutes (25 July 1865): Guarantee Society archives.

20 Bankers Guarantee and Trust Fund, trustees' minute book (March 1865–March 1866): Guildhall Library MS 14982/1. (In 1919 the Fund was acquired by the Alliance Assurance Co., now the Sun Alliance and London Insurance Group.)

21 London Joint Stock Bank, board minutes (15 November 1860, 4 April 1867, 2 January 1868): Midland Bank archives, Q6, Q7.

22 *BM* (June 1871), pp. 566–8.

23 e.g. S. MUTHESIUS, *The High Victorian Movement in Architecture 1850–1870* (Routledge & Kegan Paul, 1972), pp. 188–202.

24 *BM* (November 1876), p. 916.

25 *BM* (April 1846), p. 27.

26 *BM* (December 1856), p. 863; *BM* (February 1857), p. 145; *BM* (January 1857), p. 145.

27 JOSEPH LOWE, 'Mercantile instruction in connection with King's College London' (unpublished prospectus, 1832). Information kindly supplied by H. A. Harvey, Archivist, King's College London.

28 F. J. C. HEARNSHAW, *Centenary History of King's College* (University of London, 1929), pp. 244–6; *BM* (February 1857), pp. 145–6.

29 *BM* (September 1863), pp. 652–3.

30 *King's College Calendar* (1873–4), pp. 109–10.

31 E. WELCH, *The Peripatetic University* (Cambridge 1973), pp. 33–4.

32 E. WELCH, 'The London Society for the Extension of University Teaching, 1875–1902', *Guildhall Studies in London History*, Vol. 3 (1977), p. 60.

33 MILLERSON, op. cit., p. 127.

34 *BM* (August 1877), pp. 622–4; *BM* (October 1877), pp. 881–2.

35 *BM* (July 1862), p. 462.

36 *BM* (November 1862), p. 769.

37 MILLERSON, op. cit., pp. 92, 121, 126.

38 *BM* (January 1863), p. 16; see also *BM* (December 1862), pp. 822, 825; *BM* (May 1863), pp. 323–5.

39 *BM* (January 1871), pp. 54–5; *BM* (February 1872), p. 168.

40 Scottish Bankers' Literary Association, minute book (1872): Institute of Bankers in Scotland.

41 R. N. FORBES, *The History of The Institute of Bankers in Scotland 1875–1975* (Institute of Bankers in Scotland, 1975), p. 6.

42 Scottish Bankers' Literary Association, report by provisional committee (14 December 1874): Institute of Bankers in Scotland.

43 FORBES, op. cit., pp. 7–9.

44 Letter book (14 March 1876): Institute of Bankers in Scotland;

BM (April 1876), p. 285; *BM* (September 1876), pp. 769–70.

45 Letter book (3 September 1875): Institute of Bankers in Scotland.

46 Letter book (17 April 1876): Institute of Bankers in Scotland.

47 Letter book (27 January 1876): Institute of Bankers in Scotland.

48 *BM* (January 1877), pp. 22–4.

49 *BM* (May 1877), pp. 419–20; see also *BM* (July 1877), p. 594; *BM* (September 1877), p. 805; *BM* (October 1877), pp. 882–3.

50 *BM* (December 1877), pp. 1029–30; see also *BM* (November 1877), pp. 958–9.

51 *BM* (July 1877), p. 594.

52 *BM* (November 1877), p. 958.

53 *BM* (March 1877), pp. 412–13.

54 *BM* (February 1878), p. 101.

55 *BM* (August 1877), p. 719; letter book (20 February 1878): Institute of Bankers in Scotland.

56 *BM* (April 1878), p. 318; *BM* (June 1878), p. 502.

57 *BM* (July 1878), pp. 559–69.

58 ibid., p. 559.

59 R. B. MARTIN's letter book (31 May 1878): Barclays Bank archives.

60 *BM* (July 1878), p. 560.

61 *BM* (August 1878), pp. 686–7.

62 *The Irish Banker* (December 1878), pp. 191–2.

63 *BM* (April 1879), pp. 308, 312.

64 Letter book (26 June 1878): Institute of Bankers in Scotland.

65 *BM* (December 1878), p. 1002.

66 *BM* (September 1876), p. 767; *BM* (December 1878), p. 1004.

67 *BM* (January 1879), p. 64; *BM* (July 1878), p. 569; IBCM (30 October 1878).

68 *The First Fifty Years of The Institute of Bankers 1879–1929* (Blades, East and Blades, 1929), p. 21.

69 IBCM (26 February 1879).

70 R. B. MARTIN's diary (1879): Holland-Martin family archives.

71 *BM* (April 1879), p. 300; *BM* (July 1879), p. 566.
72 *BM* (April 1879), p. 304.
73 MILLERSON, op. cit., p. 121; H. HOWITT, *The History of the Insti-*

tute of Chartered Accountants in England and Wales 1880–1965 (Heinemann, 1966), p. 8.
74 *BM* (May 1879), p. 386.

3 PROFESSIONAL INSTITUTE OR PRESSURE GROUP ? 1879–1895

1 CRICK and WADSWORTH, op. cit., p. 397; S. G. CHECKLAND, *Scottish Banking. A History, 1695–1973* (Collins, 1975), pp. 471–3.
2 *BM* (January 1879), p. 19; *BM* (April 1879), pp. 293–4.
3 *BM* (January 1879), pp. 68–9; CRICK and WADSWORTH, op. cit., p. 228.
4 North and South Wales Bank, GEORGE RAE papers (23 January and 27 March 1899): Midland Bank archives, M159/73–4.
5 *BM* (February 1880), p. 95.
6 *BM* (May 1879), p. 392.
7 *BM* (April 1879), p. 300; *BM* (June 1879), p. 461; *BM* (July 1879), p. 594; *BM* (December 1879), p. 1011.
8 *BM* (December 1878), pp. 1002–4; *BM* (August 1879), pp. 64–101.
9 FORBES, op. cit., p. 11; CHECKLAND, op. cit., p. 471.
10 *BM* (October 1879), pp. 837–43.
11 *BM* (June 1879), pp. 461–83; *BM* (July 1879), p. 594; *JIB* (July 1880), pp. 526–7.
12 *BM* (July 1879), p. 594; IBCM (24 September, 19 November 1879); *BM* (November 1879), pp. 985–6.
13 IBCM (5 May, 3 June 1879); *BM* (April 1880), p. 321.
14 IBCM (3 June, 29 October 1879); *JIB* (June–November 1879).
15 IBCM (24 September, 11 December 1879); *BM* (January 1890), pp. 61–2.
16 IBCM (11 December 1879, 11 April 1880).
17 IBCM (22 and 31 July 1879).
18 FORBES, op. cit., pp. 10–11; *BM* (May 1879), pp. 391–2.
19 FORBES, op. cit., p. 11.
20 IBCM (17 October 1879).
21 IBCM (17 October 1879); MILLERSON, op. cit., pp. 122–3.
22 *JIB* (November 1879), pp. 158–63; *BM* (September 1880), p. 757; IBCM (17 October 1879).
23 IBCM (12 July 1880); *BM* (September 1880), pp. 750–1.
24 *JIB* (November 1880), pp. 720–1.
25 IBCM (20 June 1881, 12 June 1882).
26 *BM* (January 1881), p. 31; IBCM (18 July 1882).
27 *JIB* (July 1880), pp. 517–22; IBCM (17 June 1880, 20 June 1881, 12 June 1882).
28 *JIB* (July 1880), pp. 520–2.
29 Companies Act (1879): 42 and 43 Vict., c.76; *JIB* (June 1879), p. 28a; *BM* (September 1879), pp. 753–7; IBCM (5 May 1879).
30 CRICK and WADSWORTH, op. cit., p. 428; North and South Wales Bank, GEORGE RAE papers: Midland Bank archives, M222.
31 The Law of Bankruptcy Act (1869): 32 and 33 Vict., c.71.
32 IBCM (8 November 1880).
33 *BM* (July 1879), pp. 533–6.
34 *BM* (February 1879), p. 263.
35 IBCM (12 July, 9 August 1880).
36 IBCM (11 October, 8 November 1880).
37 Association of English Country Bankers, committee minute book (1874–5): National Westminster

Bank archives; see also M. KITA, 'The Scottish Banking Invasion of England 1874–1882', *Soka Economic Studies Quarterly*, Vol. 7 (1977), pp. 29–50.

38 IBCM (13 December 1880).

39 IBCM (13 December 1880).

40 IBCM (20 June, 8 July 1881, 5 April 1883).

41 *JIB* (October 1881), pp. 479–81; *JIB* (December 1882), pp. 519–40; IBCM (17 June 1880, 10 January, 9 May 1881); *BM* (April 1880), p. 321; *BM* (March 1882), p.206; *BM* (October 1926,) p. 465.

42 *BM* (April 1881), p. 307; IBCM (5 November 1884, 4 February 1885, 1 December 1886, 15 February 1888).

43 e.g. H. PARRIS, *Government and the Railways in Nineteenth-Century Britain* (Routledge and Kegan Paul, 1965), pp. 18–27.

44 North and South Wales Bank, GEORGE RAE papers (20 April 1881): Midland Bank archives, M222.

45 North and South Wales Bank, GEORGE RAE papers (16 May 1881): Midland Bank archives, M222.

46 IBCM (3 May, 7 June 1883, 2 January 1884); *BM* (May 1893), pp. 279–80.

47 *BM* (April 1883), pp. 398–400; IBCM (3 October 1883).

48 e.g. *BM* (December 1877), pp. 1029–30.

49 Worcester City and County Bank, board minutes (18 December 1885): Lloyds Bank archives, 351.

50 Capital and Counties Bank, circulars book (15 November 1888): Lloyds Bank archives, 1969; Lloyds Bank, reference committee minutes (13 October 1890): Lloyds Bank archives, 730; Martin and Co., minute book (29 June 1893): Barclays Bank archives.

51 Liverpool Union Bank, board minutes (27 September 1892): Lloyds Bank archives, 95.

52 *BM* (January 1889), p. 59.

53 *Questions on Banking Practice*, ed. W. TALBOT AGAR (1885, revised editions 1887, 1889, 1892, 1898); IBCM (7 October 1885).

54 *BM* (October 1892), pp. 481–2.

55 IBCM (6 February, 5 March, 3 December 1884, 18 February 1891).

56 IBCM (6 July 1887); Union Bank of Scotland, CHARLES GAIRDNER papers (18 July 1888): Bank of Scotland archives.

57 *BM* (October 1888), p. 1102; *BM* (January 1889), p. 59.

58 *BM* (October 1888), p. 1102.

59 *JIB* (June 1887), p. 313.

60 *JIB* (July 1880), p. 517; *JIB* (June 1886), pp. 390–1; *JIB* (June 1894), p. 350.

61 *JIB* (June 1893), p. 279; *JIB* (June 1896), p. 292.

62 IBCM (19 March 1890, 18 February 1891, 20 December 1893, 27 June, 19 September, 17 October 1894).

63 *JIB* (June 1892), p. 410.

64 IBCM (18 February 1891, 18 April 1894).

65 CRICK and WADSWORTH, op. cit., pp. 38–9; *JIB* (January 1891), p. 6.

66 C. A. E. GOODHART, *The Business of Banking, 1891–1914* (Weidenfeld and Nicolson, 1972), pp. 4, 26.

67 *BM* (October 1892), pp. 479–87.

68 *BM* (January 1893), pp. 89–93; *BM* (March 1895), pp. 379–80; *JIB* (May 1895), pp. 330–2.

4 A VOICE FOR THE MEMBERSHIP 1895–1914

1 *BM* (April 1879), pp. 300–1.
2 IBCM (17 October 1879).
3 CRICK and WADSWORTH, op. cit., pp. 34–7.
4 *BM* (January 1892), p. 70.
5 *BM* (June 1892), pp. 909–10.
6 *BM* (January 1897), pp. 43–7.
7 *BM* (January 1897), p. 42.
8 CRICK and WADSWORTH, op. cit., pp. 34, 37.
9 *BM* (May 1909), p. 736.
10 *BM* (November 1886), p. 942; London Joint Stock Bank, board minutes (19 June 1902): Midland Bank archives, Q12; *BM* (December 1894), pp. 728–31.
11 *JIB* (May 1912), pp. 263–6.
12 *JIB* (December 1905), p. 523.
13 H. POLLINS, *Britain's Railways. An Industrial History* (David and Charles, 1971), p. 82.
14 *Glasgow Evening News* (26 August 1887); see also *Glasgow Herald* (15 October 1886).
15 *BM* (January 1892), p. 71.
16 ANDERSON, op. cit., pp. 108–10; POLLINS, op. cit., p. 133.
17 *BM* (June 1907), pp. 863–5.
18 *BM* (January 1897), pp. 49–50; see also ANDERSON, op. cit., pp. 80–2; FORBES, op. cit., p. 11; CHECKLAND, op. cit., pp. 511–12.
19 *JIB* (December 1905), pp. 522–4.
20 *BM* (October 1896), pp. 511, 727; *BM* (December 1907), p. 570.
21 *BM* (May 1909), pp. 736–7; *Careers for Men, Women and Children* (1911), quoted in *BM* (May 1911), p. 719.
22 *BM* (May 1899), p. 733.
23 IBCM (28 September 1898).
24 MILLERSON, op. cit., p. 168; HOWITT, op. cit., p. 183; *The Chartered Institute of Secretaries 1891–1951* (Chartered Institute of Secretaries, 1951), p. 6.

25 IBCM (22 May 1907).
26 *Legal Decisions Affecting Bankers*, ed. J. R. PAGET, Vol. 1 (The Institute of Bankers, 1900).
27 IBCM (26 May 1897, 18 May 1898, 16 May 1900, 17 February 1902, 21 October 1903).
28 IBCM, report of the examinations sub-committee (18 December 1906).
29 *BM* (December 1905), p. 736; IBCM (22 May 1907).
30 *BM* (November 1907), p. 600.
31 *BM* (December 1908), pp. 749–50; IBCM (8 July, 23 September 1908).
32 IBCM (11 May 1880, 7 May 1884, 21 March, 18 April 1894).
33 IBCM (27 June, 14 November, 19 December 1894); *JIB* (June 1895), p. 353.
34 IBCM (20 February 1895); *JIB* (June 1896), p. 298.
35 *BM* (February 1905), pp. 243–4.
36 IBCM (20 May, 21 October 1896, 22 September, 20 October 1897).
37 *Journal of the Institute of Bankers in Ireland* (January 1899), pp. 1–17.
38 *BM* (February 1898), pp. 252–4; *BM* (December 1898), pp. 712–14.
39 *JIB* (June 1906), p. 273; see also MILLERSON, op. cit., p. 75.
40 IBCM, report of the sub-committee on provincial lectures (13 June 1908).
41 IBCM (14 February 1906); *BM* (February 1905), pp. 243–4.
42 ANDERSON, op. cit., p. 56.
43 *JIB* (Supplement 1909), pp. 130–6; SAYERS, op. cit., p. 193.
44 IBCM (15 March 1899, 21 January, 18 March 1903, 26 October 1910).
45 CRICK and WADSWORTH, op. cit., pp. 436–43; *BM* (October 1920).

46 *BM* (November 1908), pp. 592–3; *BM* (June 1909), pp. 901–2.

47 IBCM, Sir Edward Holden's statement to The Institute of Bankers (26 June 1912).

48 IBCM (11 June 1912).

49 IBCM, Sir Edward Holden's statement (26 June 1912).

50 IBCM, G. H. Pownall's memorandum (30 April 1913).

51 *The First Fifty Years* . . ., p. 51;

IBCM (12 March, 30 April 1913).

52 IBCM (18 December 1912, 20 May 1913).

53 IBCM (30 April 1913).

54 IBCM (13 December 1911, 24 January 1912).

55 IBCM (17 September, 15 October 1913, 11 February, 22 April, 17 June 1914).

56 *BM* (December 1913), pp. 779–80.

5   INTO THE MELTING POT 1914–1927

1 SIR EDWARD HOLDEN, speech to shareholders of London Joint City and Midland Bank (29 January 1919); *BM* (January 1920), p. 51; CHECKLAND, op. cit., p. 559.

2 London Joint City and Midland Bank, *Monthly Review* (March 1919), p. 1; B. R. MITCHELL and PHYLLIS DEANE, *Abstract of British Historical Statistics* (Cambridge University Press, 1962), p. 442.

3 *BM* (April 1920), p. 580.

4 *BM* (March 1920), p. 376; *BM* (April 1920), p. 580.

5 *Report of the Treasury Committee on Bank Amalgamations* (1918), Cd 9052.

6 CRICK and WADSWORTH, op. cit., pp. 360–4, 404–6; CHECKLAND, op. cit., pp. 561–3.

7 Information kindly supplied by D. B. Nash, Deputy Head of the Department of Printed Books, Imperial War Museum. See also *BM* (December 1915), p. 763; *JIB* (December 1915), p. 477.

8 *BM* (December 1915), p. 764.

9 ANDERSON, op. cit., p. 56.

10 *BM* (February 1906), p. 247; *BM* (September 1918), p. 240.

11 SIR EDWARD HOLDEN, speech to shareholders of London City and Midland Bank (29 January 1915);

BM (March 1917), p. 399.

12 IBCM (24 April 1918, 1 January 1919, 17 March 1920, 20 September 1922).

13 IBCM (21 April 1915).

14 *JIB* (March 1919), pp. 76–7; IBCM (21 March 1917, 22 May 1918).

15 *BM* (September 1915), p. 377; *BM* (December 1915), pp. 732–4.

16 *Chartered Institute of Secretaries*, p. 54; HOWITT, op. cit., p. 68.

17 IBCM (26 September 1917, 17 October 1917, 19 December 1917, 24 April 1918, 19 March 1919); *BM* (December 1917), pp. 664–5.

18 *BM* (September 1918), p. 240.

19 *JIB* (June 1919), p. 185; membership details kindly provided by Jon Robinson, National Union of Bank Employees.

20 *JIB* (February 1923), p. 93.

21 *BM* (December 1918), p. 572.

22 *BM* (November 1914), p. 633; *BM* (July 1922), p. 58.

23 SIR EDWARD HOLDEN, speech to shareholders of London Joint City and Midland Bank (29 January 1919).

24 *JIB* (May 1920), pp. 154–5.

25 *BM* (December 1915), p. 764; *BM* (February 1918), p. 241; *BM* (May 1918), p. 657.

26 *BM* (May 1914), p. 767.

27 *BM* (May 1927), p. 782.
28 *BM* (January 1920), pp. 31–5, 51–2; *BM* (September 1920), pp. 310–11; CHECKLAND, op. cit., pp. 582–5.
29 *BM* (November 1921), pp. 575–7.
30 IBCM (21 January, 18 February 1920).
31 IBCM (19 October 1921); *JIB* (April 1922), pp. 148–9; *JIB* (May 1922), p. 195; *JIB* (June 1922), pp. 267–8.
32 *JIB* (June 1922), p. 259; IBCM (21 June, 20 December 1922).
33 *JIB* (October 1920), p. 234; *JIB* (October 1922), pp. 300–1.
34 IBCM (19 March 1924); *JIB* (April 1924), pp. 171, 193–8.
35 *BM* (January 1920), p. 93.
36 *JIB* (April 1920), pp. 124–6; *The Banker* (April 1927), p. 281; *BM* (April 1927), p. 614.
37 *JIB* (April 1920), p. 134.
38 e.g. *JIB* (April 1920), pp. 142–4; *BM* (June 1920), p. 845.
39 *BM* (April 1920), p. 597.
40 *JIB* (June 1923), p. 272.

41 *BM* (June 1923), p. 896.
42 IBCM (17 October 1923, 18 June 1924).
43 *BM* (May 1924), pp. 730–1; *BM* (November 1926), p. 646.
44 *The Banker* (September 1926), p. 250.
45 *The First Fifty Years . . .*, p. 10.
46 IBCM (20 September 1922, 18 April, 19 September, 21 November 1923).
47 IBCM (20 February, 16 April, 18 June, 17 September 1924, 18 March, 20 May, 18 November 1925, 13 January, 17 March, 21 April, 19 May 1926, 16 February, 16 May, 18 May, 15 June, 14 December 1927).
48 *JIB* (April 1924), pp. 208–11; e.g. also IBCM (16 January 1924).
49 IBCM (18 May 1927, 13 January 1926); *JIB* (December 1926), pp. 557–9.
50 *BM* (April 1930), p. 582.
51 IBCM (19 December 1923); *BM* (July 1926), p. 91.
52 *JIB* (April 1924), p. 211.

6 CONSOLIDATION AND REFORM 1927–1945

1 R. A. BUCHANAN, 'The Professionalization of British Engineering in the 19th Century' (unpublished paper, Social History Society Conference, 1978).
2 *BM* (April 1930), p. 582; *The Banker* (December 1942), p. 99.
3 *The Banker* (June 1929), p. 152; *The Banker* (August 1929), pp. 172–3; *The Banker* (July 1933), pp. 60–1; *The Banker* (December 1933), p. 238.
4 *The Banker* (January 1936), p. 7; *The Banker* (December 1942), pp. 159–66.
5 MITCHELL and DEANE, op. cit., pp. 447–8.
6 CHECKLAND, op. cit., pp. 578–9; [A. H. ALLMAN], *Williams*

Deacon's 1771–1970 (Williams Deacon's, 1970), pp. 157–9.
7 *The Banker* (May 1935), pp. 96–9; *The Banker* (June 1935), pp. 205–6; R. McKENNA, speech to shareholders of Midland Bank (29 January 1932).
8 *JIB* (November 1935), p. 421.
9 *The Banker* (October 1935), p. 33.
10 *The Banker* (January 1931), p. 38.
11 *JIB* (October 1936), p. 411.
12 IBCM (17 April, 17 July, 18 December 1929, 19 February 1930, 16 March 1932).
13 IBCM (19 December 1934); *JIB* (February 1935), pp. 147–8.
14 *JIB* (October 1930), p. 393; *JIB* (May 1931), p. 255; *JIB* (October

1931), p. 403; *JIB* (June 1932), p. 377.

15 *JIB* (April 1935), p. 214; *JIB* (October 1936), pp. 404–5; *JIB* (December 1936), pp. 492–3.

16 IBCM (20 March 1929); *BM* (July 1929), p. 83; *JIB* (May 1933), pp. 294–5.

17 IBCM (21 November 1928); *JIB* (May 1933), p. 295; IBCM (17 May 1933, 16 October 1935). See also *JIB* (June 1938), pp. 266–7.

18 *JIB* (November 1933), p. 420; IBCM (15 June 1938, 19 July 1939).

19 IBCM (17 October 1934); *The Banker* (December 1937).

20 IBCM (18 December 1912, 19 May 1920).

21 IBCM (17 October 1928); *JIB* (October 1931), pp. 404–5; IBCM (20 March, 19 June 1935); *JIB* (June 1939), p. 291.

22 IBCM (21 May 1930); *JIB* (October 1936), pp. 408–9.

23 *JIB* (December 1938), p. 418.

24 IBCM (18 May, 19 October 1938, 16 August 1939); *JIB* (November 1938), p. 383; *Chartered Institute of Secretaries*, p. 67.

25 IBCM (19 November 1930); *JIB* (January 1933), p. 1; *JIB* (April 1935), p. 210; *JIB* (June 1936), p. 374.

26 *JIB* (November 1928), pp. 478–9.

27 *JIB* (June 1930), p. 310; *JIB* (June 1932), p. 376; *JIB* (June 1934), p. 316; *JIB* (June 1939), p. 293; *JIB* (December 1936), p. 496.

28 *JIB* (June 1936), p. 360.

29 *Financial News* (7 November 1935).

30 IBCM (16 October 1935, 12 January, 18 August, 20 October 1937, 16 August 1939); *JIB* (June 1935), pp. 360–1; *JIB* (June 1937), pp. 288–9; *JIB* (October 1937), p. 338; *JIB* (June 1938), p. 268; *JIB* (November 1938), p. 385; *BM* (January 1938), pp. 118–19.

31 *The Banker* (December 1937), p. 196.

32 *The Banker* (January 1938), pp. 52–3.

33 IBCM (19 October 1938); *JIB* (November 1938), pp. 383–4; *JIB* (December 1938), pp. 418–19.

34 A. W. TUKE and R. J. H. GILLMAN, *Barclays Bank Limited 1926–1969* (Barclays Bank, 1972), p. 48.

35 IBCM (15 November 1939, September 1940, 21 May 1941).

36 *The Banker* (March 1942), p. 142; *JIB* (April 1940), p. 76; *The Banker* (December 1942), pp. 99–101; *BM* (August 1942), p. 82.

37 e.g. IBCM (September 1942, October 1943).

38 IBCM (March 1942, 21 October 1942, 15 November 1944).

39 *JIB* (July 1946), p. 145.

40 IBCM (15 November 1944, 16 May 1945).

41 *The Banker* (August 1943), pp. 77–8.

42 *BM* (May 1944), pp. 333–4. See also *The Banker* (August 1944), pp. 83–6.

43 IBCM (15 November 1944, 21 March 1945); *JIB* (April 1945), pp. 55–63; *JIB* (July 1945), pp. 120–5.

44 *The Banker* (May 1945), p. 94.

7 OUTWARD BOUND 1945–1960

1 *The Banker* (April 1948), pp. 21–4.

2 *BM* (April 1948), p. 306.

3 HOWITT, op. cit., pp. 109–10.

4 *BM* (December 1952), p. 470; see also *The Banker* (July 1948), p. 26.

5 *The Banker* (February 1949), p. 94.

6 e.g. W. S. STANTON, 'The Midland Bank Training Schools', *The Banker* (March 1943), pp. 183–6.

7 CHECKLAND, op. cit., p. 651.

8 *The Banker* (September 1948), p. 160.

9 *The Banker* (November 1948), pp. 96–100; IBCM (19 October 1949, 18 October 1950); *JIB* (February 1951), pp. 37–9; *Education and Training in Banking* (Institute of Bankers in Scotland, 1950).

10 *The Banker* (June 1950), p. 147.

11 *The Banker* (September 1950), pp. 160–1.

12 *The Banker* (April 1954), p. 188.

13 IBCM (18 December 1946); *JIB* (January 1947), pp. 2–4.

14 *JIB* (April 1948), pp. 35–6.

15 IBCM (21 January 1948, 16 April 1952); *JIB* (December 1951), p. 264; *JIB* (June 1952), p. 180.

16 *JIB* (April 1948), p. 36.

17 IBCM (14 April 1954, 15 April 1959).

18 *JIB* (July 1948), p. 85; *JIB* (June 1952), p. 181; IBCM (17 March 1948, 17 January 1951).

19 IBCM (14 April 1954).

20 IBCM (19 October 1955, 15 February 1956, 3 April 1957).

21 IBCM (19 October 1955); *JIB* (June 1958), p. 144.

22 e.g. IBCM (3 October 1956).

23 *JIB* (June 1958), p. 145.

24 IBCM (15 July 1959, 17 February, 18 May 1960).

25 IBCM (21 February 1951, 20 February 1952); *BM* (April 1954); IBCM (20 May, 21 October 1953, 20 January 1954).

26 IBCM (21 October 1959).

27 *JIB* (June 1958), pp. 145–6.

28 IBCM (18 May 1949, 8 May 1957, 20 May 1959).

29 IBCM (19 February 1936, 19 November 1947).

30 *JIB* (September 1960), p. 227.

31 MILLERSON, op. cit., pp. 141–2.

32 IBCM (21 March 1951, 21 March, 3 October 1956, 7 May 1958).

33 MILLERSON, op. cit., p. 141; IBCM (20 April 1960); see also CHECKLAND, op. cit., p. 690.

34 *JIB* (July 1946), pp. 162–3.

35 IBCM (10 September 1947).

36 *JIB* (July 1948), p. 87; *The Third Twenty-Five Years* (The Institute of Bankers, 1954), p. 5; *BM* (May 1957), p. 467.

37 W. J. THORNE, 'One Man's University', *JIB* (May 1959), p. 125.

38 *The Third Twenty-Five Years*, pp. 4–5.

39 IBCM (17 July 1946, 16 July 1947); *The Third Twenty-Five Years*, p. 5.

40 *JIB* (July 1948), pp. 84–5.

41 IBCM (19 June 1946).

42 IBCM (25 June 1952, 16 September 1953); *BM* (January 1954), pp. 7–8.

43 IBCM (16 September 1953).

44 *JIB* (December 1948), pp. 167–75.

45 IBCM (16 September 1953).

46 *The Third Twenty-Five Years*, p. 6; see also *JIB* (June 1938), pp. 270–7.

47 IBCM (17 November 1954, 20 July 1960); E. CARPENTER, *The Institute of Bankers Today* (The Institute of Bankers, 1961), p. 11.

8 THE TESTS OF MODERN BANKING 1960–1979

1 *The London Clearing Banks* (Committee of London Clearing Bankers, 1978), p. 1.

2 ibid., pp. 48, 161–2.

3 Carpenter, op. cit., p. 1.

4 *London Clearing Banks*, p. 166.

5 ibid., p. 157.

6 IBCM (19 October 1960).

7 IBCM (19 October 1966); see also p. 155.
8 *London Clearing Banks*, p. 157.
9 IBCM (18 October 1961, 20 February, 16 October 1963, 19 April 1967, 23 April 1969, 15 July 1970).
10 IBCM (18 May, 17 October 1966).
11 IBCM (19 February 1969, 18 February 1970); *JIB* (February 1977), pp. 10–11.
12 IBAR (1975–6, 1977–8).
13 *JIB* (August 1963), pp. 265–71.
14 IBCM (19 February 1964, 12 July 1965).
15 *JIB* (February 1978), p. 22.
16 IBAR (1976–7, 1977–8).
17 e.g. IBCM (17 October 1962).
18 IBCM (19 February 1964).
19 IBCM (19 February 1964).
20 IBCM (19 April 1967); IBAR (1975–6).

21 *The Institute's Post-Qualifying Activities* (The Institute of Bankers, 1974), pp. 16, 21.
22 W. J. A. HARRIS, *Home Study Students* (University of Manchester, 1972).
23 IBCM (21 November 1968); *JIB* (June 1969), p. 162.
24 e.g. IBAR (1976–7).
25 *Education: a Framework for Expansion* (December 1972), Cmnd 5174.
26 *Report by the Wilde Committee* (The Institute of Bankers, 1973), p. 10.
27 *The Institute's Post-Qualifying Activities*, pp. 11–15.
28 IBAR (1973–4), p. 9.
29 IBAR (1975–6), p. 10.
30 E. GLOVER, 'Furthering Education', *The Banker* (December 1976).
31 ibid.
32 IBAR (1976–7).

9   CONCLUSION: NEW DIRECTIONS IN BANKING EDUCATION

1 *Report by the Wilde Committee*, p. 17.
2 *JIB* (December 1976), pp. 234–5; see also *First Policy Statement* (Business Education Council, 1976), and *Initial Guidelines on the Implementation of Policy* (Business Education Council, 1977).
3 IBAR (1975–6), p. 9.
4 *JIB* (February 1978), p. 40.
5 *JIB* (June 1977), p. 119.
6 *JIB* (April 1978), pp. 77–8.
7 *BM* (February 1851), p. 72.

8 *BM* (July 1878), p. 560.
9 *Report by the Wilde Committee*, pp. 9, 34.
10 *BM* (March 1895), pp. 379–80.
11 *The Institute's Post-Qualifying Activities*, pp. 12, 20.
12 [*Proceedings of the*] *First World Conference of Banking Institute Secretaries* (Institute of Bankers in Scotland, 1975), pp. 32–3.
13 F. BACON, *The Elements of the Common Lawes of England* (1630).

APPENDICES

APPENDIX 1.1 Salaries of bank officials in the nineteenth century:
Prescott and Co., London, 1841–89

Year	Clerks' salary scale (£)*			Apprentices' salary (£)
	top	median	bottom	
1841	310	135		30
1842	315	135	100	30
1843	315	140	105	30
1844	315	140	105	30
1845	245	135	100	30
1846	245	135	100	30
1847	245	135	110	30
1848	245	135	110	30
1849	250	140	110	35
1850	250	140	110	35
1851	250	152.5	115	30
1852	255	145	105	35
1853	265	155	100	45
1854	265	155	100	35
1855	275	152.5	90	35
1856	275	152.5	90	35
1857	280	150	95	35
1858	285	160	100	40
1859	285	160	100	40
1860	290	165	100	50
1861	290	165	95	35
1862	295	175	105	35
1863	300	160	85	35
1864	300	160	85	35
1865	315	175	95	35
1866	315	175	95	35
1867	315	175	85	35
1868	325	175	100	45
1869	325	175	100	45
1870	340	190	115	40
1871	345	200	120	35
1872	310	140	115	35
1873	310	140	115	35
1874	320	150	105	45
1875	320	150	105	35
1876	330	160	110	45

* Excluding Christmas bonus.

APPENDIX 1.1 (*continued*)

Year	Clerks' salary scale (£)*			Apprentices' salary (£)
	top	median	bottom	
1877	330	155	110	35
1878	340	165	120	45
1879	340	165	120	35
1880	350	170	125	45
1881	300	175	125	35
1882	300	175	125	45
1883	300	175	115	35
1884	310	185	125	35
1885	310	185	125	45
1886	320	185	125	55
1887	310	185	105	55
1888	310	195	115	65
1889	310	195	115	65

* Excluding Christmas bonus.
Source: Prescott and Co., salary book, 1841–89:
        National Westminster Bank archives, 5014

APPENDIX 1.2 Salaries of bank officials in the nineteenth century:
Dimsdale and Company, London, 1865–91

Year	Clerks' salary scale (£)			Apprentices' salary (£)
	top	median	bottom	
1865	280	155	90	30
1866	280	160	90	30
1867	280	180	90	30
1868	300	190	100	40
1869	300	190	110	30
1870	300	190	110	30
1871	300	170	85	30
1872	300	190	85	30
1873	300	185	95	40
1874	300	185	95	30
1875	300	170	85	30
1876	280	165	85	30
1877	280	150	85	No further
1878	280	155	90	entries
1879	280	160	80	
1880	280	150	80	
1881	300	155	70	
1882	300	160	80	
1883	330	152	80	
1884	330	145	80	
1885	330	130	80	
1886	330	135	80	
1887	330	135	65	
1888	330	140	65	
1889	330	139	80	
1890	330	150	80	
1891		140	70	

Source: Dimsdale and Company, salary book, 1865–91:
National Westminster Bank archives, 1567

APPENDIX 1.3 Salaries of bank officials in the nineteenth century:
Huddersfield Banking Company, head office staff,
1873–96

Year	Manager's salary (£)	Clerks' salary scale (£)			Apprentices' salary (£)
		top	median	bottom	
1873	2000	500	175	70	25
1874	2000	500	160	70	35
1875	2000	500	160	70	35
1876	2000	500	165	70	35
1877	2000	750	190	70	35
1878	2000	750	200	80	35
1879	2000	750	235	110	35
1880	2000	750	235	70	35
1881	2000	750	250	70	35
1882	2000	850	250	80	35
1883	1100	600	275	90	35
1884	1200	600	275	70	35
1885	1300	600	250	70	35
1886	1400	600	200	70	35
1887	1500	600	200	70	35
1888	1500	600	150	70	35
1889	1500	650	160	80	35
1890	1500	700	175	70	35
1891	1500	750	190	70	35
1892	1500	750	200	70	35
1893	1500	750	140	50	35
1894	1500	750	150	70	35
1895	1500	550	165	70	35
1896	1500	650	120	70	35

Source: Huddersfield Banking Company, salary book, 1873–96:
Midland Bank archives, Acc 48/3

APPENDIX 2 Fidelity guarantee insurance: policies issued to bank officials by the Guarantee Society, 1848–70

Year (to 30 June)	Number of proposals accepted	Number of defaulters	Premium income (£)	Net claim payments (£)	Claim payments as percentage of premiums
1848	730	4	11,990	1,081	9.0
1849	849	5	15,052	1,899	12.6
1850	951	6	18,758	1,898	10.1
1851	1,044	9	21,007	4,508	21.5
1852	1,171	11	24,244	4,896	20.2
1853	1,368	13	27,225	6,666	24.5
1854	1,490	15	30,617	7,090	23.2
1855	1,668	18	34,313	7,511	21.9
1856	1,912	21	38,615	11,337	29.4
1857	2,125	22	43,542	11,497	26.4
1858	2,343	23	48,559	11,499	23.7
1859	2,562	29	54,130	13,568	25.1
1860	2,814	31	60,047	15,106	25.2
1861	3,113	32	66,268	15,576	23.5
1862	3,432	37	73,524	20,265	27.6
1863	3,845	37	81,789	20,195	24.7
1864	4,557	43	91,604	23,446	25.6
1865	5,217	49	99,919	25,179	25.2
1866	5,578	50	103,887	26,196	25.2
1867	5,786	54	107,348	26,444	24.6
1868	5,921	62	110,358	32,047	29.0
1869	6,014	65	112,676	34,150	30.3
1870	6,136	67	114,838	36,999	32.2

Source: Guarantee Society archives, results book, 1848–70

Year	Fellows	Associates
1879	250	402
1880	311	421
1881	350	473
1882	362	489
1883	370	520
1884	381	534
1885	391	563
1886	405	571
1887	414	590
1888	430	611
1889	428	606
1890	438	602
1891	439	635
1892	441	659
1893	437	642
1894	427	642
1895	417	646
1896	409	633
1897	400	626
1898	407	620
1899	400	819
1900	400	842
1901	388	896
1902	392	954
1903	394	1,007
1904	418	1,094
1905	421	1,215
1906	399	1,289
1907	394	1,386
1908	390	1,606
1909	386	1,719
1910	386	1,865
1911	375	2,020
1912	380	2,234
1913	378	2,484
1914	400	2,796

The Institute of Bankers
ndidates for
ions, 1879–1977

Members	Total	Candidates: Banking Diploma examinations
1,292	1,944	—
1,399	2,131	46
981	1,804	22
907	1,758	34
860	1,750	35
793	1,706	40
779	1,733	53
814	1,790	60
886	1,890	131
980	2,021	125
1,057	2,091	158
1,194	2,234	168
1,315	2,389	210
1,424	2,524	256
1,591	2,670	334
1,719	2,788	362
1,869	2,932	442
1,922	2,964	441
2,099	3,125	516
2,322	3,349	644
2,451	3,670	801
2,646	3,888	951
2,909	4,193	1,231
3,274	4,620	1,506
3,560	4,961	1,764
3,832	5,344	1,916
4,097	5,733	2,211
4,489	6,177	2,544
4,887	6,667	2,817
5,252	7,248	3,180
5,686	7,791	3,489
6,095	8,346	3,761
6,374	8,769	3,923
6,664	9,278	4,155
6,851	9,713	4,152
7,346	10,542	4,366

Year	Fellows	Associates	Members
1915	394	2,711	7,336
1916	407	2,584	7,418
1917	423.	2,482	7,609
1918	436	2,428	7,880
1919	430	2,349	7,762
1920	429	2,244	7,477
1921	471	2,381	9,257
1922	483	2,694	12,093
1923	471	3,059	14,157
1924	610	3,549	16,825
1925	620	4,088	20,304
1926	619	4,775	21,079
1927	642	5,542	22,173
1928	722	6,370	22,842
1929	707	7,188	25,518
1930	707	8,125	24,182
1931	707	8,791	24,530
1932	689	9,392	23,966
1933	754	9,953	23,329
1934	750	10,474	22,971
1935	753	11,064	22,789
1936	750	12,008	23,066
1937	807	12,550	23,570
1938	877	13,310	24,120
1939	871	13,394	23,385
1940	841	12,920	22,682
1941	806	12,536	24,008
1942	770	12,232	25,309
1943	743	12,284	26,465
1944	730	12,384	27,831
1945	725	12,561	29,419
1946	741	12,744	28,608
1947	782	12,800	27,702
1948	755	12,754	23,676
1949	765	13,154	24,226
1950	786	13,796	24,134
1951	800	14,246	23,801
1952	881	14,829	23,748
1953	904	15,353	24,236

ontinued)

Total	Candidates: Banking Diploma examinations	Candidates: Executor and Trustee Diploma examinations	Candidates: Total
10,441	2,262		
10,409	1,282		
10,514	906		
10,744	1,218		
10,541	1,500		
10,150	3,274		
12,109	4,698		
15,270	6,699		
17,687	8,157		
20,984	10,167		
25,012	13,442		
26,473	11,508		
28,357	12,395		
29,934	13,400		
31,413	16,224*		
33,014	17,114*		
34,028	17,184*		
34,047	15,842*		
34,036	15,300*		
34,203	14,235*		
34,606	14,027		
35,824	14,346	542	14,888
36,927	14,382	1,505	15,887
38,307	15,329	1,860	17,189
37,650	14,753	1,814	16,567
36,443	6,902	672	7,574
37,350	5,978	347	6,325
38,311	5,782	247	6,029
39,492	4,558	237	4,795
40,945	4,297	254	4,551
42,705	4,723	316	5,039
42,093	5,673	399	6,072
41,284	10,239	615	10,854
37,185	12,019	765	12,784
38,145	12,990	914	13,904
38,716	13,178	1,049	14,227
38,847	12,563	808	13,461
39,458	11,709	736	12,445
40,493	11,921	645	12,566

Year	Fellows	Associates	Members
1954	917	15,708	24,823
1955	914	16,065	24,674
1956	930	16,494	24,790
1957	943	16,780	25,148
1958	953	16,770	25,717
1959	991	17,129	27,647
1960	1,038	17,375	30,202
1961	1,074	17,474	33,460
1962	1,120	17,886	36,498
1963	1,132	18,849	38,138
1964	1,170	19,976	40,723
1965	1,209	21,025	43,921
1966	1,249	22,008	47,020
1967	1,333	23,049	47,419
1968	1,386	24,590	49,038
1969	1,526	25,962	51,063
1970	1,656	27,135	53,316
1971	1,769	28,404	55,482
1972	1,827	29,106	53,447
1973	1,879	29,972	55,629
1974	1,982	31,575	62,692
1975	2,204	32,817	72,602
1976	2,277	33,469	72,943
1977	2,344	36,949	73,761

*Totals include candidates for qualifying examinations
†From 1955 onwards candidates for the Banking Diploma and Trustee Diploma sat common Part I papers

ntinued)

Total	Candidates: Banking Diploma examinations	Candidates: Trustee Diploma examinations†	Candidates: Total
41,448	13,500	598	14,098
41,653	12,148	375	12,523
42,214	12,700	371	13,071
42,871	12,870	297	13,167
43,440	15,696	374	16,070
45,767	17,321	334	17,655
48,615	19,735	313	20,048
52,008	25,351	316	25,667
55,504	28,957	359	29,316
58,119	35,668	674	36,312
51,869	39,131	827	39,958
66,155	42,649	963	43,612
70,277	41,255	1,056	42,311
71,801	43,482	1,177	44,659
75,014	44,556	1,274	45,830
78,551	44,288	1,303	45,591
82,107	45,441	1,251	46,692
85,655	47,876	1,198	49,074
84,380	48,852	1,167	50,019
87,480	50,269	1,095	51,364
96,249	54,504	1,096	55,600
107,623	63,126	1,177	64,303
108,694	63,631	1,149	64,780
113,054	61,676‡	1,187	62,683‡

˙he decline in 1977 (and also the relative decline in 1976) in the number of candidates
tering for the Banking Diploma examinations is explained by the introduction in 1975
the new Stage 1 scheme based on public sector business studies examinations, and the
idual phasing-out of the Institute's Part I examinations.

APPENDIX 4 Local centres of The Institute of Bankers

Date of formation	Local centre	Date of formation	Local centre
1894	Liverpool and District Bankers' Institute (affiliated to The Institute of Bankers in 1913)	1926	Peterborough
		1927	Gloucester
			Eastbourne
			Cambridge
1895	Manchester and District Bankers' Institute (affiliated to The Institute of Bankers in 1965)		Reading
			Bedford
		1929	Lincoln
			Yeovil
1913	Sheffield	1930	Jersey
	Leicester		East Kent
	Newcastle upon Tyne		Richmond and Kingston
	Bradford	1931	Cornwall
	Birmingham		York
1914	Leeds		Grimsby
	Bristol		Portsmouth
1922	Nottingham		Tunbridge Wells
1923	Derby	1933	Guildford
	Swansea	1934	East Hertfordshire
	Cardiff	1937	Huddersfield
1924	Bournemouth	1939	Taunton
	Plymouth	1947	Halifax
	Brighton		Torbay
	Ipswich	1948	Hereford
	Blackpool		Chelmsford
	North Wales (East)		Worcester
	Norwich		High Wycombe
1925	North Wales (West)		Croydon
	Southampton		North Cumbria
	Cleveland	1949	Shrewsbury
	Hull		Slough
	Exeter		Ilford
	Bath	1950	North Devon
1926	Chatham and Maidstone	1951	Coventry
	North Staffordshire		London (West End)
	Northampton	1952	Berwick and District Bankers' Association (jointly with the Institute of Bankers in Scotland)
	Chester		
	South-East Essex		
	Oxford		

Date of formation	Local centre	Date of formation	Local centre
1952	Scarborough	1965	South Lancashire
	Wolverhampton	1966	Harrogate
	City of London		Luton
1953	London (Western Boroughs)	1967	Kampala
			Swindon
1954	North London	1968	Harrow and Wembley
1955	Bromley and North Kent		North Cheshire
1956	London (Northern Boroughs)	1969	Lusaka
			Southport
1958	South-East London	1970	Darlington
1960	Worthing		Hastings
	Singapore		Cyprus
	Nairobi	1971	Crawley
1961	East Lancashire		Newport and Gwent
	Malta	1972	Dyfed
	Preston		Wigan
	Sunderland and Durham		Winchester and Salisbury
1962	South Cumbria	1973	Chichester
1963	South Yorkshire		Guernsey
	Accra		Lancaster and Morecambe
	Hong Kong	1977	West Hertfordshire

Date of inception	Name of prize
1879	The Institute of Bankers Prize Essay
1893	Beckett Memorial Prize
1895	Gwyther Prize
1903	George Rae Prize
1905	Gwyther Prize
1908	Charles Reeve Prize
1918	Edward Jones Prize
1921	Whitehead Prize
1921	Whitehead Prize
1929	The Institute Prize
1930	Whitehead Prize
1930	Whitehead Prize
1930	Frank Steele Prize
1930	Frank Steele Prize
1930	Frank Steele Prize
1930	Frank Steele Prize
1936	John Caulcott Prize
1936	Bank of England Prize Essay
1952	Frederick Hyde Prize
1953	Lombard Association Prize
1962	F. C. Clegg Prize
1965	Transatlantic Banking Scholarship
1966	Council Prize
1970	Bank of England European Banking Scholarsh (replacing the Bank of England Prize Essay)
1970	Council Prize
1976	Council Prize

e Institute of Bankers

*Eligibility for prize (highest marks in
examination papers unless otherwise stated)*

Aggregate marks (Part II)
French (optional paper)
Practice of banking (Part II)
Monetary theory and practice (Part II)
English (Part I)
Spanish (optional paper)
Finance of foreign trade and foreign exchange (Part II)
Italian (optional paper)
An outstanding contribution to the literature
    of banking, finance or monetary economics (open to
    Fellows and Associates only)
Law relating to banking (Part II)
Accountancy (Part II)
Economics (Part I)
Economic geography (Part I)
General principles of law (Part I)
Structure of accounts (Part I)
Aggregate marks in Trustee Diploma (Part II)
Award for best essay on some aspect of central banking by member of
    staff of a commercial bank
Aggregate marks in Banking Diploma (Part II, Section 2) and interview
Finance of foreign trade and foreign exchange (Part II)
Aggregate marks in economics, economic geography,
    monetary theory and practice (Part II)
(a) Aggregate marks (Part II)
(b) Minimum five years service in banking
(c) Maximum age 32 years
(d) Submission of thesis
(e) Interview selection
French, German, Italian, Russian, Spanish (optional papers)
(a) Maximum age 34 years
(b) On staff of a commercial bank in UK
(c) Conversant with at least one major European language other than
    English
Investment, taxation (optional papers)
Elements of banking (Part I)

APPENDICES

APPENDIX 6 Presidents of The Institute of Bankers

1879–83   Sir John Lubbock, Bt, MP, FRS, DCL, LLD, *Robarts, Lubbock & Co.*
           (afterwards Lord Avebury)
1883–5   Richard Biddulph Martin, MP, *Martin & Co.*
           (afterwards Sir Richard Biddulph Martin, Bt, MP)
1885–7   Joseph Herbert Tritton, *Barclay, Bevan, Tritton & Co.*
1887–9   John William Birch, *Mildred, Goyenche & Co.*
1889–91   Sir Robert Nicholas Fowler, Bt, MP, *Dimsdale, Fowler, Barnard and Dimsdale*
1891–3   Thomas Salt, MP, *Lloyds Bank*
           (afterwards Sir Thomas Salt, Bt)
1893–5   Thomas Bedford Bolitho, MP, *Bolitho, Williams, Foster, Coode, Grylls & Co.*
1895–7   The Hon. Henry Dudley Ryder, *Coutts & Co.*
           (afterwards The Earl of Harrowby)
1897–9   Lt.-Col. Robert Williams, MP, *R. and R. Williams, Thornton Sykes & Co.*
           (afterwards Col. Sir Robert Williams, Bt)
1899–
   1902   The Lord Hillingdon, *Glyn, Mills, Currie & Co.*
1902–4   Joseph Herbert Tritton, *Barclays Bank*
1904–7   John Spencer Phillips, *Lloyds Bank*
1907–9   Sir Felix Schuster, Bt, *Union of London and Smiths Bank*
1909–12   The Hon. Frederick Huth Jackson, *Fredk Huth & Co.*
1912–14   The Viscount Goschen, *London County Westminster & Parr's Bank*
1914–16   Lord Inchcape of Strathnaver, GCMG, KCSI, KCIE, *National Provincial Bank of England*
           (afterwards The Earl of Inchcape)
1916   George Henry Pownall, *Williams Deacon's Bank*
1917–19   Sir Richard Vassar Vassar-Smith, Bt, DL, JP, *Lloyds Bank*
1919–21   Walter Leaf, Litt.D, D Litt., *London County Westminster & Parr's Bank*
1921–3   Sir Charles Stewart Addis, KCMG, LLD, *Hong Kong & Shanghai Banking Corporation*
1923–5   Sir Herbert Hambling, Bt, JP, *Barclays Bank*
1925–7   Sir John Ferguson, KBE, *Lloyds Bank*
1927–9   Frederick Hyde, *Midland Bank*
1929–31   Robert Martin Holland-Martin, CB, *Martins Bank*
1931–3   Brig.-Gen. Sir Arthur Maxwell, KCB, CMG, DSO, *Glyn Mills & Co.*
1933–5   Francis Lawrence Bland, JP, *Barclays Bank*
1935–7   Sir John Caulcutt, KCMG, *Barclays Bank* (DCO)
1937–9   Reginald Appleby Wilson, *Lloyds Bank*

[230]

1939–46	Sir Charles Lidbury, *Westminster Bank*
1946–8	Sir Clarence Thomas Albert Sadd, CBE, DL, JP, *Midland Bank*
1948–50	The Lord Balfour of Burleigh, DCL, DL, JP, *Lloyds Bank*
1950–2	Frederick Cecil Ellerton, *Barclays Bank* (afterwards Sir Cecil Ellerton)
1952–4	Arthur Hinton Ensor, *Lloyds Bank*
1954–6	Sir George Erskine, CBE, *Morgan Grenfell & Co.*
1956–8	Thomas Maltby Bland, TD, DL, *Barclays Bank*
1958–60	The Viscount Monckton of Brenchley, PC, KCMG, KCVO, MC, QC, CB, OBE, *Midland Bank*
1960–2	Sir Eric A. Carpenter, OBE, *Williams Deacon's Bank*
1962–4	Sir Edward James Reid, Bt, OBE, *Baring Brothers & Co.*
1964–6	Duncan Alexander Stirling, *Westminster Bank*
1966–8	Frederick Seebohm, TD, *Barclays Bank* (now The Lord Seebohm, TD)
1968–9	Sir Cuthbert Barwick Clegg, TD, JP, *Martins Bank*
1969–70	Leonard Charles Mather, CBE, Hon. FIB, *Midland Bank*
1970–2	Andrew Hunter Carnwath, *Baring Brothers & Co.* (now Sir Andrew Carnwath, KCVO, DL)
1972–4	Richard George Dyson, *Barclays Bank International*
1974–6	Sir John Prideaux, OBE, DL, *National Westminster Bank*
1976–7	Charles John Montgomery, CBE, *Lloyds Bank*
1977–	Malcolm George Wilcox, MBE, *Midland Bank*

APPENDIX 7 Deputy Chairmen of the Council of The Institute of
Bankers

1910–11	G. Marjoribanks, *Coutts & Co.*
1911–12	J. W. Cross, *London and Provincial Bank*
1912–13	T. Aitken, *Bank of Scotland*
1913–14	J. G. Nairne, *Bank of England*
1914–15	W. Smart, *Standard Bank of South Africa*
1915–16	T. B. Moxon, *Lancashire & Yorkshire Bank*
1916–17	R. Martin-Holland, CB, *Martins Bank*
1917–18	C. F. Higginson, *National Bank*
1918–19	H. Bell, *Lloyds Bank*
1919–20	H. L. M. Tritton, *Barclays Bank*
1920–1	Brig.-Gen. A. Maxwell, CMG, DSO, *Glyn Mills, Currie & Co.* (afterwards Brig.-Gen. Sir Arthur Maxwell)
1921–2	Sir Herbert Hambling, Bt, JP, *Barclays Bank*
1922–3	J. J. Meagher, *William's Deacons Banks*
1923–4	Sir William Carruthers, *Barclays Bank*
1924–5	Sir John Ferguson, KBE, *Lloyds Bank*
1925–6	F. Hyde, *Midland Bank*
1926–7	Sir Alfred E. Lewis, *National Provincial Bank*
1927–8	G. C. Cassels, *Bank of Montreal*
1928–9	J. F. Darling, CBE, *Midland Bank*
1929–30	J. W. H. Axtell, *National Provincial Bank*
1930–1	J. Barugh, *National Provincial Bank*
1931–2	H. F. Frankl, *Midland Bank*
1932–3	R. B. Pughe-Morgan, *Barclays Bank*
1933–4	W. F. Spalding, *Hongkong & Shanghai Banking Corporation*
1934–5	Sir John Caulcutt, KCMG, *Barclays Bank* (DCO)
1935–6	R. A. Wilson, *Lloyds Bank*
1936–7	E. Godward, *Bank of Australasia*
1937–8	Sir Charles Lidbury, *Westminster Bank*
1938–9	E. Cornwall, *National Provincial Bank*
1939–45	C. H. Scott, *William's Deacons Bank*
1945–6	Sir Clarence T. A. Sadd, CBE, JP, DL, *Midland Bank*
1946–7	M. J. Cooke, *The National Bank*
1947–9	F. C. Ellerton, *Barclays Bank* (afterwards Sir Cecil Ellerton)
1949–50	C. R. Robson, *Midland Bank*
1950–1	R. W. Jones, *Westminster Bank*
1952–3	Sir George Erskine, CBE., *Morgan Grenfell & Co.*
1953–5	W. F. Crick, CBE, Hon. FIB, *Midland Bank*
1955–6	T. M. Bland, TD, DL, *Barclays Bank*

1956–9	P. T. D. Guyer, *Lloyds Bank*
1959–61	H. W. Norris, *Westminster Bank*
1961–3	E. R. Walker, *Midland Bank*
1963–5	H. E. Darvill, *Barclays Bank*
1965–7	G. M. Warry, *Lloyds Bank*
1967–9	L. C. Mather, CBE, Hon. FIB, *Midland Bank*
1969–70	A. H. Carnwath, *Baring Brothers & Co.* (now Sir Andrew Carnwath, KCVO, DL)
1970–1	R. G. Dyson, *Barclays Bank International*
1971–3	E. C. Muxlow, *Yorkshire Bank*
1973–5	J. A. Cave, *Midland Bank*
1975–6	C. J. Montgomery, CBE, *Lloyds Bank*
1976–7	M. G. Wilcox, MBE, *Midland Bank*
1977–	D. Vander Weyer, *Barclays Bank*

APPENDIX 8 Treasurers of The Institute of Bankers

1879–82	Richard Biddulph Martin, MP
1882–96	John Biddulph Martin
1896–1915	Richard Biddulph Martin, MP (in 1904 became Sir Richard Martin, Bt, MP)
1915–44	Robert Martin Holland, CB (from 1917 name changed to Robert Holland-Martin)
1944–53	Robert Vere Buxton, DSO
1953–60	Christopher J. Holland-Martin, MP
1960–3	Edward Norman-Butler, TD
1963–7	Clifford Whiteley
1967–	Leonard J. Walton

APPENDIX 9 Secretaries/Secretary-Generals of The Institute of Bankers

1879–81	George Dayrell Reed
1881–1905	William Talbot Agar, JP
1905–35	Ernest Sykes, Hon. FIB
1935–59	Maurice Megrah, QC, Hon. FIB
1959–71	Henry Eason, CBE, JP, Hon. FIB
1971–	Geoffrey Herbert Dix, OBE

APPENDIX 10 Honorary Fellows of The Institute of Bankers –
Past and Present

The Council shall have power to elect, as Honorary Fellows, men of distinction in the
practice or literature of banking, mercantile law, political economy, or other kindred
subjects.

CONSTITUTION OF THE INSTITUTE OF BANKERS

*Sir Mackenzie Chalmers
*Sir John Paget
*Ernest Sykes
*Dr Harold Stonier (USA)
*The Lord Chorley, QC, JP
  The Lord Cobbold, PC, GCVO
  W. F. Crick, CBE
  Henry Eason, CBE, JP
  L. C. Mather, CBE
  Maurice Megrah, QC
  The Rt Hon. The Lord O'Brien of Lothbury, GBE, PC
*The Viscount Radcliffe, PC, GBE
  Professor R. S. Sayers
  B. S. Wheble, CBE
  D. E. Wilde, CBE

* deceased

INDEX